Sustainable Development Goals in the Republic of Korea

This book explores the attempts of the Republic of Korea in its effort to achieve the UN's Sustainable Development Goals (SDGs) by 2030. It addresses 6 of the 17 goals – clean water, affordable and clean energy, decent work and economic growth, sustainable cities and communities, climate action, and partnership – and defines specific national strategies. For each strategy, the contributors define the research indicators they selected, then analyze and examine the extent to which Republic of Korea has met the SDG concerned. They draw these conclusions from national and international reports, government documents and policy papers on SDGs. South Korea's experience in sustainable development and green programs will contribute to the planning of long-term development strategies for developing countries.

Tae Yong Jung is a professor at the Graduate School of International Studies, and the Deputy Executive Director of the Institute for Global Sustainability, Yonsei University. He was a professor at the KDI School and worked in many international institutes.

Routledge Studies on Asia in the World

Routledge Studies on Asia in the World will be an authoritative source of knowledge on Asia studying a variety of cultural, economic, environmental, legal, political, religious, security and social questions, addressed from an Asian perspective. We aim to foster a deeper understanding of the domestic and regional complexities which accompany the dynamic shifts in the global economic, political and security landscape towards Asia and their repercussions for the world at large. We're looking for scholars and practitioners – Asian and Western alike – from various social science disciplines and fields to engage in testing existing models which explain such dramatic transformation and to formulate new theories that can accommodate the specific political, cultural and developmental context of Asia's diverse societies. We welcome both monographs and collective volumes which explore the new roles, rights and responsibilities of Asian nations in shaping today's interconnected and globalized world in their own right.

The Series is advised and edited by Matthias Vanhullebusch and Ji Weidong of Shanghai Jiao Tong University.

Find the full list of books in the series here: www.routledge.com/Routledge-Studies-on-Asia-in-the-World/book-series/RSOAW

Chinese State Owned Enterprises in West Africa
Triple-embedded globalization
Katy N. Lam

Water Policy and Governance in South Asia
Empowering Rural Communities
M. Anwar Hossen

China and EU
Reform and Governance
Edited by Jing Men and Annika Linck

Sustainable Development Goals in the Republic of Korea
Edited by Tae Yong Jung

Sustainable Development Goals in the Republic of Korea

Edited by
Tae Yong Jung

LONDON AND NEW YORK

First published 2018
by Routledge
2 Park Square, Milton Park, Abingdon, Oxon OX14 4RN

and by Routledge
711 Third Avenue, New York, NY 10017

Routledge is an imprint of the Taylor & Francis Group, an informa business

© 2018 selection and editorial matter, Tae Yong Jung; individual chapters, the contributors

The right of Tae Yong Jung to be identified as the author of the editorial material, and of the authors for their individual chapters, has been asserted in accordance with sections 77 and 78 of the Copyright, Designs and Patents Act 1988.

All rights reserved. No part of this book may be reprinted or reproduced or utilised in any form or by any electronic, mechanical, or other means, now known or hereafter invented, including photocopying and recording, or in any information storage or retrieval system, without permission in writing from the publishers.

Trademark notice: Product or corporate names may be trademarks or registered trademarks, and are used only for identification and explanation without intent to infringe.

British Library Cataloguing-in-Publication Data
A catalogue record for this book is available from the British Library

Library of Congress Cataloging-in-Publication Data
A catalog record for this book has been requested

ISBN: 978-1-138-47889-3 (hbk)
ISBN: 978-1-351-06747-8 (ebk)

Typeset in Galliard
by Apex CoVantage, LLC

Contents

List of figures — viii
List of tables — xi
List of abbreviations, acronyms, and symbols — xii
List of contributors — xv
Acknowledgement — xix

PART I
SDGs in Republic of Korea's context — 1

1 Introduction — 3
   IN-KOOK PARK

2 Methodology for evaluating ROK's progress in the SDGs — 7
   TAE YONG JUNG, JUNG HEE HYUN, AND DAHYUN KANG

   Literature on the SDGs 7
   Factor analysis for index building 9
   Methods and scope of study 11
   Example of index-building using factor analysis 15

3 Brief overview of sustainable development policies — 21
   SUNG JIN KANG, YONG JUN BAEK, AND YOON JIN KANG

   Introduction 21
   Brief overview of sustainable development policies 22
   Institutional framework to achieve sustainable development 30
   Conclusion 31

PART II
Analysis on SDGs in Korea   35

4 Goal 6: clean water   37
HYUN JUNG PARK, JAEWAN KIM, AND THOMAS TAEK SUNG KIM

Introduction 37
Assessment of water-related SDG targets and indicators
   in the ROK context 39
Data and methodology 55
Analysis results 55
Conclusion 59

5 Goal 7: affordable and clean energy   65
TAE YONG JUNG, MINKYUNG HUH, AND JONGWOO MOON

Introduction 65
Analysis on the performance of the ROK Goal 7 by target 66
Results from factor analysis 77
Conclusion 79

6 Goal 8: decent network and economic growth   85
SUNG JIN KANG, SUN LEE, AND SEO KYUNG LIM

Introduction 85
Relevant policy overview 86
Data for economic growth trend 89
Empirical results 101
Conclusion and implications 105

7 Goal 11: sustainable city and communities   110
JAEMIN SONG AND EUN WOO LEE

Introduction 110
Relevant policy overview 111
Data 113
Results 113
Conclusions and implications 133

8 Goal 13: climate action   138
TAE YONG JUNG, HANBEE LEE, AND DOHYUN PARK

Introduction 138
Trends in achieving Goal 13 in ROK 140
Conclusion 155

9 Goal 17: partnership for the goals   158
   JOOYOUNG KWAK, EUNGKYOON LEE, AND STEVEN KYUM KIM

   *Sustainable Development Goals (SDGs) and
      global partnership 158
   History of non-state partnerships for sustainable
      development 164
   Partnerships in action for waste reduction and
      resource recovery 170
   Conclusion 175*

PART III
Conclusion   179

10 **Conclusion**   181
   SUNG JIN KANG AND JUNG HEE HYUN

   Index   187

Figures

2.1	Seoul's network and environment development over time	17
3.1	Milestones of ROK's sustainable development efforts	23
4.1	Water-related policy overview (1960–2000)	38
4.2	Trends of GDP, urbanization, water coverage, and sanitation coverage	39
4.3	Population with access to tap water on premises (%)	40
4.4	Interrupted water services	41
4.5	Population without access to public sanitation systems	42
4.6	Violation rate of wastewater discharging facilities (2004–2013)	45
4.7	Annual average water quality of four major rivers (BOD, mg/L)	46
4.8	Release of hazardous chemicals	47
4.9	Water-use efficiency (industrial and agricultural)	48
4.10	Leakage rate of water supply systems	49
4.11	Average monthly precipitation (1981–2010)	50
4.12	Ramsar wetlands in the ROK (1997–2016)	52
4.13	ODA in water sector (2002–2013)	53
4.14	Trend of SDG 6 target by factor	57
4.15	Index for SDG 6	58
4.16	Conceptual framework of SDG 6	59
5.1	Overview of energy-related policies (1950–2000)	66
5.2	Access to electricity (%)	67
5.3	Share of renewable energy (%)	69
5.4	Overview of renewable energy basic plan	69
5.5	Overview of renewable energy-related policies	71
5.6	Overview of energy conservation and efficiency policies	71
5.7	Energy intensity (ton of oil equivalent per US dollar 2010)	75
5.8	Foreign direct investment in electricity and gas sector (million USD 2010)	77
5.9	Index for SDG 7	79
6.1	National policies relevant to SDG 8	86

Figures ix

6.2	Detailed policies for SDG 8	88
6.3	Growth rates of GDP per capita and GDP per employed person (annual %)	91
6.4	Informal employment rate by non-agricultural industry and gender (%)	92
6.5	Domestic material consumption per GDP and capita	94
6.6	Gender wage gap (%)	95
6.7	Unemployment rate by age group (%)	95
6.8	Unemployment rate by male and female (%)	96
6.9	Sustainability of work indicators	97
6.10	Share of tourism contribution to GDP and employment	98
6.11	Number of commercial bank branches	98
6.12	Number of automated teller machines	99
6.13	Proportion of adults (15 years and older) with electronic finance services	99
6.14	OECD aid for trade commitments and disbursements (LDCs)	100
6.15	OECD public expenditure (%)	101
6.16	Sub-goal trend by factor 1	103
6.17	Sub-goal trend by factor 2	104
6.18	Sub-goal trend by factor 3	104
6.19	Index for SDG 8	105
7.1	Urban and rural population	111
7.2	Overview of local sustainable development policies	112
7.3	Population living in slums (%)	117
7.4	Share of public transportation (%)	119
7.5	Map of greenbelt in Seoul metropolitan area	120
7.6	Decadal trend in land consumption rate to population growth rate	120
7.7	Number of municipalities with urban planning	121
7.8	Heritage management budget	122
7.9	Number of persons affected per 100,000 people by disaster	123
7.10	Property loss per GDP due to disaster	124
7.11	Disaster management system in ROK	125
7.12	Waste generation per capita	126
7.13	Recycling ratio	127
7.14	Mean values of PM10 in cities (population weighted)	127
7.15	Size of public space	129
7.16	Green space per person in selected cities	129
7.17	Number of sexual assault cases	130
7.18	Ratio of victims of crime	130
7.19	Trend of targets by factor 1	132
7.20	Trend of targets by factor 2	132
7.21	Index for SDG 11	133

8.1	Flow of natural disaster and climate change countermeasures	140
8.2	Deaths caused by natural disasters (2006–2015)	141
8.3	Total GHG emissions (excluding LULUCF), selected years	144
8.4	GHG emissions reduction target for 2030 (million tons)	146
8.5	Share of climate finance of total ODA (%)	151
8.6	Climate-related development finance	152
9.1	Governance framework for partnership	163
9.2	Emergence of international partnership	167
9.3	Causal chain for partnership's contributions to waste reduction and resource recovery	175
10.1	Index for SDG 6 by administration	183
10.2	Index for SDG 7 by administration	184
10.3	Index for SDG 8 by administration	184
10.4	Index for SDG 11 by administration	185

Tables

2.1	Index development of clusters	16
3.1	List of plans and policies corresponding to the 17 SDGs	27
4.1	Freshwater withdrawals from renewable freshwater resources	49
4.2	Data sources and basic statistics of key variables	56
4.3	Factor loadings and index weights for SDG 6	57
5.1	RPS targets	72
5.2	Factor loadings and index weights for SDG 7	78
6.1	Variables and year coverage used in SDG 8 index	90
6.2	Material footprint	93
6.3	Youth not in employment, education or training (NEET) % by age group	96
6.4	First factor extraction statistics	102
6.5	Orthogonal varimax rotation factors	103
6.6	Factor loadings and index weights for SDG 8	103
7.1	Variables used for SDG 11 index	114
7.2	Housing welfare road map	116
7.3	Key housing quality indicator	117
7.4	Comparisons of PM10 concentration of Seoul with other cities	127
7.5	Factor loadings and index weights for SDG 11	131
8.1	Countermeasures against Natural Disasters Act	143
8.2	Evaluation of The First Climate Change Response Strategy Plan	145
8.3	Climate change contents included in scholastic curriculum	147
9.1	Goal 17 targets and indicators	159
9.2	Member organizations of the Korea Civil Society Network on SDGs	170
9.3	Government incentives for waste reduction	173

Abbreviations, acronyms, and symbols

Abbreviations and acronyms

ATM	automated teller machine
BOD	biochemical oxygen demand
BOK	Bank of Korea
BAU	business as usual
CFCs	chlorofluorocarbons
CO_2	carbon dioxide
COD	chemical oxygen demand
COP	Conference of the Parties
CSD	Commission of Sustainable Development
CSO	civil society organization
DAC	Development Assistance Committee
DMC	Domestic material consumption
EDCF	Economic Development Cooperation Fund
EIP	eco-industrial park
EU	European Union
FDI	foreign direct investment
FiT	feed-in-tariff
FSF	first-start finance
GCF	Green Climate Fund
GCI	global competitiveness index
GDP	gross domestic product
GHG	greenhouse gas
GGGI	Global Green Growth Institute
GNI	gross national income
IAEG–SDG	UN Inter-Agency and Expert Group on SDG Indicators
ICT	information, communication, technology
IEA	International Energy Agency
ILO	International Labor Organization
IMM	international market mechanism
INDC	intended nationally determined contribution
IWRM	integrated water resources management

Abbreviations, acronyms, and symbols

K-EXIM	Export–Import Bank of Korea
KDB	Korea Development Bank
KEPCO	Korea Electric Power Corporation
KGGTF	Korea Green Growth Trust Fund
KOICA	Korea International Cooperation Agency
KRW	Korean won
KWWA	Korean Water and Wastewater Works Association
LA21	Local Agenda 21
LAWASIA	The Law Association for Asia and the Pacific
LDC	least developed countries
LGGC	Local Green Growth Commission
LNG	liquefied natural gas
LSAK	Local Sustainability Alliance of Korea
MDB	Multilateral Development Bank
MDG	Millennium Development Goal
MF	material footprint
MOI	means of implement
MOE	Ministry of Environment
MOFA	Ministry of Foreign Affairs
MOTIE	Ministry of Trade, Industry, and Energy
MKE	Ministry of Knowledge Economy
NDC	nationally determined contribution
NEET	not in education, employment, or training
NGO	non-governmental organization
NPS	non-point source
NSSD	national strategy for sustainable development
ODA	official development assistance
OECD	Organization for Economic Co-operation and Development
OGPC	Office for Government Policy Coordination
PCGG	Presidential Commission on Green Growth
PCSD	Presidential Commission of Sustainable Development
R&D	Research and development
ROK	Republic of Korea
RPS	renewable portfolio system
SBSTA	subsidiary body for scientific and technological advice
SDG	Sustainable Development Goal
SE4All	Sustainable Energy for All
SIDS	small-island developing states
SME	small and medium enterprises
SMP	system marginal price
TTS	total suspended solids
UN	United Nations
UNEP–DHI	United Nations Environment Programme–DHI
UNFCCC	United Nations Framework Convention on Climate Change
UNSTATS	United Nations Statistics Division

USD	US dollar
WCED	World Commission on Environment and Development
WDI	World Development Indicator
WEF	World Economic Forum
WEM	water and environmental management
WRI	world resource institutes
WTTC	World Travel and Tourism Council

Symbols and unit

$\mu g/m^3$	density of particulate matter
°C	Celsius
J	Joule
Mtoe	million tonnes of oil equivalent
toe	tonne of oil equivalent
PM10	particulate matter less than 10μm
%	percentage
m^3	cubic meter
ha	hectare
km^2	square kilometer
ton	tonne
mg/l	milligram per liter
kg/day	kilogram per day

Contributors

Yong Jun Baek is a Ph.D. candidate at the Graduate School of Energy and Environment, Korea University. His research interests focus on renewable energy policies and low carbon development in developing countries in Africa. He is continuing his research in the promotion of renewable energy policies and the transfer of low carbon technologies. He holds an MA from Yonsei University.

Minkyung Huh is a research associate at the Institute for Global Sustainability, Yonsei University. Her research interests focus on climate change and renewable energy policy for sustainable development. She is studying a comparative analysis on how renewable energy policies to cope with climate change lead to the transition to a low carbon economy. She received her MA from Yonsei University.

Jung Hee Hyun is a research associate at the Institute of Sustainable Development, Korea University. Her research interests are climate finance and the use of capital market-based instruments in addressing the impacts of climate change. She received a BA from Barnard College, Columbia University, and an MA from Yonsei University.

Tae Yong Jung is currently a professor at the Graduate School of International Studies and Deputy Executive Director of the Institute for Global Sustainability, Yonsei University. He was a professor at the KDI School, Principal Climate Change Specialist at the Asian Development Bank, Deputy Executive Director of the Global Green Growth Institute, and Senior Energy Economist at the World Bank. He was Project Leader in Climate Policy at the Institute for Global Environmental Strategies of Japan and Senior Fellow at Korea Energy Economics Institute. He holds a BA from Seoul National University and an MA and Ph.D. from Rutgers, the State University of New Jersey.

Dahyun Kang is a research associate at the Institute of Global Sustainability, Yonsei University. Her research interests are the socio-economic implications of climate change and environmental policy in the context of green growth and sustainable development.

Sung Jin Kang is currently a professor in the Economics Department, an adjunct professor in KU-KIST Green School, and a director of the Institute for Sustainable Development at Korea University. His main fields of research are issues on sustainable development such as green growth, climate change, and economic development, including foreign direct investment, poverty reduction, and foreign aid. He has published several articles and books on international economics and the field of development economics. He holds a BA and MA from Korea University and a Ph.D. from Stanford University.

Yoon Jin Kang is a research associate at the Institute for Global Sustainability, Yonsei University. Her research interests lie primarily in the fields of environment and economic development, with a focus on urban impacts such as tackling issues of anthropogenic climate change and low-carbon development, linking these issues to sustainable development topics in developing nations.

Jaewan Kim is a research associate at the Institute of Global Sustainability, Yonsei University. Her research interests focus on the environmental valuation of non-market goods and services through various techniques in the field of climate change and sustainable water resource management. She holds a BA from Yonsei University and an MA from Imperial College, London.

Jooyoung Kwak is Associate Professor of International Business at Yonsei University. She completed her Ph.D. at Massachusetts Institute of Technology, majoring in international development and regional planning. She has published in the area of business–government relations, particularly in the context of emerging markets.

Steven Kyum Kim is a Ph.D. candidate in Public Administration at Korea University. His research interest includes environmental and spatial justice and environmental governance. He received his BS in Urban and Regional Planning from Cal Poly Pomona and his MPP from the KDI School of Public Policy and Management.

Thomas Taek Sung Kim is a Ph.D. candidate in Economics at Ohio State University. His research interest is applied micro econometrics, focusing on issues related to development and labor economics. He received his BA and MA in Economics from Yonsei University.

Eun Woo Lee is a research associate at Smart City Research Center at the University of Seoul. Her research interests focus on sustainability of urban area and resilience of cities, especially how cities in Korea have developed sustainability in the framework of SDGs and how the indicators of SDGs have been connected.

Eungkyoon Lee is Professor at Korea University. He obtained a Ph.D. in Public Policy from Massachusetts Institute of Technology. His research interests include environmental regulation, regulatory compliance, climate change, and energy policy. He has published research articles in *Environmental Science &*

Policy, Journal of Public Administration Research & Theory, Regulation & Governance, and a number of international journals.

Hanbee Lee is a research associate at the Institute for Global Sustainability, Yonsei University. Her research interests focus on climate change governance. She studies how the structure and patterns of combating climate change vary according to the different socio-political systems in Northeast Asia.

Sun Lee is a Ph.D. candidate in the Department of Economics at Korea University. She was a researcher at the Korea Environment Institute (KEI). Her research is focused on economic development and environmental economics, including sustainability assessment of social infrastructure and its services, happiness and industrial analysis, etc. She holds an MA in Economics from Korea University.

Seo Kyung Lim is a research associate at the Institute for Global Sustainability, Yonsei University. Her research interests focus on environmental economics. She studies quantitative analysis of climate change and sustainability issues, primarily based on microeconomic and statistical approaches.

Jongwoo Moon is a research associate at the Institute for Sustainable Development, Korea University. His research interests focus on the areas of renewable energy policies and carbon pricing schemes. He studies how technology, renewable policies, and carbon prices change investment decisions in renewable energy and the landscape of the electricity market. He holds an MA from the School of Advanced International Studies, Johns Hopkins University.

Dohyun Park is Climate Change Specialist at the Korea International Cooperation Agency (KOICA), the national grant ODA agency of the Republic of Korea. He works on climate change policy and its implementation, aiming at supporting sustainable growth for developing countries, especially in Asia and the Pacific region. His research interest is in low carbon energy, climate finance, and carbon trading mechanisms in the context of Sustainable Development Goals. He received his MA from the KDI School of Public Policy and Management.

Hyun Jung Park has intensive international working experience in the areas of water, climate change, sustainable development, and disaster management. She is currently Vice-Director of the Institute of Climate Change Action and is responsible for international cooperation, focusing on an integrated approach to address dynamic and complex environmental issues. She was Programme Management Officer for the Sustainable Development Mechanisms Programme at the United Nations Framework Convention on Climate Change (UNFCCC). She was invited to participate as a visiting fellow with the Research Program (Environment, Population and Health) in the POSCO fellowship of East West Center in Honolulu, USA. She received her M.C.P from Seoul National University and Ph.D. from Georgia State University.

In-Kook Park is currently President, Korea Foundation for Advanced Studies. He has been a high-level diplomat in both the Korean government and the UN. He was Deputy Foreign Minister, Ministry of Foreign Affairs, ROK; Permanent Representative of the ROK to the United Nations; and Chairman, Preparatory Process of the UN Conference on Sustainable Development. He was heavily involved in UN–SDG processes. He holds a BA and an MA from Seoul National University.

Jaemin Song is currently an associate professor in the Department of Urban Planning and Design at the University of Seoul, and is a director general for the International Urban Development Collaboration at Seoul Metropolitan Government. Before joining the university, she worked as a climate change specialist at the World Bank. Her areas of interest include climate change resilient cities, low carbon cities, and sustainable urban development in developing countries. She holds a BS and an MS from Seoul National University and a Ph.D. from Massachusetts Institute of Technology.

Acknowledgement

We sincerely acknowledge the support from the Institute for Global Sustainability of Yonsei University, Global Energy Technology Policy Professional Program of Korea University, Smart City Research Center of University of Seoul and Korea Foundation for Advanced Studies.

Part I
SDGs in Republic of Korea's context

1 Introduction

In-Kook Park

Since the need for 'sustainable development' was first raised by the United Nations Human Environment Council in 1972, it took more than 40 years for SDGs to be formulated. In the history of sustainable development, 1972 is an important milestone that marks the establishment of the United Nations Environment Program (UNEP) through the Stockholm Declaration and the publication of *The Limits to Growth* in support of the need for sustainable development. *The Limits to Growth* warned that existing human activities could have a very devastating effect on the environment (Meadows et al. 1972) and stressed that if such economic activity continued, it would be fatal to future generations. Discussions for resolving this problem have required dialogue at the national and international levels. Through the UN Human Environment Conference, the UN not only addressed the world about the environmental degradation caused by economic development but also established the UNEP to promote international cooperation. Although the UNEP was only a mere program and was not implemented in a full-fledged governance regime, it was still significant as the beginning of a full-scale sustainable development agenda.

In 1987, the World Commission on Environment and Development (WCED), led by former Norwegian Prime Minister Gro Halel Brundtland, was established and produced a report titled *Our Common Future*. This report presented the conceptual framework of sustainable development. This report is remarkable in that it defined sustainable development as not being confined to environmental protection, but as a multifaceted approach that takes economic, social, and human factors into consideration. Though these three factors were not considered as important at that time, it is noteworthy that the Brundtland report raised these three factors as essential for sustainable development. For the purposes of "human activity, development, and better life" mentioned in the report, the UN published Agenda 21 in 1992 (United Nations 1992, p. 16). Although Agenda 21 has been criticized as unrealistic for incorporating too many agendas, it is significant for not only presenting a common goal and vision for sustainable development but for also dealing with economic and social development, in addition to environmental preservation (e.g. child welfare, human rights, and women's capacity building). *Our Common Future* is considered to be the forbearer of the current SDGs framework. Moreover, considering that this is the agenda that the

UN and its member countries proactively initiated after the end of the Cold War, it could be considered as an agenda for a new era of international development cooperation. Despite the widespread expectation that ODA and international cooperation would increase on a large scale at the end of the Cold War, I personally observed a dramatic decrease in ODA, and the international community has recognized this as a big crisis. This, in turn, accelerated the formulation of Agenda 21, which then led to the establishment of the MDGs. Furthermore, Agenda 21 has profoundly impacted the formulation of the agenda for sustainable development in each member country of the UN. Particularly, it provided the motivation for cooperation between civil society and the government in establishing a common agenda for sustainable development. For instance, in the ROK, Agenda 21 allowed the PCSD to be established and the basic law on sustainable development to be enacted under the Dae-Jung Kim administration.

Meanwhile, in September of 2000, at the dawn of a new millennium, heads of state and government gathered together at the United Nations Headquarters in New York, building on a decade of important UN conferences and summits, to adopt the United Nations Millennium Declaration (United Nations 2015). The Declaration encouraged nations to build a new global partnership to reduce extreme poverty and set out a series of eight time-bounded targets with a deadline of 2015 that have become known as the MDGs. Based on the belief that globalization at present has brought about very uneven distribution in the world, heads of state and government recognized that developing countries and countries with economies in transition face special difficulties in responding to the central challenge. They believed that only through broad and sustained efforts to create a shared future could globalization be made fully inclusive and equitable. Thus, efforts must include policies and measures, at the global level, that correspond to the needs of developing countries and economies in transition and are formulated and practiced with their effective participation. Consequently, MDGs contain certain fundamental values essential to international relations in the twenty-first century (UN General Assembly 2015).

But progress has been uneven across regions and countries, leaving millions of people behind, especially the poorest and those disadvantaged due to sex, age, disability, ethnicity, or geographic location (UN Department of Public Information 2012). If China had not made such significant progress in implementing the MDGs, the results of those goals could have been even worse. Moreover, the 2007–2008 financial crisis negatively impacted overall economic performance and exacerbated income inequality, hitting the most vulnerable the hardest. This is where SDGs are expected to play an important part. Based on the achievements and limitations of MDGs, the international community began discussing the establishment of SDGs during the preparation of the Rio +20 Summit in 2012. At its sixth plenary meeting, on June 22, 2012, the United Nations Conference on Sustainable Development adopted the outcome document, entitled *The Future We Want*. SDGs will guide policy and funding for the next 15 years, beginning with the historic pledge on September 25, 2015 that stressed everything from zero poverty, zero hunger, good health, quality education, gender equality, clean water and sanitation, and affordable clean energy, to decent work and economic growth, innovation, reduced inequalities, sustainable cities, responsible consumption, climate action, unpolluted oceans and land, and partnerships to achieve the goals.

According to the SDGs, sustainable development is defined as "meeting the needs of the present without compromising the ability of future generations to meet their own needs" (WCED 1987). All current activities for development are viewed as a process of change that takes future needs into consideration through institutional improvements, technology, resources, and environmental protection. Development considering the needs of the future will be made possible only when the three major axes – 'social development, economic growth, environment preservation' – are harmonized. Moreover, the SDGs were proposed to achieve a balanced development of those three pillars.

From 2013, the UN began working on establishing the SDG framework for full-fledged negotiations through the Open Working Group, Sustainable Development Solutions Network (SDSN), and High Level Political Forum (HLPF) on Sustainable Development. The then secretary-general, Ki-Moon Ban, is said to have played a pivotal role in developing the SDG framework (UN Department of Public Information 2016). Also during his tenure of office, Mr. Ban presided over the Paris Climate Change Conference, considered a triumph for people, the planet, and for multilateralism, and a stepping-stone to advance the 2030 Agenda for Sustainable Development.

The UN chose 17 goals in 2014 for the final draft, and the SDGs, with 17 goals and 169 targets covering a broad range of sustainable development issues, emerged. At first, the SDG had ten goals, which was fewer than the current 17 SDG goals because too many goals were considered too difficult for the common people to memorize and understand. It was also due to fact that if the goals were considered too ambitious, there might be difficulty achieving them by 2030. The SDGs highlight several new values, such as inclusiveness, universality, and equality, along with the existing MDGs that emphasize poverty eradication. The SDGs also strengthen the goals of sustainable economic growth and environmental conservation as well as social development. This is the result of efforts by many stakeholders to participate in discussions over a relatively long period of time and strike a balance between the three pillars of sustainable development (UN News Center 2015).

Each country, and the global community, faces a different level of challenges that could be tackled, depending on the priority of the agenda and issues under the framework of the SDGs. The next task is how to monitor and evaluate the performance of effective implementation of SDGs in order to achieve a sustainable society locally, nationally, regionally, and globally.

The objective of this edited book is to analyze the ROK's efforts towards realizing sustainable development prior to and after its commitment to the 2030 Agenda. It describes the social, economic, and environmental conditions of the ROK, identifying the SDGs most relevant to these conditions and demonstrating institutions, policies, and stakeholders for the implementation of those goals.

This book especially suggests unique statistical measures to analyze systematically compiled data for those environmentally focused SDGs and examines the trajectory of the ROK's past and future in achieving the SDGs.

This book is organized into ten chapters. Of the UN's 17 SDGs, it focuses on some of the more environmental goals of the SDGs, discussing clean water, affordable and clean energy, decent work and economic growth, sustainable cities and communities, climate action, and partnership for the SDGs in the ROK. The following chapters discuss the ROK's current performance and its integration of sustainable development objectives into the national framework from the perspective of domestic measures, and how to prepare a roadmap for the design of SDGs strategies; in addition, they provide a set of efficient definitions and the implementation of national strategies – key barriers and opportunities – to support the focus areas of the SDGs that are all related and interconnected.

References

Meadows, Donella H., Dennis L. Meadows, Jorgen Randers and William W. Behrens. 1972. *The Limits to Growth*. New York: Universe Books.

United Nations. 1992. "United Nations Conference on Environment & Development Rio de Janerio, Brazil, 3 to 14 June 1992 Agenda 21." Accessed November 13, 2017. https://sustainabledevelopment.un.org/content/documents/Agenda21.pdf

United Nations. 2015. "Millennium Development Goals (MDGs) and Beyond 2015." Accessed November 13, 2017. www.un.org/millenniumgoals/bkgd.shtml

United Nations Department of Public Information. 2012. "The Millennium Development Goals Report." Accessed November 13, 2017. www.un.org/millenniumgoals/pdf/Press%20Release%20MDG%20Report%202012.pdf

United Nations Department of Public Information. 2016. "Ban Ki-Moon Announces Common Ground Initiative with Advertising's 'Big Six' to Support SDGs." Accessed December 5, 2017. www.un.org/sustainabledevelopment/blog/2016/06/ban-ki-moon-announces-common-ground-initiative-with-advertisings-big-six-to-support-sdgs/

United Nations General Assembly. 2000. "Resolution Adopted by the General Assembly." Accessed November 14, 2017. www.un.org/millennium/declaration/ares552e.pdf

United Nations News Center. 2015. "Sustainable Development Goals Kick off with Start of New Year." Accessed November 13, 2017. www.un.org/sustainabledevelopment/blog/2015/12/sustainable-development-goals-kick-off-with-start-of-new-year/

World Commission on Environment and Development. 1987. "Report of the World Commission on Environment and Development: Our Common Future." Accessed December 10, 2017. www.un-documents.net/our-common-future.pdf

2 Methodology for evaluating ROK's progress in the SDGs

Tae Yong Jung, Jung Hee Hyun, and Dahyun Kang

The vast literature on SDGs describe it as a multi-dimensional concept that is captured by numerous predefined sub-targets and indicators. Yet, a quantitative methodology designed to evaluate the performance of SDGs across countries based on a common scale is not available in the analysis of the SDGs. Thus, this study suggests a statistical method application – Factor Analysis (Principal Component) – to create indexes to be used as a comprehensive and unique evaluative measure of ROK's past and future trajectory in achieving the SDGs. This chapter introduces and elaborates on the methodologies used in past SDGs research, finding that very limited rigorous empirical analysis has been completed.

Literature on the SDGs

Research on sustainable development has moved beyond defining and conceptualizing this relatively new concept, which was introduced in 1980s, towards concrete analysis, interpretation, and projections for the future. Since the Brundtland Report, many studies have attempted to define sustainable development in different ways and to suggest different approaches for various applications. Pearce (1988) defines 'sustainability' as making things lasting, permanent, and durable. According to this definition, 'sustainable development' implies two main concepts: sustaining and augmenting the natural environmental system, and sustaining economic development. Likewise, Pearce (1988) provided a more integrated perspective by defining sustainable development as economic change based on natural capital stock. Under this assumption, it is important to guarantee equity in sharing the limited capital between and within generations, economic resilience to external shocks, and uncertainty of the natural environment.

Mebratu (1998) reviewed a wide variety of definitions on sustainable development (SD), finding that many definitions have been biased towards institutional and stakeholders' advantages. Historically, SD studies originated from the acknowledgement that ecology was the foundation of civilization and other important social transformation. Yet, the framework of the current definitions of SD remains narrow since specific groups or organizations have conducted studies to articulate their interests. Desta (1998) expected that more logically coherent analyses on SD, focusing on larger contexts, would overcome the influence of institutional and group interest.

The concept of SD became more mainstream when Jeffrey Sachs welcomed SDGs while concluding the Millennium Development Goals (MDGs) in 2012 (Sachs 2012). He declared that the world could no longer deny the urgency of sustainable development. While MDGs focused on issues of developing countries such as poverty or hunger, the scope of the SDGs is global, focusing on the combination of economic development, environmental sustainability, and social inclusion, called the "Triple Bottom Line" approach. SDG also suggests the importance of governance cooperation at all levels – from local to global and private to public. Joshi et al. (2015) assessed the role of governance for the successful implementation of SDGs by utilizing a module named International Futures (IF) – widely used for global forecasting by UNDP and many other organizations. He found that the level of governance is not only desirable by itself, but also a necessary means to accomplish the other SDGs in the long run.

Meanwhile, empirical studies evaluating how well SDGs have been executed in country-specific cases, especially in the ROK, are rare. One of a few empirical studies conducted by Hwang and Kim (2016) surveyed young Koreans from 15 to 24 years old about their basic understanding and the capacity of SDGs in the country. The qualitative study used the survey response to explore various policy implications for adolescents to successfully participate in SDG implementation. The results suggest building a foundation for increasing the rights and roles of youth in the future, capacity training of youth for leading SDGs, and aligning the youth policy to the SDGs framework. This study is one of the first to rigorously collect data looking for empirical implications for SDGs in the ROK. Kim and Sorin (2016) surveyed pre-school teachers' recognition of the importance of SD education. They observed that teachers who participated in the sustainable development education programs increasingly placed more importance on the issue. The teachers realized the necessity of SD education in early childhood since the understanding of SD concepts are tied to future development of the economy, environment, and society.

Another method for conducting empirical studies on SDGs has been building comprehensive indexes. SDGs include an official indicator set of 17 goals and 169 targets. In addition, the inter-agency expert group suggests 230 indicators. It is difficult for the public to approach and evaluate the current status of SDGs implementation in a glance. Suggesting an index that includes and evaluates overall SDGs can enable the observation of the current status in a more convenient way. Sachs et al. (2017) presented a country-level SDG index for all developing and developed countries that measures SDG achievements in all 17 goals using national cross-country data. This index served as a metric to preliminarily rank countries to assess their current progress with SDGs. They collected various data across countries that were "technically sound, quantitative and useful for policy-making, sufficiently up-to-date data at the country level, and the data for which UN members stated to be available" (Sachs et al. 2017). To aggregate collected data into one SDG index, they firstly assign percentile to each variable of each country according to the score of the variable. Each goal and every variable are assigned identical weight by assuming policymakers are committed to treating all SDGs equally. Using the identical weights, they derived an SDG index for each country. This methodology, however, merely complements the official monitoring process of SDGs.

Prakash et al. (2016) also built an index to assess the SDGs for 124 cities in the US. Among all indicators proposed by the UN Inter-Agency and Expert group, only indicators that have sufficient up-to-date data at the metropolitan statistical area (MSA) level were included in the analysis. The authors assigned a score using a scale of 0 to 100 to each variable, calculated the arithmetic mean within each SDG, and then calculated the final mean across all SDGs to create one index. This methodology also assumed that each goal was weighted equally. The US SDG Cities index over all metropolitan areas were presented and ranked. The top scoring metropolitan statistical area, Provo-Orem in Utah, showed 55.45% to go for the best possible outcome of SDGs, which means that even for the area with the highest score, much progress remains.

An index study for SDGs for the ROK is rare. Park (2016) conducted one of a few studies to look for an ideal monitoring system for successful implementation of SDGs in the ROK. The research additionally suggested the development of a national index framework that considers both efficiency of data collection and balance over economic–social–environmental values. Current Korean national indexes such as national core index, life quality index, and e-national index were first introduced and compared to SDGs indicators. The comparison found that while social and economic values are well represented by existing indexes, environmental values and indexes rarely include other variables except for SDG indicators. In addition, in creating an index, the study emphasized the importance of considering the way a global index and IAEG–SDGs deal with this issue. Lastly, it is important to consider uniqueness of the country as much as common components when considering methodology.

Factor analysis for index building

Differing from former SDGs and index-creating studies, the present study suggests a more practical method to create a SDG index based on empirical data. Factor analysis will be used as the main tool to create a SDG index in our study. Factor analysis is a statistical method to explain variability among observed and correlated variables in terms of a potentially lower number of unobserved variables called factors.

The origins and development of factor analysis was introduced in a paper by Vincent (1953). Factor analysis was first introduced as an analytical tool for psychology in the early 1900s by Spearman's papers in the *American Journal of Psychology* (Spearman 1904a, 1904b), and has since become a famous statistical method applied to other fields of study. Factor analysis started with one-factor type simply because it was believed that there was only one cause that influenced the variances in a set of variables. But Spearman suggested the word 'factor' and even calculated the value of factor loadings in a way identical to its current methods. However, he did not provide any further arrangement to formularize the factor analysis method. In 1909, Sir Cyril Burt, using the concepts in Spearman's paper, introduced a proper formula explaining factors and factor loadings. At the time, Spearman and Sir Cyril Burt mentioned and proposed incomplete concepts of multiple factors, which was theoretically suggested in 1916 by Sir Godfrey Thomson. Finally, Carey (1914), one of Spearman's students, presented a technique for testing a table of correlations for the presence of multiple factors. Since then, factor analysis has been used as a powerful statistical tool in various fields of study.

There are many empirical analyses utilizing factor analysis to explore correlations within data sets across disciplines. Maiz et al. (2000) studied heavy metal availability in polluted soils. Factor analysis was conducted to explore two possible correlations between (1) the metal contents in the soil and the grass and (2) the level of different sequential fractions and the metal contents in the grass. Ludvigson and Ng (2007) researched the relationship between risk and return in the US stock market using factor analysis for large data sets to comprehensively explain three new factors: 'volatility,' 'risk premium,' and 'real.' While existing literature about the risk–return relationship focused more on modeling the conditional mean and variance with small amount of data, this study overcame the problem and made two important methodological contributions. First, it successfully evaluated the potential role of omitted information by capturing latent factors. Second, they proposed significant out-of-sample forecasting power that has proved to be methodologically stable over time.

As exampled in the studies above, factor analysis can be used for exploratory purposes to explain latent dimensions that clarify observed information with fewer variables or representative variables. But factor analysis can also be used for confirmatory purposes. When researchers impose certain constraints on factors or factor loadings, communality concerns can be addressed. In this chapter, the confirmatory factor analysis is used to analyze the multitrait–multimethod matrix. In selecting this method, Fabrigar et al.'s (1999) study – which suggests standards for selecting between factor analysis and principal component analysis (PCA), and between varimax rotation and quartimin rotation – was noted. In this book, the varimax rotation method was selected to follow each factor analysis. Henry F. Kaiser (1958) first introduced the varimax rotation, which is an orthogonal rotation of axes of factors to maximize the variance of factors on all variables. The core difference with other factor rotation methodologies is that the varimax rotation encourages the identification of corresponding variables with a single factor.

Although there are numerous areas of research in which factor analysis can play an analytical role, the purpose for utilizing this methodology is to create a representative index that can comprehensively explain numerous variables. Nardo et al. (2005) introduced the theoretical bases of important tools for creating composite indicators. Indicators created by factor analysis are also included in their paper. Our empirical study of creating an SDG index for ROK most closely follows the theoretical model of their work. Indicators explaining market regulation can also be calculated by factor analysis as shown by Nicoletti et al. (2000). They focused on the relative relation between the level of regulations and market characteristics. Many detailed indicators are aggregated into a summary variable showing the level of market regulations. It is used to analyze regulatory frameworks across OECD countries and various sets of regulations.

Tarantola et al. (2002) also conducted principle component analysis to create the new internal market index (IMI). They intended to evaluate the impacts of internal market policies of the European Union, such as the free circulation of goods, services, capital, and workers within the EU. They collected data for possible outcome variables of the internal market policies and ran principal component analysis with a purpose similar to this study to look for proper weights for each outcome variable. The IMI of five countries, the newest member states, has grown faster than the IMI of the EU, which means that the newcomers have benefited from the internal market structure.

Methods and scope of study

Collection of data

Yearly time-series data were collected according to the official list of SDG indicators composed by the UN Inter-Agency and Expert group. Each SDG has 3 to 19 sub-goals that specify each goal; each sub-goal also has up to three indicators that can be used to evaluate the sub-goal. A total of 81 indicators for the environmental SDGs were chosen and studied for this book.

We made a distinctive decision for unavailable indicators. They are either replaced by one or more other proxy variables that could logically approximate the indicators or are dropped from the analysis. There are three reasons some indicators were not available.

- *Some indicators are qualitative. For example, sub-goal 6.5 is 'Implement integrated water resource management,' and its indicator is 'Degree of integrated water resource management implementation.' This indicator is basically measured by subjective evaluation. Although it might have qualitative implications, its ability to be quantitatively analyzed is limited.*
- *Some indicators have no data for the ROK. For example, the indicator suggested for sub-goal 6.b is 'Proportion of local administrative units with established and operational policies and procedures for participation of local communities in water and sanitation management.' Although centrally managed data by the Ministries could be easily accessed, unfortunately the challenges for standardized data managed by local governmental offices are much more substantial.*

- *Some indicators lack time-series data. Even if the exact data for an indicator was found, there were many cases where only a few years of the time-series was available. Since we intended to run factor analysis, a minimum number of time-series information was required. Variables lacking sufficient time-series data were dropped or replaced. The determination for the minimum number of time-series data was made individually for each SDG, varying from 20 to 36 years.*

Data processing

Some of the data collected included missing points. Either the data started from a later time or had missing values in between. For variables that were kept but still have some missing values, imputation methodologies were conducted to fill in missing points. Since there is no satisfactory method to impute panel data that preserves both the variance of the data and time related properties, this study used a combination of two imputation methods. Once the two imputation methods were conducted, the mean value of the two results replaced the missing values of the indicators. The two methods used for the imputation process are as follows.

Linear interpolation imputation

Linear interpolation imputation is firstly used for estimating the missing values. It is briefly defined as the estimation of missing values of one variable based on its linear relationship with another variable. For example, to estimate missing value x_0 between known values x_1 and x_2 in a vector X and the known vector Y, with y_0, y_1, and y_2 corresponding to x_0, x_1, and x_2, respectively. Then we can estimate x_0 by the following calculation.

$$\frac{x_0 - x_1}{y_0 - y_1} = \frac{x_2 - x_1}{y_2 - y_1}$$

Since x_0 is the only unknown value in the equation, we can easily estimate the value for x_0 by assuming that both X and Y vectors are linear polynomials.

Regression based imputation

The second imputation method used was a regression-based imputation. A simple regression model is used with the variable of the estimate missing values as the dependent variable. The composition of independent variables varied according to the dependent variable, to best estimate the fitted value of the regression.

Data normalization

After the imputation process, we standardized each variable so that it had mean ($\bar{x}$) and standard deviation (σ), 0 and 1, respectively. Each data point was calculated based on the standardization method calculation as shown below.

$$x' = \frac{x_a - \bar{x}}{\sigma}$$

Since the transformation of a real value into normalized data points could create negative values, the final index values for each SDG can be negative in certain years. If more than one indicator was prescribed to the sub-goals in each SDG, variables were aggregated according to each chapter's authors.

Additionally, to set all variables into a common range, data rescaling methods were applied on certain variables. Most of the data were in percentage form. These variables were kept as is while the other variables, which were on different scales, were also brought in line with the 0–100 range.

Factor analysis

Factor analysis explores the joint variations within the observed variables in response to unobserved latent variables. The observed variables are assumed as linear combinations of the potential factors and error terms. Factor analysis aims to find independent latent variables. The objective of applying the factor analysis is that the information gained about the interdependencies between observed variables can be used later to reduce the set of variables in a dataset. At the initial stage, there are too many variables to conduct research, and in fact, there is no prior information on the relationship among observed variables. Then, the relationship among unobserved latent variables can be identified by a minimum number of factors. Factor analysis is not used to any significant degree in physics, biology, and chemistry, but it is used very heavily in psychometrics personality theories, marketing, product management, operations research, and finance, where unobserved variables may play an important role in understanding the social phenomena or human behavior being studied.

Factor analysis works with data sets where there are large numbers of observed variables thought to reflect a smaller number of underlying/latent variables. It is one of the most commonly used interdependency techniques; it is used when the relevant set of variables shows a systematic interdependence and the objective is to find the latent factors that create a commonality. In some disciplines, factor analysis and another statistical method, principal component analysis (PCA), are used interchangeably. Principal component analysis is typically used if the goal of the analysis is to simply reduce correlated observed variables to a smaller set of important independent composite variables. The PCA's eigenvalues are essentially inflated component loadings of factor analysis.

In this study, factor analysis is used to explore the latent relationship while reducing the number of variables of the research. Technically, with imputed, standardized, and representative indicator variables for each sub-goal, we ran a factor analysis for each SDG. The main purpose of conducting a factor analysis was to determine the proper weights for sub-goals under each SDG so an index for each SDG could be created based on the actual data of the ROK. The brief process of factor analysis was as follows (Harman 1976).

$$\frac{X-\mu}{\sigma^2} = Z = LF + \epsilon \tag{1}$$

X is a matrix of sub-goal indicator variables under one SDG.
μ is a matrix of mean variables of the sub-goal indicators.
σ^2 is a matrix of variance of the sub-goal indicators.
F is a matrix of factors, unobserved random variables.
L is a matrix of factor loadings, unobserved constants.
ϵ is a matrix of error terms.

The analysis holds the following assumptions.

- *F* and ϵ are independent.
- $E(F) = 0$
- $Cov(F) = I$ *(identity matrix, assuming factors are not correlated)*.

We square each side of equation (1), then since $Cov(F) = E[(F-E(F))(F-E(F))^T] = E(FF^T) = I$, we have equations (2) and (3).

$$ZZ^T = L(FF^T)L^T + \epsilon\epsilon^T = LL^T + \epsilon\epsilon^T \tag{2}$$

$$\left[\epsilon\epsilon^T\right]^2 = \left(ZZ^T - LL^T\right)^2 \tag{3}$$

We find LL^T, a set of factor loadings that minimizes the square error terms.

Creating an index

From the literature review, the weighting of most indexes simply takes the sum or the average of the components, hence giving the appearance of equal weights. In theory this is incorrect, as it implies that each component is equally important. Several studies address this issue by proposing the use of principal components analysis. While an accepted statistical method, it is purely data driven and the weights have no conceptual interpretation. Lack of a conceptual agreement on which is more important among the Sustainable Development Goals over another variable is the main problem behind the weighting issue.

The results of the factor analysis loading of each factor for each indicator variable were used to calculate the weighting of the index for this study. Factor loading indicates how well the unobserved factor explains the corresponding indicator variable. Therefore, the higher the factor loading, the better the factor explains corresponding indicator variables. The highest factor loadings for each indicator variable were selected and squared. The value of squared factor loading is the weight for the indicator. Finally, the weighted sum of all indicator variables becomes an index for the SDG.

Example of index-building using factor analysis

For a more intuitive understanding of how factor and principal component analysis is used for index building, a study conducted on Seoul's (the ROK capital) urban development pathway using this methodology will be explained as an example. This study's goal was to identify the unique urban development pattern of Seoul using a set of 100 time-series indicators categorized into urbanization's 'preconditions,' 'enablers,' and 'outcomes.' Under these three categories, eight clusters[1] were predetermined. Within each data set, the Kaiser–Meyer–Olkin (KMO) test was performed for sampling adequacy. To identify whether the indicators measure the same aspect, or in other words to measure the internal consistency of the indicators, Cronbach's Coefficient Alpha was also calculated for each data set.

Factor analysis was then conducted for each cluster set and served as a method of identifying the most relevant variables by transforming correlated original variables into a new set of uncorrelated variables using the covariance matrix and/or correlation matrix. Once the irrelevant and overlapping variables were dropped, the original set of 100 variables was reduced to 54 variables, where each cluster included fewer than ten variables. Ultimately, each cluster would serve as its own index, in which the factor loadings of variables would become its weight in the index. Examples of the results from this process can be seen in Table 2.1 for four of the seven clusters.

These indexes not only serve as a metric to evaluate Seoul's unique urban development pathway across the years but also highlight the indicators (variables) that are the most influential based on empirical findings. For example, Seoul's network development was most influenced by bus transit, which is intuitively and theoretically accurate for Seoul.

When the index was used to see the time-variant progress of the city, interesting results were found by which to make conclusions about and see implications of Seoul's urban development pathway. As shown in Figure 2.1, the results of the 'Network' and 'Environment' clusters were charted using the raw data, weighted based on the cluster index, with the base year at 2010.

The network graph shows that Seoul's network has continued to grow (the indicators are all positive variables). Meanwhile, for the environment cluster, most indicators were negative variables, creating a downward sloping line that shows

Table 2.1 Index development of clusters

Precondition		Utilities		Network		Government	
Dependence ratio	20.60%	Electricity supply	6.50%	Road (km)	7.10%	Local bond	13.10%
Population	17.90%	Renewable energy	14.40%	Auto transit	11.90%	Citizen per one public servant	14.70%
Persons per household	17.80%	City gas sales	13.90%	Bus transit	12.50%	Seoul budget	13.70%
Lowest temp	0.70%	Petroleum sales	7.00%	Subway transit	7.80%	Enviro budget	15.80%
Green area	20.00%	Water pipe length	7.40%	Taxi transit	11.50%	Social budget	15.80%
Rivers + streams	8.70%	Water leakage rate	12.90%	Flight passengers	12.00%	Infra budget	16.50%
# of trees	14.30%	Household water	13.20%	AirMail freight	9.10%	Culture art budget	10.40%
		Waste collection	11.70%	Parking lots	7.50%		
		Citizen burden of waste cost	13.00%	Bike lane	9.80%		
				Internet use	10.60%		

Source: Jung (2016).

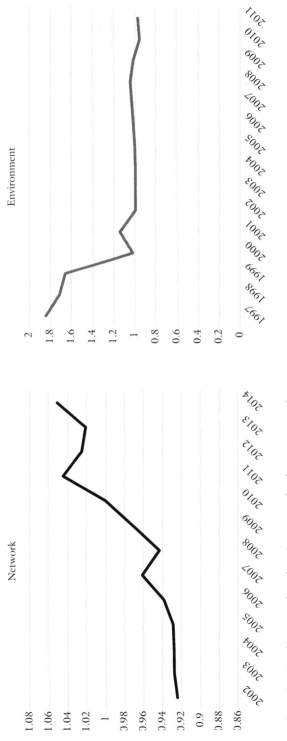

Figure 2.1 Seoul's network and environment development over time

the environmental quality improved. The rapidly improved environment of Seoul can be explained by action taken in July 1997 by the Ministry of Environment that designated Seoul, Incheon, and other parts of Gyeonggi-do Province as air quality control areas, pursuant to the National Clean Air Conservation Act. Additionally, the Seoul Local Air Environment Standard was created in March 1998. These actions drastically improved air quality and the overall environment of Seoul.

This study on Seoul's urban development is meaningful, in that it empirically analyzes a megacity in Asia and can serve as a benchmark study for developing Asian countries still in the process of managing and growing their cities. This common methodology can also be used to analyze and cross-compare the case of other megacities in Northeast Asia (i.e. Incheon, Tokyo, Yokohama, Beijing, Shanghai), just as it can be applied to studies such as the one presented in this book.

The aim of this edited book is to create an index for each SDG that enables us to gain insight on the current overall progress of SDG implementation in the ROK. In our analysis, we have chosen to analyze only the environmentally focused SDGs. The SDGs analyzed using a common quantitative method in this study are as follows.

> SDG 6. Ensure availability and sustainable management of water and sanitation for all.
> SDG 7. Ensure access to affordable, reliable, sustainable, and modern energy for all.
> SDG 8. Promote sustained, inclusive, and sustainable economic growth, full and productive employment, and decent work for all.
> SDG 11. Make cities and human settlements inclusive, safe, resilient, and sustainable.

The following goals were evaluated without using factor analysis due to the less quantitative nature of the indicators.

> SDG 13. Take urgent action to combat climate change and its impacts.
> SDG 17. Strengthen the means of implementation and revitalize the Global Partnership for Sustainable Development.

Note

1 'Preconditions' was a cluster on its own; the 'enabler' category included *government, utilities, network*, and *education* clusters; 'outcomes' included *economic, environment*, and *social* clusters.

References

Burt, C. 1909. "Experimental Tests of General Intelligence." *British Journal of Psychology 1904–1920*, 3.1–2: 94–177.

Carey, N. 1914. "Factors in the Mental Processes of School Children." *British Journal of Psychology 1904–1920*, 7.3: 453–490.

Fabrigar, L. R. et al. 1999. "Evaluating the Use of Exploratory Factor Analysis in Psychological Research." *Psychological Methods*, 4.3: 272.

Harman, H. H. 1976. *Modern Factor Analysis*. Chicago: University of Chicago Press.

Hwang, S., and N. Kim. 2016. "Analysis on Life-Quality and Supporting Policy for Adolescents for Accomplishment of Sustainable Development Goals." Report of ROK Institute for Youth Development: 1–415.

Joshi et al. 2015. "Improving Governance for the Post-2015 Sustainable Development Goals: Scenario Forecasting the Next 50 Years." *World Development*, 70: 286–302.

Jung, T. Y. 2016. "Indexing Seoul's Urban Development Pathway Using Factor Analysis (PCA)." Presentation at KU–KIST Green School Global Conference on Climate Change, Jeju, October 21.

Kaiser, H. F. 1958. "The Varimax Criterion for Analytic Rotation in Factor Analysis." *Psychometrika*, 23.3: 187–200.

Kim, J., and C. Sorin. 2016. "Pre-Service Teachers' Understanding of Education for Sustainable Development: Analysis of Reflection Journals Collected from the 'Early Childhood Education for Sustainable Development' Class." *Early Childhood Education Research and Review*, 20.5: 59–80.

Ludvigson, S. C., and Serena Ng. 2007. "The Empirical Risk – Return Relation: A Factor Analysis Approach." *Journal of Financial Economics*, 83.1: 171–222.

Maiz, I., et al. 2000. "Evaluation of Heavy Metal Availability in Polluted Soils by Two Sequential Extraction Procedures Using Factor Analysis." *Environmental Pollution*, 110.1: 3–9.

Mebratu, D. 1998. "Sustainability and Sustainable Development: Historical and Conceptual Review." *Environmental Impact Assessment Review*, 18.6: 493–520.

Nardo, M. et al. 2005. "A Tools for Composite Indicators Building. Joint Research Centre European Commission." Institute for the Protection and Security of the Citizen Econometrics and Statistical Support to Antifraud Unit, Ispra.

Nicoletti, G., S. Scarpetta, and O. Boylaud. 2000. "Summary Indicators of Product Market Regulation with an Extension to Employment Protection Legislation." *OECD Economics Department Working Papers*, No. 226, OECD Publishing.

Park, Y. 2016. "Search of Monitoring System for Implementation of Sustainable Development Goals." *Journal of International Development Cooperation*, 2: 45–76.

Pearce, D. 1988. "Economics, Equity and Sustainable Development." *Futures*, 20.6: 598–605.

Prakash, M. et al. 2016. "Preliminary US Cities Sustainable Development Goals Index." Sustainable Development Solutions Network.

Sachs, J. D. 2012. "From Millennium Development Goals to Sustainable Development Goals." *The Lancet*, 379.9832: 2206–2211.

Sachs, J., Schmidt-Traub, G., Kroll, C., Durand-Delacre, D., and Teksoz, K. 2017. "*SDG Index and Dashboards Report 2017.*" New York: Bertelsmann Stiftung and Sustainable Development Solutions Network (SDSN). Accessed July 26, 2017. http://unsdsn.org/resources/publications/sdg-index-and-dashboards-report-2017/

Spearman, C. 1904a. "General Intelligence: Objectively Determined and Measured." *The American Journal of Psychology*, 15.2: 201–292.

Spearman, C. 1904b. "The Proof and Measurement of Association Between Two Things." *The American Journal of Psychology*, 15.1: 72–101.

Tarantola, S., M. Saisana, and A. Saltelli. 2002. "Internal Market Index 2002: Technical Details of the Methodology." European Commission Joint Research Centre, Italy.

Vincent, D. F. 1953. "The Origin and Development of Factor Analysis." *Applied Statistics*: 107–117.

3 Brief overview of sustainable development policies

Sung Jin Kang, Yong Jun Baek, and Yoon Jin Kang

Introduction

From the early 1960s to the late 1990s, the ROK has achieved remarkable economic growth. Before the 1960s, the ROK was a war-ridden country receiving aid from the international community. However, successful export-oriented industrialization policies transformed the underdeveloped country into a modern industrialized economy (Moon 2006). Although rapid economic growth improved the standard of living greatly, it came at a high price. The hard push on economic development led to the negligence of environmental problems and pollutions that continued until the 1990s.

While the ROK government focused on economic growth, the international community began discussions on the adverse impacts of the economic growth-oriented model. In 1972, the Club of Rome published *Limits to Growth*, which argued that economic growth is putting a heavy strain on the environment; thus, countries should pursue a zero-growth strategy to protect the environment (Meadows et al. 1992). Although this shocking claim could be accepted by already developed countries, it was not welcomed by developing countries that urgently needed economic development. Despite the different perspectives, this report triggered the initial discourse on the limits of traditional growth models.

While the international community was building upon the discourse on sustainable development, the ROK was slow to make the transition. Since the early 1960s, four decades of accelerated economic growth led to the deterioration of natural scenic sites and ecosystems and the rapid increase of environmental pollution. Only after a series of environmental disasters did society realize the pressing environmental issues and began to show interest.

Initially, the local government actively participated in implementing sustainable development policies. At the Earth Summit in 1992, the local governments agreed to develop and implement policies according to Local Agenda 21 (LA21). In 1996, the Ministry of Environment (MOE) was appointed as the focal point for establishing and coordinating the nation-wide action plan for Rio Agenda 21 (ROK 2009). The ROK government eagerly focused on achieving sustainable development by establishing the Presidential Commission of Sustainable Development (PCSD) in 2000 and enacting several laws to guide the national sustainable development strategy. However, coordinating and achieving sustainable development is not an easy task as it encompasses three broad dimensions: economy; society; and environment.

This chapter presents the ROK government's effort to pursue sustainable development over the past two decades. A series of legal frameworks were established and the interests of multiple stakeholders have been rigorously coordinated by the ROK government to achieve SDGs. Following a historical overview of ROK's efforts for implementing sustainable development, this chapter concludes with policy implications for the new administration, which bears the heavy burden of nurturing the heritage of past governments.

Brief overview of sustainable development policies

Pre-establishment of national sustainable development strategies

Early environmental concerns were brought forth by rural residents seeking monetary compensation from adverse health and degradation of the land caused by industrial pollution. By the 1980s, the environmental movement had made a significant shift towards a broader anti-pollution base. The democratization of the late 1980s marked a shift in the governance approach from protesting industrial corporations and autocratic government-oriented problem solving towards a more conciliatory approach towards mainstream environmentalism that focused on advocacy and collaboration with government and industry to influence public policy (Ku 2009).

Sustainable development in the ROK has a history that spans over two decades, starting with involvement at the 1992 Earth Summit. The discourse started with a bottom-up approach in which local governments and civil society organizations (CSO) collaborated on LA21 as a part of achieving local autonomy and promoting the environmental movement. The result of these efforts was the establishment of the Local Councils for Sustainable Development in 1995 (ROK 2016b). This early success of the environmental movement was recognized as a successful global case at the 2002 World Summit on Sustainable Development (Yoon 2016).

As of 1995, the local governments had developed policies to implement Rio Agenda 21, and a year later, the MOE was selected to establish and coordinate a nation-wide action plan for Rio Agenda 21 (ROK 2009). Since then, several Local Commissions of Sustainable Development (LCSDs) have been established by the local governments; by 2016, 100 out of 243 local governments had set up LCSD (Cho-Ahn et al. 2017). Furthermore, the ROK government enacted several laws and established commissions to oversee the sustainable development efforts. The important dates are presented in Figure 3.1.

In 2000, President Dae-jung Kim established the PCSD, and the National Environmental Vision for the New Millennium was implemented as the national master plan for sustainable development. The PCSD was responsible for coordinating

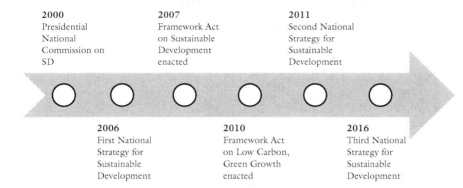

Figure 3.1 Milestones of ROK's sustainable development efforts
Source: Author's design.

and designing nation-wide sustainable development policies and strategies. Furthermore, reports from special committees were compiled to develop sectoral strategies and harmonize the different perspectives of various related ministries (ROK 2016b).

First National Strategy for Sustainable Development (2006–2010)

In 2005, President Moo-hyun Roh announced the National Vision for Sustainable Development to pursue a national growth that balances the three dimensions of sustainable development: economy; society; and environment. Then, in the following year, the PCSD published the First National Strategy for Sustainable Development (NSSD) and its implementation plans. For the four decades prior to the First NSSD, the national development plan was focused on economic development, while efforts for environmental preservation and social integration were almost non-existent. Therefore, the ROK government realized the necessity of developing the environment and social dimensions along with the economy, which was reflected in the First NSSD.

The First NSSD was based on the concept of sustainable development to meet the needs of the present without compromising the ability of the next generation. Based on the Sustainable Development Act, national strategies are to be established every five years for over 20 years (PCSD 2006). The First NSSD had four main strategies of sustainability: natural resource management; social integration and national health; sustainable economic growth; and coping with climate change and environmental conservation. These strategies were further broken down into 48 tasks.

The implementation tasks of the First NSSD were undertaken through two stages; first, they were selected from the 2002 World Summit on Sustainable Development;

and second, they were revised for the context of the ROK. Additionally, the implementation of the plan was evaluated annually at the department level and was reported to the PCSD, which played a critical role in mediating between stakeholders and coordinating inter-department involvement with both government and non-government actors in the development of a national strategy (Huh 2014).

The emphasis on civic participation in the First NSSD reflected not only the importance of the social dimension of sustainable development, but also the presidential commitment towards participatory governance. The PCSD and First NSSD brought together the policy recommendations from 22 government departments, which were reviewed in consultation with civic experts and academics. Before the final declaration, a public review process was conducted as well (KEI 2014).

Furthermore, the ROK government's strong desire to contribute to the international effort on sustainable development can be seen from the enactment of the Framework Act on Sustainable Development in 2007. Due to the enactment, the legal foundation of PCSD was changed from a Presidential Decree to the Framework Act on Sustainable Development, which greatly enhanced the authority and status of the PCSD (ROK 2016b).

In 2008, with the incoming of President Myung-bak Lee's administration, a new approach towards sustainable development was carried out under the new national vision of 'Low Carbon, Green Growth.' In 2010, the Framework Act on Low Carbon, Green Growth was enacted. Based on this law, the Presidential Commission on Green Growth (PCGG) was established with the purpose of creating environmentally friendly industries and jobs. Accordingly, the PCSD became the Commission of Sustainable Development (CSD), which is a ministerial committee under MOE. Afterwards, PCGG published the First Five-Year Plan for Green Growth (2009–2013) with the purpose of pursuing the highest level of low carbon green growth in the ROK.

The First Five-Year Plan for Green Growth was based on the green growth vision of ROK becoming the seventh and then the fifth most advanced green country by 2020 and 2050, respectively. In order to achieve this vision, three strategies and ten policies were selected. The first strategy is climate change adaption and energy independence, with the goals of efficient reduction of greenhouse gases (GHG), reduction of oil reliance, and the improvement of climate change adaptation capacity. The second strategy is seeking a new growth model with the goals of developing and commercializing green technologies, developing environmentally friendly industries, restructuring the current industrial organization, and creating a foundation for a green economy. The third strategy focuses on improving the standard of living and becoming a role model in green growth among the international community (Joint Work of Relevant Ministries 2009).

Second National Strategy for Sustainable Development (2011–2015)

In 2011, the Second NSSD was established based on the evaluation of the First NSSD. Several areas for improvement were identified, and eventually four strategies and 25 tasks were set for Second NSSD. The goals are to improve social equity, to improve the income of vulnerable classes, to create more jobs, to implement a new growth paradigm for efficient use of natural resources, and to achieve sustainable development through qualitative growth (Joint Work of Relevant Ministries 2011).

During President Lee's administration, the national vision was focused on green growth, which resulted in national resources being geared towards achieving green growth. Reflecting the belief that previous economic growth was achieved at the cost of the environment, the Global Green Growth Institute (GGGI) was established as a non-governmental organization (NGO) in 2010. Later, the organization would convene as an international organization with the support of 18 member countries in 2012. GGGI framed environmental challenges as economic policy issues, taking a more expansive look at how countries can address development and environmental concerns through more efficient use of resources based within the context of individual countries. GGGI convenes local partners and governments with academia, CSOs, industry, and other governments to share the know-how of successful best practices around the world (GGGI 2015).

In 2014, the Second Five-Year Plan for Green Growth was published under a new vision of creating a lively society through harmonious development of the economy and environment. While the First Green Growth Plan was focused on setting the ground for green growth, the Second Green Growth Plan focuses on achieving outcomes. Based on the revision of the First Green Growth plan, the targets of each strategy have been reduced; thus, there are three strategies and five implementation policies (Joint Work of Relevant Ministries 2014). The first strategy is setting the foundation for low carbon economic and social structures. The second strategy is to achieve a creative economy through integration of green technology and ICT. The third strategy is to establish a safe living environment from climate change.

In 2015, while the ROK government was working towards achieving sustainable development, the UN members gathered to agree on the 2030 Agenda for Sustainable Development. This ambitious agenda contained 17 goals and 169 targets, going much further than the MDGs by targeting entrenched sources of poverty and creating the conditions for sustainable growth and development for both developing and developed countries. The ROK has made commitments to incorporate SDGs into the national discourse in order to create a framework for domestic and international implementation (ROK 2016b).

The primary ministries responsible for the implementation of SDGs are currently the MOE, Ministry of Foreign Affairs (MOFA), the Office for Government Policy Coordination (OGPC), and Statistics Korea (ROK 2016a). The responsible government bodies are working across sectors and with CSOs to engage in multi-stakeholder discussions in the development of strategies and policies for SDGs.

Third National Strategy for Sustainable Development (2016–2035)

In 2016, the Third NSSD was established and aligned to meet the SDGs. Thus, the Third NSSD was developed with the vision of harmonious development of environment, economy, and society. In order to achieve this vision, four main strategies, 13 sub-strategies, and 50 tasks were selected. Another key characteristic of the Third NSSD is the alignment to meet SDGs that suit local conditions, such as reduction of GHG emissions and increasing the portion of renewable energy, equality of sexes, and disaster control (Joint Work of Relevant Ministries 2016).

The first strategy is to preserve a healthy land and environment, which has three sub-strategies – securing high-quality environmental services, expanding the value of ecosystem services, and guaranteeing clean water – and ten tasks for implementation. The second strategy is to create an integrated safe society where social polarization is reduced, health management system is improved, and the social safety net is strengthened. The third strategy is to create inclusive economic innovation, where inclusive growth is encouraged, policies for recycling of resources is strengthened, and an environmentally friendly and safe energy system is created. The fourth strategy is to become a globally responsible country by improving support to developing countries and actively responding to climate change.

Under President Geun-hye Park's administration, green growth is no longer a top priority; the priority has shifted to the third goal of an inclusive creative economy. The creative economy goal has 12 policy targets that seek to create more sustainable economic growth by nurturing 'job expansion' and 'inclusive growth' in new environmentally friendly industries (Chung 2016). Efforts are being made in areas that bring together ICT and green technologies, including the development of and training for skills linked to green technology industries (OECD 2017).

Furthermore, the last goal for global prosperity focuses on international cooperation in strengthening partnerships for achieving SDGs. The eight policy targets focus on integrating international cooperation and development support as the primary tool for the ROK's global implementation of SDGs. Formally an aid recipient, the country ascended into the OECD Development Assistance Committee (DAC) in 2010, becoming an aid donor country. Under the Second Strategic Plan for International Development Cooperation (2016–2020), SDGs are integrated into the ODA policy vision (ROK 2016b). Initiatives such as the Better Life for Girls, Saemaul Undong for rural development, Scientific and Technological Innovation for Better Life, and Safe Life for All offer innovative pathways for sharing the knowledge and experience of the ROK to enhance the effectiveness of ODA in the SDGs period and beyond (ROK 2016a).

The country also has numerous acts, policies, and plans, in addition to mid- and long-term policy plans and frameworks that correspond to the SDGs. These policies and programs include the GHG emissions trading scheme and the Three-Year Plan for Economic Innovation, which aims to reform the public sector, promote a 'creative economy,' and boost domestic demand (ROK 2016b).

Table 3.1 List of plans and policies corresponding to the 17 SDGs

Sustainable Development Goals	Relevant government policies
Goal 1. End poverty in all its forms everywhere	• The Second Five-Year Plan for Green Growth • The Fifth Comprehensive Mid-term Plan for Environmental Protection • The Fourth Comprehensive Plan for National Environment • The Three-Year Plan for Economic Innovation • The Third Plan for Low Fertility and Ageing Society
Goal 2. End hunger, achieve food security and improved nutrition, and promote sustainable agriculture	• The Second Five-Year Plan for Green Growth • National Climate Change Adaptation Measures • The Third National Biodiversity Strategy • The Three-Year Plan for Economic Innovation
Goal 3. Ensure healthy lives and promote well-being for all at all ages	• The Second Five-Year Plan for Green Growth • The Fifth Comprehensive Mid-term Plan for Environmental Protection • The Fourth Comprehensive Plan for National Environment • The Second Master Plan for Public Transportation • The Three-Year Plan for Economic Innovation • The Fourth Health Plan
Goal 4. Ensure inclusive and equitable quality education and promote lifelong learning opportunities for all	• The Second Five-Year Plan for Green Growth • The Sixth Plan for Industrial Technology Innovation • The Plan for Realization of Creative Economy • Comprehensive Plan for Environment and Health • The Three-Year Plan for Economic Innovation • The Fourth Comprehensive Plan of Policies for Persons with Disabilities
Goal 5. Achieve gender equality and empower all women and girls	• The Sixth Plan for Industrial Technology Innovation • The Fourth Master Plan for Women's Policy • The Three-Year Plan for Economic Innovation
Goal 6. Ensure availability and sustainable management of water and sanitation for all	• National Climate Change Adaptation Plan • The Fifth Comprehensive Mid-term Plan for Environmental Protection • The Fourth Comprehensive Plan for National Environment • Revised Plan of the Fourth Comprehensive Plan for National Territory

(*Continued*)

Table 3.1 (Continued)

Sustainable Development Goals	Relevant government policies
Goal 7. Ensure access to affordable, reliable, sustainable, and modern energy for all	• The Second Five-Year Plan for Green Growth • The Fourth Master Plan for New Renewable Energy • The Second Master Plan for Energy • National Climate Change Adaptation Plan
Goal 8. Promote sustained, inclusive and sustainable economic growth, full and productive employment and decent work for all	• The Three-Year Plan for Economic Innovation • The Second Five-Year Plan for Green Growth • The Sixth Plan for Industrial Technology Innovation • The Plan for Realization of Creative Economy
Goal 9. Build resilient infrastructure, promote inclusive and sustainable industrialization and foster innovation	• The Second Five-Year Plan for Green Growth • The Second Master Plan for Energy • The Sixth Plan for Industrial Technology Innovation • The Three-Year Plan for Economic Innovation
Goal 10. Reduce inequality within and among states	• The Second Master Plan for International Development Cooperation • The Second Five-Year Plan for Green Growth • The Second Master Plan for Energy • The Fifth Comprehensive Mid-term Plan for Environmental Protection • The Third National Biodiversity Strategy • The Plan for Realization of Creative Economy • The Fourth Comprehensive Plan of Policies for Persons with Disabilities
Goal 11. Make cities and human settlements inclusive, safe, resilient and sustainable	• The Second Master Plan for Public Transportation • The Second Five-Year Plan for Green Growth • National Climate Change Adaptation Plan • The Fifth Comprehensive Mid-term Plan for Environmental Protection • The Revised Plan of the Fourth Comprehensive Plan for National Territory • Guideline for Evaluation of Sustainability and Living Infrastructure of Cities
Goal 12. Ensure sustainable consumption and production patterns	• The Second Five-Year Plan for Green Growth • The Fourth Master Plan for New Renewable Energy • The Second Master Plan for Energy • The First Master Plan for Resource Circulation • The Fifth Comprehensive Mid-term Plan for Environmental Protection

Goal	Plans
Goal 13. Take urgent action to combat climate change and its impact	• The Second Five-Year Plan for Green Growth • The Second Master Plan for Energy • The Fifth Comprehensive Mid-term Plan for Environmental Protection • National Climate Change Adaptation Plan • The Third National Biodiversity Strategy
Goal 14. Conserve and sustainably use the oceans, seas, and marine resources for sustainable development	• The Revised Plan of the Fourth Comprehensive Plan for National Territory • The Fourth Comprehensive Plan for Marine Environmental Protection • The Five-Year Basic Plan for Fisheries Resource Management
Goal 15. Protect, restore and promote sustainable use of territorial ecosystems, sustainably manage forests, combat desertification, and halt and reverse land degradation, and halt biodiversity loss	• The Second Five-Year Plan for Green Growth • National Climate Change Adaptation Plan • The Fifth Comprehensive Mid-term Plan for Environmental Protection • The Third National Biodiversity Strategy
Goal 16. Promote peaceful and inclusive societies for sustainable development	• The Second Five-Year Plan for Green Growth • The Fifth Comprehensive Mid-term Plan for Environmental Protection • The Three-Year Plan for Economic Innovation
Goal 17. Strengthen the means of implementation and revitalizing the global partnership for sustainable development	• The Second Five-Year Plan for Green Growth • The Sixth Plan for Industrial Technology Innovation • National Climate Change Adaptation Plan • The Fifth Comprehensive Mid-term Plan for Environmental Protection • The Third National Biodiversity Strategy • The Plan for Realization of Creative Economy • The Revised Plan of the Fourth Comprehensive Plan for National Territory

Source: ROK (2016b).

Institutional framework to achieve sustainable development

Commission on sustainable development

In the early 1990s, LA21 was established as a strategy to achieve sustainable development from the grass-roots level. Various opinions from diverse stakeholders, ranging from local citizens to NGOs, could be integrated into the sustainable development policies. In 1994, the first pilot program was introduced in Ansan city, which quickly spread to different cities across the country. A partnership among the community leaders, local communities, and NGOs in various cities was formed to coordinate their efforts for LA21 (MOE 2006). Afterwards, in 1996, the ROK government assigned the MOE as a focal point to coordinate the sustainable development policies and strategies in the country.

National institutions of the PCSD and the Local Sustainability Alliance of Korea (LSAK) were established in 2000 to govern the activities at the local and national level. In 2007, legislative support was given to the PCSD with the enactment of the Framework Act on Sustainable Development. The legislation took over five years of consensus building with diverse stakeholders in government, business, and civil society. It requires the government to develop a 20-year strategy for sustainable development and to create an action plan every five years. The appointed PCSD chair was recommended by civil society, and the commission members included affiliates from government, civil society, and business (Yoon 2016). The LSAK provided an institutional platform for a national network of LCSDs, supporting capacity building in policies and implementation through forums, conferences, and best-practices awards in collaboration with the MOE (ROK 2016b).

After the establishment of the Framework Act for Green Growth, the PCSD became a ministerial level committee under the MOE. Until 2010, the PCSD and LCSD had been communicating and working closely to design sustainable development from the grass-roots level. The LCSD was particular important as it played a key role in implementing SDGs at the local level. The LCSDs have been developing a process to further promote sustainable development over the last 20 years, and currently implement policies directly related to the SDGs at the local level by analyzing and aligning existent projects in the context of the SDGs.

The LCSD is an organization where the local government, CSO, and private sector gather to set and implement sustainable development plans. The organizational structure includes the general assembly, delegation with representatives from local government, CSO and private sector, steering committee, and the secretariat. Agenda Implementation Sub-Committees consist of around 100~150 members, and the members of the steering committee are selected by the sub-committees. However, after the PCSD was degraded to CSD, the communication and cooperation among the two organizations has been minimal. This is largely due to the organizational obstacle where the channel of communication is controlled by the Environmental Cooperation Team under the MOE, leading to limited cooperation (CSD 2016).

Green growth committee

In 2009, President Lee proclaimed a new vision for national development based on low carbon and green growth. The new president advocated green growth with a focus on the win–win strategy of economic growth without environmental damage (Lee and Yun 2011). The PCGG was launched in 2009 in support of the National Strategy for Green Growth. There are four subcommittees under the PCGG: Green Growth Strategy; Climate Change Countermeasure; Energy; and Green Technology and Industry. The subcommittees of the PCGG have been reorganized over time, starting with three subcommittees in the first phase (2009) that were reorganized into four subcommittees in the second phase (2010) and third phase (2011). The secretariat is also established to undertake administrative duties and support the work of the PCGG.

The Framework Act on Low Carbon, Green Growth provides a legal foundation for the establishment of the PCGG. The enactment of the law has three major objectives. First, promote sustainable development by effectively dealing with climate change and energy issues. Second, establish a governance system to implement green growth, through the PCGG. Lastly, promote low-carbon green growth by establishing various institutions (GGGI 2015).

Furthermore, to enforce green growth initiatives in local regions, the local governments were to establish Local Green Growth Commissions (LGGC). This organizational structure is similar to that of the PCSD and LCSD. The role of LGGC is to coordinate and promote green growth initiatives at the local level. As of 2013, the government organizational restructuring moved PCGG from a presidential committee to prime ministerial committee.

Green growth initiatives can complement sustainable development, but the existing green growth strategies alone are not sufficient for achieving sustainable development. The green growth strategies do not pay enough attention to the social aspect of sustainable development. Social development issues range from absolute and relative poverty, income inequality, the enhancement of capabilities, and social integration to various kinds of social conflicts (Kang 2012). In the near future, green growth should transform itself as a comprehensive development strategy that can deal with many different issues. As the first step, the ROK government should merge the PCGG and the CSD, which are pursuing similar goals separately without coordinating their efforts.

Conclusion

This chapter provides an overview of sustainable development policies and the institutional framework established by each administration to achieve sustainable development. Since the 1960s, the ROK has experienced unprecedented economic growth, but unlike international communities, little focus has been given to social and environmental issues, which are the two dimensions of sustainable development. As an underdeveloped country, top policy priority was given to economic growth, and discussions on environmental and social development were largely neglected.

However, since the Rio conference in 1992, the ROK has been actively participating in international discussions on sustainable development. As previously mentioned, by 1995 the local governments had developed policies to implement Rio Agenda 21, and a year later, the MOE was selected to establish and coordinate a nation-wide action plan for Rio Agenda 21.

In 2000, as the local governments were working independently, President Dae-jung Kim established PCSD as the head committee to govern overall sustainable development activities within the country, and already three NSSD had been published. Also, the government's strong desire to contribute to the international effort on sustainable development can be seen from the enactment of Framework Act on Sustainable Development in 2007, which was later superseded by the Act on Sustainable Development in 2010.

In order to deal with critical environmental issues, the PCGG was established in 2008, and two Five-Year Plans for Green Growth were published. The government has rigorously pursued sustainable development for the past two decades. However, despite various government efforts, there are several areas to overcome to achieve sustainable development.

First, there are still many obstacles to overcome to solve the environmental issues at stake. Historically, the manufacturing sector led rapid economic growth, which resulted in high levels of GHG emissions. Currently, as the service sector of the economy is growing, GHG emissions are expected to reduce accordingly, but the emission level is still showing an increasing trend. In other words, the decoupling of GHG emissions and economic growth has yet to occur in the ROK. The reason is that economic growth is still heavily reliant on heavy and chemical industries, which were key drivers for past economic growth. Therefore, the ROK faces a difficult challenge of pursuing environmentally friendly economic growth by transforming heavy and chemical industries into low carbon industries.

Second, the ROK government has put much effort towards sustainable development, but the results of these efforts are not clearly visible. In other words, monitoring and assessment are required to check whether the goals have been met. For example, the UN is providing various indicators on SDGs that can be used to perform detailed assessments on current government plans. The quality of the national plans should be guaranteed through periodic assessments. Therefore, as a part of the assessment, the following chapters examine the ROK government's achievements in selected SDGs.

References

Cho-Ahn, C., O. Kwon, E. Kim, M. Lee, and D. K. H. Yoon. 2017. "Korean Civil Society Report for 2017 HLPF on Sustainable Development. Seoul: Korea Civil Society Network on SDGs." Accessed September 2, 2017. https://

sustainabledevelopment.un.org/index.php?page=view&type=111&nr=14506&menu=138&template=1706
Chung, S. Y. 2016. "The Localization of the SDGs in South Korea." Presentation at Sustainable Development Goals in Asia and Europe. Localising the 2030 Agenda for Sustainable Development, Bucharest, Romania. Accessed September 20, 2017. www.asef.org/projects/themes/sustainable-development/3761-sustainable-development-goals-in-asia-and-europe-localising-the-2030-agenda-for-sustainable-development
Commission of Sustainable Development (CSD). 2016. "Report on National Sustainable Development ('12~'14): Assessment of National Strategy of Sustainable Development and Evaluation Indicators." [In Korean.] Accessed July 28, 2017. http://webbook.me.go.kr/DLi-File/091/023/012/5618404.pdf
Global Green Growth Institute (GGGI). 2015. "Korea's Green Growth Experience: Process, Outcomes and Lessons Learned." Accessed July 30, 2017. http://webbook.me.go.kr/DLi-File/091/023/012/5618404.pdf
Huh, T. 2014. "Dynamics and Discourse of Governance for Sustainable Development in South Korea: Convergent or Divergent." *Journal of Environmental Policy and Planning* 16.1: 95–115. doi:10.1080/1523908X.2013.819779
Joint Work of Relevant Ministries. 2009. "Five-Year Plan for Green Growth (2009–2013)." [In Korean]. Accessed August 27, 2017. www.greengrowth.go.kr/download/0713-2full.pdf
Joint Work of Relevant Ministries. 2011. "Second National Strategy for Sustainable Development: 2011–2015." [In Korean]. Accessed August 20, 2017. http://ncsd.go.kr/app/board/infoAcademicData/view.do?bbsSeq=5157
Joint Work of Relevant Ministries. 2014. "Second Five-Year Plan for Green Growth." [In Korean]. Accessed August 27, 2017. www.greengrowth.go.kr/download/140603-2full.pdf
Joint Work of Relevant Ministries. 2016. "Third National Strategy for Sustainable Development: 2016–2035." [In Korean]. Accessed August 20, 2017. http://ncsd.go.kr/app/board/infoResearchReport/view.do?bbsSeq=7177
Kang, S. J. 2012. "Green Growth and Sustainable Development in G20: Performance and Prospects." In *The International Monetary System, Energy and Sustainable Development*, edited by S. J. Kang and Y. C. Park, 273–293. New York: Routledge.
Korea Environment Institute (KEI). 2014. "Measuring Progress for Sustainable Development." *Greenable Volume 2, 2014.* Seoul: KEI.
Ku, D. 2009. "The Emergence of Ecological Alternative Movement in Korea." *Korean Social Science Journal*, 2: 1–32.
Lee, J., and S. Yun. 2011. "A Comparative Study of Governance in State Management: Focusing on the Roh Moo-hyun Government and the Lee Myung-Bak Government." *Development and Society*,40.2: 289–318.
Meadows, D. H., D. L. Meadows, and J. Randers. 1992. *Beyond the Limits: Global Collapse or a Sustainable Future*. London: Earthscan.
Ministry of Environment (MOE). 2006. "Choice for Sustainable Development: Local Agenda 21 in Korea." Accessed September 22, 2017. www.me.go.kr/home/file/readDownloadFile.do?fileId=2269&fileSeq=1
Moon, T. H. 2006. "Sustainable Development in Korea, Key Issues and Government Response." *International Review of Public Administration*, 11.1: 1–18. doi:10.1080/12294659.2006.10805074

Organisation for Economic Co-operation and Development (OECD). 2017. *OECD Environmental Performance Reviews: Korea 2017*. Paris: OECD.

Presidential Commission of Sustainable Development (PCSD). 2006. "National Strategy for Sustainable Development." Accessed August 20, 2017. http://ncsd.go.kr/app/board/infoResearchReport/view.do

Republic of Korea (ROK). 2009. "18th–19th Session of the Commission on Sustainable Development (CSD): National Report." Accessed August 2, 2017. www.un.org/esa/dsd/dsd_aofw_ni/ni_pdfs/NationalReports/korea/full_report.pdf

Republic of Korea (ROK). 2016a. "2016 National Voluntary Review – Executive Summary." The Government of the Republic of Korea. Accessed August 2, 2017. https://sustainabledevelopment.un.org/content/documents/10446Executive%20Summary%20Review_ROK.pdf

Republic of Korea (ROK). 2016b. "Year One of Implementing the SDGs in the Republic of Korea: From a Model of Development Success to a Vision for Sustainable Development." Accessed August 2, 2017. https://sustainabledevelopment.un.org/content/documents/10632National%20Voluntary%20Review%20Report%20(rev_final).pdf

Yoon, D. 2016. "Starting Strong on the SDGs in Asia: Readiness in South Korea." (Discussion Paper for the International Forum for Sustainable Asia and the Pacific). Japan: Institute for Global Environmental Strategies (IGES). Accessed September 12, 2017. http://pub.iges.or.jp/modules/envirolib/view.php?docid=6682

Part II
Analysis on SDGs in Korea

4 Goal 6: clean water

*Hyun Jung Park, Jaewan Kim, and
Thomas Taek Sung Kim*

Introduction

Water is indispensable for life on earth, so the term 'water for life' has been widely used to highlight the importance of water in sustaining the well-being of humans and ecosystems. This term was further recognized by the International Decade for Action 'Water for Life' proclaimed by the United Nations General Assembly in an effort to more effectively achieve internationally agreed upon water-related goals.[1] Water-related goals include access to water, sanitation, and hygiene, which are often considered as a group due to their interdependence in the context of public health and international development programs.[2] Environmental sustainability, one of the Millennium Development Goals (MDG 7), included two critical water-related targets: improved access to 'safe drinking water' and 'basic sanitation.'

Although there has been significant global progress on water-related goals, many challenges and problems remain.[3] Due to increasing climate change risks, there is growing instability in water resources and systems. Water demand associated with urbanization and economic growth rapidly deplete water resources. Water scarcity intensifies water conflict or weakens water cooperation. Socio-economic inequality and poverty make it difficult to achieve water-related goals, particularly adequate and equitable access to sanitation services. Due to technical and administrative difficulties in managing and controlling processes, the diffusion of water pollutants and hazardous materials are still key challenges in improving the water quality.

The 'Water for Life' decade ended in 2015. A post-2015 development agenda (Sustainable Development Goals: SDGs) was adopted, which included a comprehensive water goal (SDG 6) to address the remaining challenges and problems. Given that water and sanitation are critical for human life and dignity, environmental integrity, and sustainable development, the UN-Water highlights the critical importance of the water goal in achieving the SDGs and specifies the linkages between the water goal and other SDGs.[4]

The water goal (SDG 6) aims to "ensure availability and sustainable management of water and sanitation for all," which is assessed on six outcome targets (SDG 6.1–6.6) and two implementation targets (SDG 6.a and 6.b) as well as 11 indicators.[5] The SDG 6 is further elaborated in the economic, social, and

38 *Hyun Jung Park et al.*

environmental pillars of sustainable development. Affordability of water services (including drinking water, sanitation, and hygiene systems) and water-use efficiency are considered in the economic pillar. Universal and equitable access to water services and the implementation of water governance are considered in the social pillar, which focuses on local participation, international cooperation, and integrated management as well as the needs of vulnerable groups. The environmental pillar is directly related to water quality, water quantity, and water-related ecosystems, which are central to ensure availability and sustainability of water services. Focusing on the water goal, this chapter explores the progress made in the ROK.

Figure 4.1 is a timeline overview of water-related policies in the ROK. The upper flow includes the main laws governing water infrastructure, resources, pollution, and water-related ecosystems. The lower flow includes relevant policies significant to the implementation of the water goal in the ROK. Until the mid-1980s, water resources were considered as a driving force[7] for economic development and a key element for urbanization, so policies promoted the development of water supply systems and multi-purpose dams through significant investments. As much as 19% of the total investment of the first Economic Development Plan was spent for water resource development (Koun 2013). As shown in Figure 4.2, water coverage has been dramatically improved, along with rapid urbanization and economic growth. However, the policies focused on water supply could not effectively address flooding, water scarcity, and water pollution, so water policies after 1990 embraced a new paradigm that includes ecosystem conservation, quality management, and demand management.

By sharing the lessons and experiences of the implementation of the water goal in the ROK, this chapter aims to promote the global effort in achieving SDG 6. Therefore, it provides: (1) evidence-based information of progress on the water targets, including internationally proposed water indicators and additional national water indicators where needed; (2) a trend of progress on the water goal, based on factor analysis; and (3) conclusions for ways forward, which include policy implications and recommendations for achieving SDG 6.

1961	1961	1966	1966	1977	1990	1999
Water Supply &Waterworks Installation Act	River Act	Specific Multi-Purpose Dams Act	Sewage Act	Environment Conservation Act	Water Quality Environmental Conservation Act	Wetland Conservation Act

1962	1965	1972	1993	1995
Five-Year Economic Development Plan	Ten-Year Planon Comprehensive Water Resource Development	Ten-Year Comprehensive National Territorial Plan	Comprehensive Measures on Provision of Clean Water	Comprehensive Measures on Water Management

Figure 4.1 Water-related policy overview (1960–2000)[6]

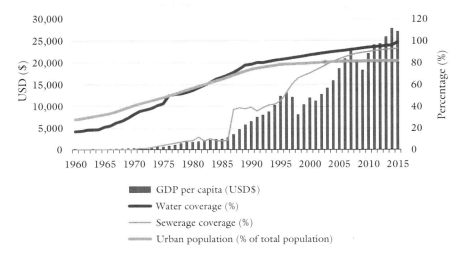

Figure 4.2 Trends of GDP, urbanization, water coverage and sanitation coverage

Source: Ministry of Environment. 1980, 1985, 1990, 1995, 2000, 2005, 2010, 2014, 2015. "The Statistics of Water Supply." [In Korean]. Accessed February through September 2017. http://stat.me.go.kr/nesis/mesp/knowledge/MorgueStatistical.do?task=I

Assessment of water-related SDG targets and indicators in the ROK context

Drinking water

Target 6.1: "By 2030, achieve universal and equitable access to safe and affordable drinking water for all."

"Drinking water" can be defined as piped or tap water on the premises that is treated and delivered in accordance with the rules and procedures of the ROK's Water Supply and Waterworks Installation Act and Management of Drinking Water Act. Tap water in the ROK generally meets[8] the national quality standards for drinking water, so it is considered safe to drink. "Safety" or "reliability" of drinking water systems can be further assessed by using data on interrupted water services due to aging water infrastructure or weather-related disasters. "Universal and equitable access to water" is assessed by using comparative data on regional installations of water supply systems. "Affordability" is assessed by using data on water tariffs relative to the financial ability of water users to pay.

The internationally proposed indicator for drinking water is the "percentage of population using safely managed drinking water services," which is redefined here as the "percentage of population with access to tap water on the premises" and simply called "water coverage." Figure 4.3 shows the trends of drinking water indicators covering the national, rural, and Seomjin River areas. As of 2015, 98.8% of Koreans have access to tap water on their premises. According to Korea Water and Wastewater Association (KWWA 2016), universal access to water services has been almost met through the strong leadership and top-down approach of the ROK government, particularly through the integration of the water sector into national economic development and a comprehensive National Water Resource Plan. Equitable access to drinking water has been continuously improved for the last ten years since waterworks facilities have been significantly expanded in rural area. However, the water supply rate in the least developed areas, such as agricultural and fishing villages in the Seomjin River area, is still relatively low (73.6% as of 2015).

Figure 4.4 displays interrupted water services during the period of 2007–2015. In terms of occurrence and duration of water cut-off, the safety of drinking water systems has improved. However, the credibility level of water quality is fairly low. Many Koreans doubt the quality of tap water and do not drink tap water directly. According to the Korean Ministry of Environment (MOE 2016b), water services are interrupted mainly due to aging water infrastructure that is associated with low quality drinking water (containing rust stain and odor), which results in the low level of water use for direct drinking (only 5.1%).

In the ROK, water prices are not expensive because the tariffs are set "below two percent of the family income for those in the lowest income decile" (KWWA 2016, p. 6), so affordability is not a significant issue in drinking water. Local governments have the primary responsibility in the development of local water pricing mechanisms. According to Koun (2013), the water pricing mechanisms

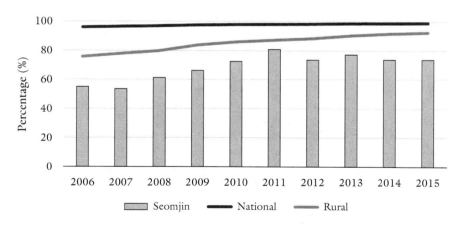

Figure 4.3 Population with access to tap water on premises (%)

Source: Ministry of Environment. 1980, 1985, 1990, 1995, 2000, 2005, 2010, 2014, 2015. "The Statistics of Water Supply." [In Korean]. Accessed February through September 2017. http://stat.me.go.kr/nesis/mesp/knowledge/MorgueStatistical.do?task=I

Goal 6: clean water 41

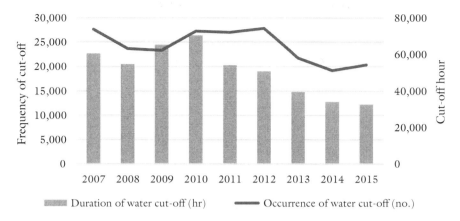

Figure 4.4 Interrupted water services
Source: Ministry of Environment. 1980, 1985, 1990, 1995, 2000, 2005, 2010, 2014, 2015. "The Statistics of Water Supply." [In Korean]. Accessed February through September 2017. http://stat.me.go.kr/nesis/mesp/knowledge/MorgueStatistical.do?task=I

only cover around 80% of the production costs, resulting in negative impacts on sustainable water management. Water prices of local governments in small towns are more expensive than those of metropolitan cities serviced by the bulk water supply system, so equitable access to affordable drinking water is not yet achieved (Lee 2016).[9]

Sanitation and hygiene

Target 6.2: "By 2030, achieve access to adequate and equitable sanitation and hygiene for all and end open defecation, paying special attention to the needs of women and girls and those in vulnerable situations."

"Access to adequate sanitation" is defined as access to public sewerage facilities and services that are installed and managed in accordance with the rules and procedures of the Korean Sewage Act for the Treatment of Sewage and Excreta. In the ROK, the population living within the 'designated sewerage treatment area' has full access to the public sewerage systems and wastewater treatment facilities, while those living outside of the designated area have limited access to public sanitation services. "Equitable sanitation" is assessed by using data on comparative access to sanitation systems in urban and rural areas, particularly focusing on the population living outside of the 'designated sewerage treatment area.'

"Open defecation" is not a problem in the ROK as nearly every household has toilet facilities. Also, many public toilets are available for free due to public toilet improvement policies promoted and implemented nationally.[10] "The needs of women and girls and those in vulnerable situations" can be further considered in the context of public toilet service.

Hygiene is more associated with personal habits or behaviors such as hand washing, bathing, and tooth brushing, so the key issue of hygiene is the impacts on health.[11] In the ROK, "access to adequate hygiene" has been improved though hygiene education for children and nation-wide hygiene campaigns and facility investments that were particularly promoted in preparation for international sporting events such as the 1986 Asian Games, 1988 Olympic Games, and 2002 FIFA World Cup. However, it is difficult to obtain the reliable trend data of hygiene, so it is not further assessed here.

The internationally proposed indicator for sanitation is the "percentage of population using safely managed sanitation services including a hand washing facility with soap and water," which can be redefined for the ROK as the "percentage of population living in the designated sewerage treatment area" simply called "sewerage coverage." According to the Korean Population and Housing Census (2015), nearly every household has a toilet (more than 99.9%) and bathing facility (more than 98.3%) in their home, so "a hand washing facility with soap and water" component of the sanitation indicator is not further assessed. From the 1980s, the sewerage demand has been increasing due to the growing concerns of water quality and recognition of public hygiene. Significant improvements from the mid-1980s to the early 2000s are associated with international sporting events held in the ROK (MOE 2016a).

The trends in population that does not have access to public sanitation systems in urban area and rural area respectively are shown in Figure 4.5. Total population living outside the designated 'sewerage treatment area' has continuously decreased due to the expansion of sewerage systems in the ROK. Even those

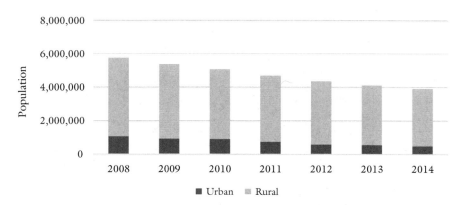

Figure 4.5 Population without access to public sanitation systems

Source: Korea Water and Wastewater Works Association (KWWA). 2014. "Wastewater Statistics." [In Korean]. Accessed March 15, 2017. https://www.kwwa.or.kr/reference/stats02_view.php?bid=pds_statiswaste&num=28856&title=2014+%C7%CF%BC%F6%B5%B5%C5%EB%B0%E8

living outside of the designated area can have limited access to sewerage treatment systems or septic tanks. However, equitable access to sanitation services is not yet achieved. For the period of 2008–2014, population without access to public sanitation systems in urban areas has rapidly declined, while only slowly decreasing in rural areas (0.81% in urban areas compared to 10.82% in rural areas, as of 2014).

To improve the hygienic convenience for females and other vulnerable groups (e.g. seniors, children, and the disabled), the number of stalls or separate toilets for female or the disabled have increased and various service facilities such as diaper changing, children's urinals, emergency bells, and free hygienic goods (soap, toilet paper, hand dryer, and sanitary pads) have been installed in public toilets (Choi 2017).[12] Recently, there have been growing demands for separate public toilets and other safety measures for females to prevent violent crimes against women.[13] The needs of vulnerable groups can be further assessed, focusing on the integration of gender and other socio-economic inequalities in the ROK's water services (including drinking water, sanitation, and hygiene systems), but the assessment is not included here due to lack of data.

Affordability is not officially considered in the international sanitation indicator. Also, sewerage tariffs are relatively[14] low in the ROK, so affordability is not further assessed here. However, there is a potential risk in ensuring sustainable management of sanitation due to the low level of cost recovery. According to the MOE (2016a), the national average cost recovery ratio in the sanitation sector is only 39.1% as of 2014. Sanitation systems consume significant energy, 98.6% of which is dependent on electricity (Lee 2017). By converting sewage sludge to fuel or improving energy efficiency, energy independence of public sewage treatment plants has been enhanced. The target of this energy independence plan is 50% by 2030 (MOE 2016a), but local governments, particularly small-sized ones, do not have capacities to implement such innovative energy plans due to their low levels of cost recovery and fiscal soundness.

Water quality

Target 6.3: "By 2030, improve water quality by reducing pollution, eliminating dumping and minimizing release of hazardous chemicals and materials, halving the proportion of untreated wastewater and increasing recycling and safe reuse globally."

"Water quality" is critical to ensure sustainable water management and water-related ecosystem health, so water quality standards and aquatic environmental standards are established in accordance with relevant regulations including Water Quality and Ecosystem Conservation Act. A variety of chemical, physical, and biological indicators are used to monitor water quality. Biochemical oxygen demand (BOD), chemical oxygen demand (COD), and heavy metals are chemical indicators, while turbidity, color, taste, and total suspended solids (TSS) are physical indicators. Fecal coliform bacteria (*E. coli*) is one of the most important biological indicators. In the ROK, many different water quality standards are set for drinking, groundwater, effluent, and other uses (e.g. swimming). Effluent standards are highly associated with point source water pollution. Thus, the government has established regulatory frameworks to manage water pollution from effluent of sewage treatment facilities and industrial plants.

To improve water quality, it is critical to manage non-point source (NPS) pollution that originates from diffused and often unidentified sources. Sources of NPS such as agricultural fields, livestock facilities, roads, construction sites, and other urban areas create pollution through rainfall or snowmelt, so NPS pollution is difficult to monitor or control and it becomes the major threat to the Korean major river watersheds.[15] To address NPS pollution, the government has shifted policy paradigms through the Second Comprehensive Plan on Non-Point Source Management (2012–2020). Based on the achievements of the First Plan (including seven designated NPS control areas and 46 NPS mitigation facilities), the Second Plan includes specific measures that take into account the key characteristics of different land uses, and innovative measures such as green storm water infrastructure or low impact development methods.[16]

Problems of "dumping" and "hazardous chemicals and materials" spills are often recognized through serious environmental incidents. The phenol contamination incident in the Nakdong River caused by an electronics company was recorded as one of the top environmental pollution incidents. It triggered significant changes in the regulatory frameworks and public awareness for water quality. To reduce such problems, the Korean government has enhanced monitoring/surveillance systems, control technologies, public relations, administrative guidance, and public–private partnerships.

Given the high level of sewerage coverage and the advanced regulatory frameworks for effluent and wastewater, the portion of "untreated wastewater" is relatively low. Industrial wastewater treatment is controlled in accordance with the Korean Water Quality and Ecosystem Conservation Act, which requires wastewater discharging facilities to have permits and/or reporting systems prior to their construction and to comply with the effluent standards.

There is a growing need for "recycling and reuse" of water through advanced treatment processes for wastewater. Recycling of treated wastewater is not yet common in the ROK. According to KWWA (2014), the population covered by advanced sewerage treatment is 82.8%, but its reuse rate is only 13.5%: half of the reclaimed water has been used on-site for cleaning, cooling, and other purposes, and the other half has been used off-site, mainly for river maintenance.

One of the internationally proposed indicators for water quality is the "percentage of wastewater safely treated," which includes total wastewater produced from domestic, commercial, and industrial water uses. In the ROK, domestic and commercial wastewater produced within the designated sewerage treatment area is treated through the public sewerage systems. The percentage of the population covered by wastewater treatment is 92.5% (KWWA 2014).

According to Yang (2014), most pollution load in the ROK's rivers comes from sewage and industrial wastewater, which represent, respectively, 78.7% and 20.7%

by volume. For effective and efficient treatment, large wastewater treatment plants and individual wastewater treatment service agencies are established. Through real-time tele-monitoring systems (so-called SOOSIRO system), a total of 936 facilities, including 248 wastewater discharging ones, 570 public sewerage treatment facilities, and 118 wastewater treatment plants are monitored in a timely fashion by the Korea Environment Corporation, as of December 2016 (KEC 2016). According to the Environmental Statistics Yearbook (2014), the pollutant load of industrial wastewater becomes low after adequate treatment processes: for example, BOD has been reduced to 19,799kg/day from 2,417,541kg/day, as of December 2012. However, Figure 4.6 shows the increasing violation rate (%) of wastewater discharging facilities despite enhanced inspection and administrative measures.

Another internationally proposed indicator for water quality is the "percentage of water bodies with good water quality." The water quality target in the ROK is determined by key characteristics, pollution sources, and water use in the river basin or lake area. Based on the advanced level of information technology (IT), the Korean government has established a National Water Quality Monitoring Program and operated comprehensive data platforms for water quality, such as a 'water information system' that includes monitoring systems in the rivers, lakes, agricultural reservoirs, and urban water infrastructures. Real-time data on water quality is also collected by 70 automatic monitoring sites in the four major rivers.[17] However, this data service does not regularly report the average conditions against the water quality target defined per river or lake, so key water quality indicators need to be selected to understand the overall trends of water quality.

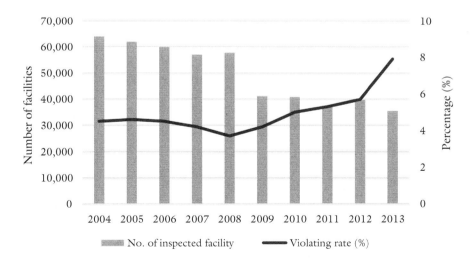

Figure 4.6 Violation rate of wastewater discharging facilities (2004–2013)

Source: Ministry of Environment. 1989, 1995, 2000, 2005, 2010, 2014, 2015. "Environmental Statistics Yearbook." [In Korean]. Accessed February through September 2017. http://stat.me.go.kr/nesis/mesp/knowledge/MorgueStatistical.do?task=I

The most common measurements of water quality are BOD and COD. The steady trends (with a range of 1–2 mg/L) of annual average BOD concentration in the major rivers can be seen in Figure 4.7; with the exception of the Nakdong River where the overall BOD level is higher. Since the adoption of the river-basin approach (including Comprehensive Measures on Water Management, 1995–2005; Water and Environmental Management Plans, 2006–2015 and 2016–2025), water quality has been improved, particularly in terms of BOD. The annual average values of COD are generally higher than those of BOD, and the "best" water quality targets (1mg/L for BOD; 3mg/L for COD) differ. The COD trends are also stable for the major rivers (except for Nakdong River) with a range of 2.6–4.7mg/L.[18] Due to the increase of insoluble materials from NPS, it is challenging to decrease the COD levels.

The ROK government has tried to reduce the release of hazardous chemicals and materials. For example, through voluntary participation in the 'stewardship-based management for area-specific risk reduction target' (SMART) program, many facilities that deal with hazardous chemicals monitor and report their production and release. Figure 4.8 demonstrates the release trend of hazardous chemicals (in line). As of 2014, only 0.0332% of the total production (54,261 tons, in bar) is released into the environment. Although they are not directly released into the water, they could be serious NPS pollutants. Water pollution incidents have occurred in all river basins and the frequency has been rising. As of 2013, there have been 157 water pollution accidents, which are caused mainly by management negligence (MOE).

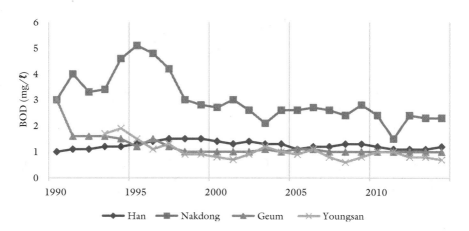

Figure 4.7 Annual average water quality of four major rivers (BOD, mg/L)

Source: Ministry of Environment. 1989, 1995, 2000, 2005, 2010, 2014, 2015. "Environmental Statistics Yearbook." [In Korean]. Accessed February through September 2017. http://stat.me.go.kr/nesis/mesp/knowledge/MorgueStatistical.do?task=I

Goal 6: clean water 47

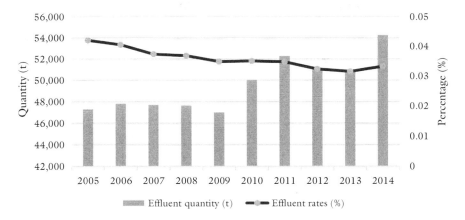

Figure 4.8 Release of hazardous chemicals
Source: Ministry of Environment. 2016c. "Chemical Emissions in 2014"

Water-use efficiency and water scarcity

Target 6.4: "By 2030, substantially increase water-use efficiency across all sectors and ensure sustainable withdrawals and supply of freshwater to address water scarcity and substantially reduce the number of people suffering from water scarcity."

"Water-use efficiency" is assessed by using percentage data (%) on municipal water consumption against withdrawal in the municipal sector or economic data on sectoral output per unit of water used (USD/m^3) in the agricultural sector and industrial sector. Due to growing concerns over water availability and competing water uses, water policy has incorporated water-use efficiency or water-saving technologies/practices, which led to the adoption of the Act on the Promotion and Support of Water Recycling. Water-use efficiency can be improved not only by demand-side management but also by supply-side management. So, water-use efficiency can be further assessed by using data on water recycling or water loss in the water supply systems.

Due to emerging climate change risks, water scarcity and uncertainty in water resources management are increasing. Drought caused by "water scarcity" is one of the most common disaster risks, which generally affects broad areas with a low level of intensity and a high level of frequency. However, not all drought incidents have been systematically monitored, so there is limited data on their impacts in terms of the number of people suffering from, areas affected by, or economic loss from drought incidents. The level of water stress is assessed by using data on water withdrawals against the total available water resources.

The internationally proposed indicator for water-use efficiency is the "percentage of change in water use efficiency over time," which includes domestic, agricultural, and industrial water-use efficiency. Agricultural and industrial water-use efficiencies show an improving trend in Figure 4.9. In the ROK, the agricultural sector is the largest water user because of irrigation-dominant practices, but its economic contribution to the GDP is small. As a result, the level of agricultural water-use efficiency is relatively low, and the difference between agricultural and industrial water-use efficiency is widening.

In the ROK, the water supply sector heavily relies on subsidies from the central government, so there are no strong incentives to manage water losses proactively. According to the Ministry of Environment (20146b), annually estimated water losses are 6.9 million tons, which is enough to support the entire nation for 50 days in 2014. To reduce water losses and deal with aging infrastructure, the Korean government has implemented a modernization plan of the water supply systems. Figure 4.10 shows incremental improvement in water loss management since 2001.

The internationally proposed indicator for water stress is the "freshwater withdrawal in percentage of available freshwater resources," disaggregated by sectoral water withdrawals (agricultural, domestic, and industrial). As shown in Table 4.1, the total amounts of available water resources and freshwater withdrawals have increased. Water stress generally starts when the total freshwater withdrawal is above 20% of the total amount of available water resources, so the level of water stress in the ROK is considered high (36.5% in 2012)[19] to meet increased water demands due to population growth and economic development.

In the ROK, the average annual rainfall is 1,274mm (57% higher than the world average), while the average annual rainfall per capita is 2,660m^3 (84% lower than the world average).[20] According to World Bank data, renewable

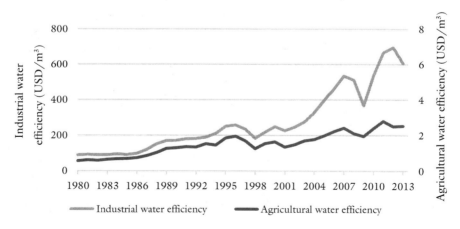

Figure 4.9 Water-use efficiency (industrial and agricultural)

Source: Ministry of Land, Infrastructure, and Transport (MOLIT), Water Resources Management Information System (WAMIS).

Goal 6: clean water 49

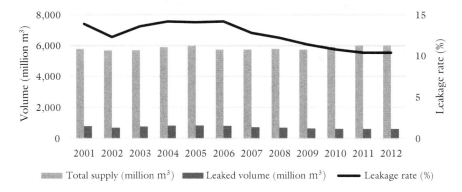

Figure 4.10 Leakage rate of water supply systems
Source: KWWA, 2016, "Republic of Korea: Transformation of the water sector (1960–2012)." (Original source: Korean Ministry of the Environment, "Statistics of Waterworks (2013).")

Table 4.1 Freshwater withdrawals from renewable freshwater resources

							(Unit: 100 million m³/yr)
		1965	1980	1994	1998	2003	2007
Total amount of water resource		1,100	1,140	1,267	1,276	1,240	1,297
Total use		51.2 (4.7%)	153 (13.4%)	301 (23.8%)	331 (25.9%)	337 (27.2%)	333 (25.7%)
Sectoral use	Domestic	2.3	19	62	73	76	75
	Industrial	4.1	7	26	29	26	21
	Agricultural	44.8	102	149	158	160	159
	Maintenance	–	25	64	71	75	78

Source: MOLIT, "Long-term comprehensive plan for water resource (2011)."

internal freshwater resource availability in the ROK has significantly reduced from 2,446m³/capita in 1962 to 1,278m³/capita in 2014.[21] Not only is there a reduction in water resource availability but increasing variations over seasons and regions are also exacerbating water stress. As shown in Figure 4.11, there is a seasonal variation in monthly precipitation. The variation level of precipitation is highly associated with droughts and floods. Trends, periodicities, and frequencies of Korean drought vary by river basin, but Lee et al. (2012) identify southern river basins as more vulnerable to severe drought and foresee longer drought duration in spring and winter. To prevent floods in the urban areas, comprehensive measures on sewerage management have been implemented since 2012. Through extension and improvement of sewer pipes and pump stations as well as separate drainage systems, rainwater management has been enhanced.

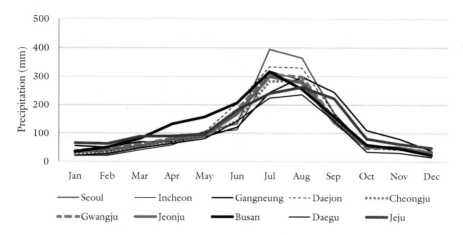

Figure 4.11 Average monthly precipitation (1981–2010)
Source: Korea Meteorological Administration (2011).

Integrated water resources management (IWRM)

Target 6.5: "By 2030, implement integrated water resources management at all levels, including through transboundary cooperation as appropriate."

Integrated water resources management (IWRM) is a framework to manage water resources in a comprehensive, participatory, and coordinated manner by incorporating relevant sectors, stakeholders, and agendas. Due to the complexities, uncertainties, and interdependencies of water-related issues, an integrated approach is needed. An enabling environment, the roles of institutions and management instruments are three cores for the IWRM approach (Bielsa and Cazcarro 2015). IWRM is based on integrated watershed management, which includes coastal areas as well as transboundary communities. In the ROK, IWRM has been adopted, but there is no national monitoring data on progress of the implementation.

One of the internationally proposed indicators for IWRM is the "degree of integrated water resources management (IWRM) implementation (0–100)," which has been globally monitored and reported by the UNEP–DHI partnership. They conducted two global comprehensive surveys in 2007 and 2011 focusing on the 14 key areas for IWRM, which include main national instruments, sub-national instruments, other national instruments, international agreements, governance systems, stakeholder participation, capacity building, management instruments and programs for water resources, monitoring and information management, knowledge sharing, financing of water resources management, infrastructure investment plans, and mobilizing financing for infrastructure. The 2011 survey results (UNEP–DHI Data Portal) show that the implementation level of IWRM in the ROK is highly advanced in most key areas, but the implementation of international agreements has not yet started.[22]

In the Korean framework of water management, the scope and roles of governance systems are dramatically expanded and a variety of instruments have been developed based on lessons learned from experience (particularly failures and problems). The first Water and Environmental Management Plan (WEM) specifies a paradigm-shift from pollution control to ecosystem integrity and water security, while the second WEM plan highlights the central roles of Integrated Watershed Management and the adoption of cost-sharing principles.[23] However, the core integration between water quantity and water quality has not fully been implemented, and there are growing concerns on the inefficient and inconsistent implementation of water policy associated with institutional fragmentism. Recently, there are collective efforts to improve institutional arrangement and regulatory frameworks, which include the adoption of the integrated Water Resources Framework Act and the balanced approach of the key principles such as water publicity, rights, security, equitable access and sustainability(Ryu 2017).

Another indicator for IWRM is the "percentage of transboundary basin area with an operational arrangement for water cooperation." There is only one transboundary basin in the ROK, which is shared with North Korea: the Imjin River in North Korea merges into the Han River in the ROK. The two governments have not yet made any agreement on water cooperation over this transboundary basin. Therefore, transboundary water cooperation in the ROK is literally zero. However, as seen in the 2005 flooding incident that was caused by massive release of upstream water in North Korea without any prior warning, people and ecosystems in transboundary river basins can be in danger if no collaborative frameworks are implemented among key stakeholders. Therefore, urgent action is needed to establish transboundary cooperation over the Han River basin, which will contribute to South–North Korean relations, peace, and sustainable development and also improve water resources management.

Water ecosystems

Target 6.6: "By 2020, protect and restore water-related ecosystems, including mountains, forests, wetlands, rivers, aquifers and lakes."

"Water-related ecosystems" are vital to sustainable water management, as water availability and quality are highly associated with ecosystems' conditions, such as biodiversity, capacity, and health. The ROK's Master Plan for Water and Environmental Management and Water Quality and Aquatic Ecosystem Conservation Act highlight the importance of water-related ecosystems and promote the conservation and restoration of critical, vulnerable, or ecologically important aquatic ecosystems. Water-related ecosystems vary, but wetlands are one of the most important ecosystems because they have a significant role in reinforcing biodiversity, resilience to weather-related disaster risks, mitigation of climate change, and groundwater recharging. Also, water conservation forest plays the key role in accumulating and purifying water resources. According to Forest Statistics (2016), water conservation forest represents 902 thousand ha, which covers 14.2% of the total forest area in the ROK.

The internationally proposed indicator for ecosystem, "percentage of change in water-related ecosystems extent over time," is redefined here by the "change in protection areas of designated wetlands over time." Wetlands represent 1,399 km² (1.39% of the total country area), and designated wetland protection areas cover 336.713 km² over 32 sites as of 2013.[24] Since 1999, when four wetlands were designated as protection areas, and in accordance with the Wetland Conservation Act, designated wetlands have increased. As shown in Figure 4.12, there are 22 wetlands (with a total area of 18,164 ha) designated by the Ramsar Convention as Wetlands of International Importance in the ROK. Although there is no trend data on change in water conservation forest caused by the conversion of forests to other land uses, the average 6,846 ha of national forests is annually reduced (Forest Statistics 2016), which results in decreasing water conservation forest.

Water cooperation

Target 6.a: "By 2030, expand international cooperation and capacity-building support to developing countries in water- and sanitation-related activities and programmes, including water harvesting, desalination, water efficiency, wastewater treatment, recycling and reuse technologies."

"International cooperation" and "capacity-building" support to developing countries is needed to achieve the global SDGs. To deal with complex water issues, collective actions are needed not only at the national level, but also at the regional and international levels. One of the major challenges for international cooperation is the lack of financial support. Without adequate infrastructure for water, sanitation and wastewater, the water SDG cannot be achieved, which calls for increased investment in water infrastructure and increased Official

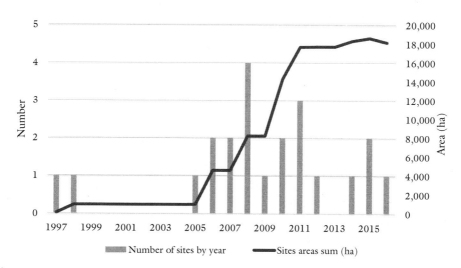

Figure 4.12 Ramsar wetlands in the ROK (1997–2016)
Source: Ramsar Statistics.

Goal 6: clean water   53

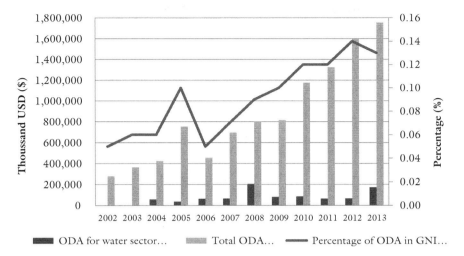

Figure 4.13 ODA in water sector (2002–2013)
Source: KOICA ODA statistics, EDCF Korea Statistics.

Development Assistance (ODA). The ROK was a ODA recipient county and the development of early water infrastructure in the 1960s and 1970s depended heavily on ODA. ODA significantly contributed to the ROK's rapid development in the water sector as well as economic growth (MOE 2015).

The internationally proposed indicator for international cooperation is the "amount of water and sanitation related Official Development Assistance (ODA) that is part of a government coordinated spending plan." Since becoming an ODA donor country, the ROK has made efforts to scale up the amount of ODA. The upward trends of total ODA and water-related ODA are shown in Figure 4.13. The adopted Strategic Plan for International Development Cooperation highlights the ROK's development experiences, its ODA system, and inclusive partnership.[25]

Water governance: local participation

Target 6.b: "Support and strengthen the participation of local communities in improving water and sanitation management."

The "participation of local community" is critical to ensure availability and sustainable management of water and sanitation. By empowering local stakeholders through participatory processes and by promoting ownership, the participation of the local community can be ensured. Local Agenda 21 (LA21), a local-driven initiative actively implemented in the ROK, has contributed to the establishment of local water partnerships and successes of river restoration projects through water governance reform (Kim 2012). Based on six case studies of local water partnerships in the ROK, Kim (2012) calls for the facilitative role of national government and cooperation between emerging and existing institutions.

The internationally proposed indicator of the "percentage of local administrative units with established and operational policies and procedures for participation of local communities in water and sanitation management" can be assessed by proxy indicators (such as the number of LA21 action plans published or implemented). According to the Ministry of Environment and Korean Council for Local Agenda 21 (2006),[26] 90% of 248 local administrative districts developed LA21 action plans and 67 local governments established non-governmental permanent secretariats of promotional organizations to promote NGO participation. The Local Sustainability Alliance of Korea (LSAK) was established as a nationwide network of around 200 Local Agenda 21 organizations, and now the LSAK has contributed to establishing the local frameworks for the SDGs.[27]

Box 4.1 Case for power of local participation: cancellation of a dam plan for the Dong River

In 1997, a plan of dam construction was proposed in the Dong River to expand water supply, reduce flood damages, and generate hydropower. However, local stakeholders and environmentalists strongly opposed this dam construction and received the backing of public opinion, which included academic, religious, and cultural groups as well as international NGOs. Strong local partnerships with various stakeholders finally led to a cancellation of this dam proposal in 2000. According to Oh (2009), the transparent processes for conflict resolution that enhanced participation of the local communities were important.

Source: pixabay.com.

Data and methodology

The coherent analytical approach of this book is to apply factor analysis (described in Chapter 2) and to develop an index for each goal. This section elaborates on the data sources and processing related to SDG 6.

Definition of indicators and data sources

To better understand the comprehensiveness and complexity of the water goal, key data and relevant information were collected from various data sources. Data was collected mostly from the Korean Ministry of Environment. The targets and indicators of SDG 6, the key variables for the analysis, and data sources of each variable are shown in Table 4.2. Due to the limited data availability, some relevant indicators were not included for the analysis. Data processing and methodological limitations are further explained later.

Data processing for factor analysis

To identify proper weights of the selected variables in terms of factor loadings used to create an index for SDG 6, a factor analysis was employed. A total of 11 variables were used for time-series analysis covering the period of 36 years (1980~2015). To standardize the impact of each target on the index, several indicators under each target were averaged into one variable by adopting row mean calculation for each year. Missing data in some variables (such as Indicators 6.3.1, 6.3.2, 6.4.1, and 6.4.2) were filled by the imputation method, which combined two different methods, regression-based imputation and interpolation.

The direction (+ or –) of each variable was determined according to its contribution to the water goal. That is, four variables were multiplied with –1 because they had negative impacts on SDG 6, which included 'illegal effluent into waterbody,' 'leakage rate,' 'abstraction rate out of renewable water resources,' and 'cost of flood damage.' Two variables were generated through specific calculations to improve their relevance to the target: (1) variable 6.3.1 'Illegal effluent into waterbody (m^3/day)' was generated by multiplying total amount of wastewater discharge with the average violation rate of facilities over the recent 20 years; (2) variable 6.6.1 'Total size of water conservation forest (ha)' was calculated by multiplying total forest area with rate of water conservation forest.

Analysis results

Results

Initial results of factor with common components resulted in factor 1 and factor 2, which are shown in Table 4.3 along with factor loadings (weight) for the five targets. Figure 4.14 represents trends of each target respectively for factor 1 and for factor 2. Figure 4.15 shows the trend of the SDG 6 index derived by applying weighted value between indicators.

The rising trend of the SDG 6 index indicates the incremental improvement of the availability and sustainable management level of water and sanitation in

Table 4.2 Data sources and basic statistics of key variables

Targets	Official indicators	Selected variables	Source
6.1	6.1.1 Proportion of population using safely managed drinking water services	Percentage of population with access to tap water on the premises (%)	Ministry of Environment/ The Statistics of Water Supply 1980, 1985, 1990, 1995, 2000, 2005, 2010, 2014, 2015
		Proportion of the least developed water coverage area (Seomjin) / National water coverage	Ministry of Environment/ The Statistics of Water Supply 1980, 1985, 1990, 1995, 2000, 2005, 2010, 2014, 2015
6.2	6.2.1 Proportion of population using safely managed sanitation services	Percentage of population using public sewage systems in the designated sewerage treatment area (%)	Ministry of Environment(2016a, p33)
6.3	6.3.1 Proportion of wastewater safely treated	(–) Illegal effluent into waterbody (m³/day)	Ministry of Environment/ Report of Industrial Wastewater 1999, 2001, 2005
	6.3.2 Proportion of bodies of water with good ambient water quality	Proportion of waterbody below 2ml/liter ('Good' by WAMIS criteria) of annual average BOD concentration (%)	Ministry of Environment/ Environmental Statistics Yearbook 1989, 1995, 2000, 2005, 2010, 2015 Ministry of Environment, 2007
6.4	6.4.1 Change in water-use efficiency over time	(–) Leakage rate (%)	Ministry of Environment/The Statistics of Water Supply 1980, 1985, 1990, 1995, 2000, 2005, 2010, 2014, 2015
		Agricultural water use efficiency (USD/m³)	Ministry of Land, Infrastructure, and Transport/ Report of Domestic Basins, 2011
	6.4.2 Level of water stress: freshwater withdrawal as a proportion of available freshwater resources	(–) Gross abstractions as percentage of total renewable resources (%)	OECD statistics/Fresh Water Abstractions
		(–) Cost of flood damage (KRW)	K-water, my water statistics

Goal 6: clean water 57

Targets	Official indicators	Selected variables	Source
6.5	6.5.1 Degree of integrated water resources management implementation (0–100)		
	6.5.2 Proportion of transboundary basin area with an operational arrangement for water cooperation	Not included for analysis	
6.6	6.6.1 Change in the extent of water-related ecosystems over time	Total size of water conservation forest (ha)	Korea Forest Service/ Forest Statistics 2016
		Total size of wetlands designated by the Ramsar Convention (ha) since 1997	Ramsar Statistics

Table 4.3 Factor loadings and index weights for SDG 6

Variables	Factor 1	Factor 2	Weight
Indicator for SDG 6.1	0.9616	−0.0716	24.16%
Indicator for SDG 6.2	0.9459	−0.2179	23.38%
Indicator for SDG 6.3	−0.1202	−0.8540	19.06%
Indicator for SDG 6.4	0.7793	0.3350	1587%
Indicator for SDG 6.6	−0.3184	0.8189	17.52%

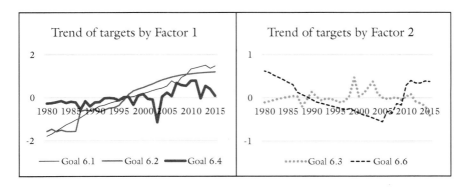

Figure 4.14 Trend of SDG 6 target by factor

the context of the ROK. Some ups and downs of the index seem associated with Korean historical situations. For example, the increase from 1986 to 1990 may reflect the efforts of the Korean government in preparation for the 1986 Asian Games and 1988 Olympic Games. During this period, water quality and

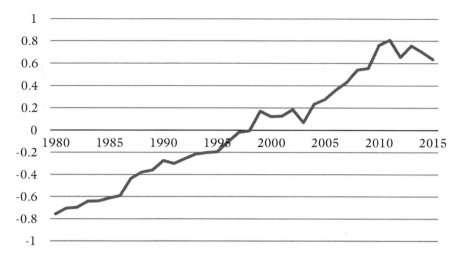

Figure 4.15 Index for SDG 6

sanitation service improved, which is consistent with results in Figure 4.14. A plateau of slow growth between 1990 and 1992 may be associated with a regression effect after rapid growth during the 1988 Seoul Olympic Games. When it comes to water ecosystems, as the area of water conservation forest has been decreasing gradually, the overall trend represents a downward direction. However, since the ROK joined the Ramsar convention in 1997, the trend of target 6.6 has switched upward since the early 2000s.

Methodological limitations

As mentioned earlier, not all internationally proposed indicators for SDG 6 were included for the analysis because of limited data availability, qualitative characteristics, or methodological standardization of some targets. Therefore, the index derived from five indicators may not fully reflect the social, economic, and environmental components of SDG 6. The limited scope of SDG 6 results in the limited evaluation of the water sector in the ROK. Some selected variables were defined by focusing on fractional issues. For example, water quality was assessed by focusing on the BOD standard, not by aggregating all water quality standards. Due to the increasing problems associated with NPS pollutants, the focus of water pollutants has shifted from BOD to total-N and total -P, but the analysis did not include this trend. As the monitoring technologies have been developed along with enhanced regulatory frameworks, intensive and comprehensive water data is available, but sampling problems remain in many data sources, which were not fully incorporated in the analysis.

Imputation is a useful method to estimate the missing data, but there are some methodological limitations. For example, most variables show stabilized trend since the 1990s, and the time-series data does not incorporate the early development of the water sector in the ROK (particularly in the 1960s and 1970s when the rapid grow of the water sector was driven by the Korean government). So, the index based on the imputed data could not reflect the overall trends of SDG 6 in the ROK and depends heavily on the recent data.

Conclusion

Figure 4.16 summarizes the conceptual framework of the water-related targets and indicators, which highlights the interlinkage of key water issues. Efficacy of water resources focusing on drinking water and sanitation is the first priority in the water sector and global water-related agenda because it is critical for human survival. The efficacy targets cannot be met unless targets associated with water quantity and water quality are achieved. In fact, water quantity/quality issues and water efficacy have interdependent relationships and their relationships become more comprehensive when the target of water-related ecosystems is involved. Although the interlinkage of all water targets is easily perceptible, it is difficult to apply an integrated approach to achieve the water targets. The Korean experience demonstrates that a fragmented approach is applied to address only top priority targets at the earlier stage of development, and an integrated approach for

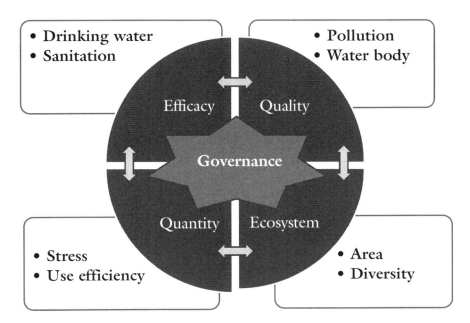

Figure 4.16 Conceptual framework of SDG 6

multiple targets is applied at the later stage to address challenges and opportunities in a coherent and balanced manner. It is critical to improve water governance since it is central to achieving the water goal. Integration, cooperation, and participation are the key targets of water governance.

Driven by a top-down command and control approach, water-related infrastructure and regulatory frameworks in the ROK have been developed along with rapid economic development, population growth, and urbanization. The supply-focused approach, however, could not fully address other emerging water issues such as water quality, social conflicts, water scarcity, and ecosystems' integrity and nexus issues associated with other sectors such as land uses, agriculture, and energy. So, the Korean government has applied a more comprehensive approach to ensure sustainable management of water resources and improve water governance.

This chapter presented progress in the ROK in ensuring availability and sustainable management of water and sanitation through evidence-based trends per the water-related SDG targets and indicators as well as the simplified SDG 6 index. Both the rising trends of positive indicators and the declining trends of negative indicators confirmed the successful implementation of the water goal in the ROK. To assess the economic, social, and environmental components of water issues in an integrated framework, the definitions of the internationally proposed SDG water targets and indicators were expanded in a comprehensive manner and modified to account for nation-specific situations and needs.

This chapter focused on the SDG 6 targets/indicators, but not all key water issues in the ROK were fully addressed. Groundwater, NPS water pollution, water governance, nexus issues, and ecosystems were outside the scope of this research due to lack of relevant data. The analytical method was not comprehensive, so the general trend of the SDG 6 index was limited in understanding the interrelation of the complex water issues. Regardless of its limitations, this chapter shared the important experience of the ROK and the key lessons learned from the implementation of the water goal, which could contribute to achieving the SDG 6 in developing countries.

Notes

1 Resolution was adopted by the UN General Assembly on December 23, 2003 (A/RES/58/217).
2 For example, the collective term of WASH (standing for Water, Sanitation, and Hygiene) is globally used by the UN (www.unicef.org/wash/3942_3952.html).
3 According to the UN MDGs report (2015), the global population who had access to improved drinking water was increased from 76% (1990) to 91% (2015), while 67% of the global population had access to improved sanitation as of 2015. This report also elaborated major challenges, including uneven successes of MDG7 across countries.
4 SDG 6 infographic on the linkages between the water targets and other SDGs/targets is presented by the UN Water (http://www.unwater.org/publications/sdg-6-infographics/).
5 The UN Sustainable Development Knowledge Platform specifies the SDG, targets and indicators (https://sustainabledevelopment.un.org/sdg6).

Goal 6: clean water

6 Note that not all water laws are included and that most laws are revised or replaced. For example, Water Quality Environmental Conservation Act (1990) was replaced by Water Quality and Ecosystem Conservation Act (2007).
7 Choi and his colleagues (2017) demonstrated the effects of increased water resource stock in Korea's GDP, based on Koyck's infinite distributed lag models.
8 According to the 2014 Environmental Statistics Yearbook, the violation rates of water standards monitored for tap water are very low (less than 0.02% or one violation per year) since 2009.
9 As of 2016, water price in Seoul is 360 won/ton, while water price in Bonghwa county (small town) is 2,000 won/ton (www.yonhapnews.co.kr/bulletin/2016/09/20/0200000000AKR20160920161600003.HTML).
10 According to Choi (2017), the total number of public toilets is 58,248 as of 2014, which is a significant increase compared to 3,185 in 1971.
11 UNICEF highlights the importance of hygiene, focusing on the consequences of hygienic behavior on health (www.unicef.org/wash/index_hygiene.html).
12 Choi (2017) presents the conditions of public toilet facilities (for example, female toilets= 45% vs. male toilets= 55%; toilets for the disabled = 93%; hand wash stands for kids = 19% installed).
13 Wikipedia reports a crime case happened in a public toilet in the ROK, "Seocho-dong public toilet murder case" (https://en.wikipedia.org/wiki/Seocho-dong_public_toilet_murder_case).
14 According to the Ministry of the Interior and Safety, average sewerage tariffs are lower than average water price (www.mois.go.kr/frt/sub/a02/publicPriceList/screen.do).
15 According to Korean Ministry of Environment, NPS is considered as the primary source for the discharged BOD load (up to 72.1% in 2020) (http://eng.me.go.kr/eng/web/index.do?menuId=269).
16 The Korean government applies preventive management and focuses on runoff volume reduction to control NPS pollution (http://eng.me.go.kr/eng/web/index.do?menuId=262).
17 Five common water quality indicators and twenty-five selected water quality indicators are monitored, and this real-time data system is operated by a partnership among five institutes (www.koreawqi.go.kr/index_web.jsp).
18 Korean Ministry of Environment has regularly updated the annual average values of BOD and COD of the major four rivers at the "Water Quality Status"(www.index.go.kr/potal/stts/idxMain/selectPoSttsIdxMainPrint.do?idx_cd=2788&board_cd=INDX_001).
19 watersaving.com provides key water data of "South Korea" and a method to measure water stress under the title of "Availability" (www.watersaving.com/en/infos/south-korea/).
20 Korea Groundwater and Geothermal Energy Association presents some key data on water resources in the title of "Groundwater state" of "Introduce in Korea" (www.kogga.or.kr/eng/korea/korea.asp).
21 World Bank provides data of "renewable internal freshwater resources per capita" for the ROK during the period of 1962–2014 (https://data.worldbank.org/indicator/ER.H2O.INTR.PC?locations=KR).
22 The UNEP–DHI partnership establishes IWRM data portal and provides the "Status of implementation" of IWRM for the "Republic of Korea" (http://iwrmdataportal.unepdhi.org/Data.html?Country=Republic of Korea).
23 Korean Ministry of Environment explains the "Master Plan for Water Environment Management (2006~2015)" as one of the major water policies (http://eng.me.go.kr/eng/web/index.do?menuId=262).
24 Korean Ministry of Environment introduces the "Protected Area Designation and Management" (http://eng.me.go.kr/eng/web/index.do?menuId=410).

25 Korea Official Development Assistance presents its "Strategic Plan" to clarify the ODA policy (www.odakorea.go.kr/eng.policy.StrategicPlan.do).
26 The Korean Council for Local Agenda 21 presents key information on LA21 in the report, "Choice for Sustainable Development: Local Agenda 21 in Korea" (www.me.go.kr/home/file/readDownloadFile.do?fileId=2269&fileSeq=1).
27 Sustainable Development Knowledge Platform provides the "Voluntary National Review 2016" of the ROK, which includes policies and enabling environment for SDGs (https://oceanconference.un.org/index.php?page=view&type=30022&nr=67&menu=3170).

References

Bielsa, J., and I. Cazcarro. 2015. "Implementing Integrated Water Resources Management in the Ebro River Basin: From Theory to Facts." *Sustainability*, 7: 441–464. doi:10.3390/su7010441. Accessed July 1, 2017. www.mdpi.com/2071-1050/7/1/441/pdf

Choi, H., M. Ryu, and S. Hong. 2017. "A Study on Effects Water Resource Stock in the Korean Economic Development Process." *The Journal of Korean Public Policy*, 19.3: 33–56. [In Korean].

Choi, S. 2017. "Korean Public Toilet Improvement Experience and Its Implications." Sejong, South Korea: KDI School of Public Policy and Management.

EDCF Korea Statistics. [In Korean]. Accessed March 5, 2017. www.edcfkorea.go.kr/site/homepage/menu/viewMenu?menuid=004002004001

Kim, K. U. 2012, "The Institutional Development and Outcomes of Water Partnerships in Korea: A Comparative Case Study Based on a Modified Institutional Analysis and Development (IAD) Framework." Ph.D. diss., London School of Economics.

KOICA ODA Statistics. [In Korean]. Accessed March 10, 2017. http://stat.koica.go.kr/ipm/os/acms/smrizeBothMltltrlList.do?imenu=Y&lang=ko

Korea Environment Corporation. 2016. "Status of the Installation of Tele-Monitoring System in Wastewater Discharging Facilities." [In Korean]. Accessed November 1, 2017. www.keco.or.kr/kr/business/water/communityid/193/view.do?p=&idx=21206&=&f=1&q=

Korea Meteorological Administration. 2011. "Climatological Normals of Korea (1981-2010)." [In Korean]. Accessed August 10, 2017. www.weather.go.kr/down/Climatological_2010.pdf

Korea Forest Service, Forest Statistics. 2016. [In Korean]. Accessed August 10, 2017. www.forest.go.kr/newkfsweb/kfi/kfs/soft/selectTotalTradeList.do?mn=KFS_02_03_03_01_01

Korean Population and Housing Census. 2015. [In Korean]. Accessed March 5, 2017. www.census.go.kr/dat/ysr/ysrList.do?q_menu=5&q_sub=7

Korean Statistical Information Service (KOSIS). [In Korean]. Accessed February 10, 2017. http://kosis.kr/statHtml/statHtml.do?orgId=106&tblId=DT_106N_06_0100054&vw_cd=MT_TITLE&list_id=106_005&seqNo=&lang_mode=ko&language=kor&obj_var_id=&itm_id=&co nn_path=E1#

Koun, H. 2013. "Water Resource Management." Korea Research Institute for Human Settlements (KRIHS). Accessed November 10, 2017. http://www.gdpc.kr/data/pkpp/6%20Water%20Resource%20Management.pdf

Korea Water and Wastewater Works Association (KWWA). 2014. "Wastewater Statistics." [In Korean]. Accessed March 15, 2017. https://www.kwwa.or.kr/refer

ence/stats02_view.php?bid=pds_statiswaste&num=28856&title=2014+%C7%CF%BC%F6%B5%B5%C5%EB%B0%E8

Korea Water and Wastewater Workers Association (KWWA). 2016. *Republic of Korea: Transformation of the Water Sector (1960–2012)*. Seoul: KWWA.

Lee, J. 2016. "Yoon Youngil Says, There Are up to 11 Times Differences in Water Prices among Local Governments. Equalization Is Needed." *Yonhap News*. September 21, 2016. [In Korean]. Accessed October 1, 2017. www.yonhapnews.co.kr/bulletin/2016/09/20/0200000000AKR20160920161600003.HTML

Lee, J., J. Seo, and C. Kim. 2012. "Analysis on Trends, Periodicities and Frequencies of Korean Drought Using Drought Indices." Water Engineering Research, 34.1: 75–89. [In Korean]. doi: http://dx.doi.org/10.3741/JKWRA.2012.45.1.75

Lee, M. 2017. "A Study on the Improvement of Energy Efficiency in Self-Supporting Energy of Sewage Treatment Facilities." M.A diss., Sejong University. [In Korean].

Ministry of Environment. 1980, 1985, 1990, 1995, 2000, 2005, 2010, 2014, 2015. "The Statistics of Water Supply." [In Korean]. Accessed February thru September, 2017. http://stat.me.go.kr/nesis/mesp/knowledge/MorgueStatistical.do?task=I

Ministry of Environment. 1989, 1995, 2000, 2005, 2010, 2014, 2015. "Environmental Statistics Yearbook." [In Korean]. Accessed February thru September, 2017. http://stat.me.go.kr/nesis/mesp/knowledge/MorgueStatistical.do?task=I

Ministry of Environment. 1999, 2001, 2005. "The Occurrence and Treatment of Industrial Wastewater." [In Korean]. Accessed February thru September, 2017. http://webbook.me.go.kr/DLi-File/pdf/2009/05/148746.Pdf

Ministry of Environment. 2007. "Overall Water Quality Deteriorated Last Year." ME press release. [In Korean]. Accessed June 20, 2017. www.kdi.re.kr/policy/ep_view.jsp?idx =86965

Ministry of Environment. 2015. *History of Korean Sewage Development*. Sejong: Ministry of Environment. [In Korean].

Ministry of Environment. 2016a. "Development of Korean Sewage Plant I." [In Korean]. Accessed February thru September, 2017. http://www.me.go.kr/home/web/policy_data/read.do?menuId=10264&seq=6831

Ministry of Environment. 2016b. "Modernization of Water Supply Systems." [In Korean]. Accessed July 10, 2017. https://me.go.kr/home/file/ readDownloadFile.do?fileId=130910&fileSeq=1&openYn=Y

Ministry of Environment. 2016c. "Chemical Emissions in 2014" [In Korean]. Accessed September 15, 2017. www.me.go.kr/home/web/board/read.do?boardId=660020&boardMasterId=1

Ministry of Environment and Korean Council for Local Agenda 21, 2006. "Choice for Sustainable Development: Local Agenda 21 in Korea." Accessed December 1, 2017. www.me.go.kr/home/file/readDownloadFile.do?fileId=2269&fileSeq=1

Ministry of Land, Infrastructure, and Transport. 2011. *Long-Term Comprehensive Plan for Water2011–2020*. Sejong. MOLIT. [In Korean].

OECD Stat. "Fresh Water Abstractions." Accessed November 10, 2017. https://stats.oecd.org/Index.aspx?DataSetCode=WATER_ABSTRACT

Oh, K. 2009. "Study on the Impacts of the Key Components of Governance on Conflict Resolution." Ph.D. diss., Inha University. [In Korean].

Ramsar Statistics. Accessed July 10, 2017. https://rsis.ramsar.org/ris-search/?f[0] =regionCountry _en_ss%3ARepublic+of+Korea&pagetab=2

Ryu, K. 2017. "Review on the Framework Act of Water Management in Korea through Comparison with the Basic Law of Water Circulation in Japan." *Journal of Water Policy & Economy*, 28: 17–34. [In Korean].

UNEP–DHI Data Portal. Accessed July 10, 2017. http://iwrmdataportal.unepdhi.org/ Data.html? Country=RepublicofKorea

World Bank Database. Accessed April 20, 2017. https://data.worldbank.org/indicator/ER.H2O.FWTL.K3?locations=KR&name_desc=true

Yang, H. 2014. "Construction of Sound Water Environment and Sustainable Water Supply System in Korea." National Institute of Environmental Research. Accessed December 1, 2017. www.me.go.kr/eng/file/readDownloadFile.do;jsessionid=zkOCH1LvPxinye4pgXgiYqFgg8hUvrbxb8Bv4AWkjHSxYF7R2zhcM-KADy21XyBhd.meweb2vhost_servlet_engine1?fileId=92576&fileSeq=1

5 Goal 7: affordable and clean energy

Tae Yong Jung, Minkyung Huh, and Jongwoo Moon

Introduction

Energy is one of the essential drivers for economic and social development. The absence of reliable and sustainable energy restricts the provision of basic services for human activities. However, fossil fuel energy use is the key contributor to climate change; thus, addressing energy challenges is closely related to global efforts to curb climate change. According to the IPCC (2014), the combustion of fossil fuel is the primary source of the CO_2 emissions that account for approximately 65% of greenhouse gas emissions globally. The United Nations General Assembly, recognizing energy services as an important driver to achieve sustainable development, adopted SDG 7 to "ensure access to affordable, reliable, sustainable, and modern energy for all by 2030" (UN General Assembly 2015). SDG 7 is composed of five outcome targets (7.1–7.3, 7.a, and 7.b) with six indicators. Sustainable Energy for All (SE4ALL Initiative), a joint initiative by the United Nations and the World Bank, encourages collective efforts and monitors the progress in achieving SDG 7 (SE4ALL 2012).

Addressing energy challenges has been an important national agenda for the economic development of the ROK since it lacks energy sources and imports most of its energy use. Since the 1960s, the ROK has achieved rapid economic growth and development, and accordingly, the ROK's primary energy consumption has increased rapidly. From the 1980s to 2010s, the primary energy supply increased more than four times. The energy use per capita is now ranked eighth in the world, according to World Bank Development Indicator. The surging energy demand has created challenges for sustainable energy, such as ensuring a stable and reliable energy supply and slowing down the pace of growing energy demand. The ROK has been introducing policy measures in all areas of sustainable energy to address the energy challenges.

Figure 5.1 shows the overview of energy policy development in the ROK. In general, the ROK's energy policy can be largely divided into three stages: the early phase of economic development (1960s–1970s), the period of fast economic growth (1980s–1990s), and the period of economic slowdown (2000s). During the early phase of economic development, the ROK focused on securing a stable and reliable energy supply. In the next stage, energy policies were introduced to

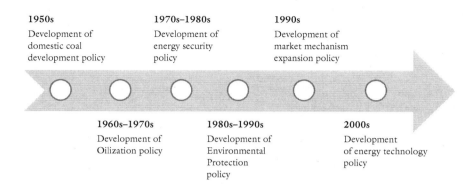

Figure 5.1 Overview of energy-related policies (1950–2000)
Source: Boo et al. 2013.

curb the surging energy demand due to the challenges of rapidly growing economic development, in addition to securing a stable energy supply. In the period of economic slowdown, the ROK's energy policy embraced the concerns about the environmental and climate change. Further development and deployment of renewable energy and low-carbon technologies have been included as important parts of national energy policies. Though many energy challenges and issues still exist, the ROK has made significant progress in establishing a policy framework for addressing the energy challenge, according to RISE.(Regulatory Indicators for Sustainable Energy (RISE) Homepage)[1]

This chapter reviews and analyzes the ROK's efforts and progress towards achieving SDG 7 based on the targets and indicators. The chapter measures the progress of each target by using the selected indicator and illustrates the ROK's relevant policy measures and efforts that contributed towards the progress. An index is also created through a factor analysis to measure the ROK's overall progress towards SDG 7. Based on the results of the factor analysis, the chapter concludes with lessons learned and recommendations to further advance progress towards SDG 7.

Analysis on the performance of the ROK Goal 7 by target

Access to electricity

- *Target 7.1: By 2030, ensure universal access to affordable, reliable and modern energy services.*
- *Indicator 7.1.1: Proportion of population with access to electricity.*

Goal 7: affordable and clean energy 67

- *Indicator 7.1.2: Proportion of population with primary reliance on clean fuels and technology.*

Ensuring access to sustainable and modern energy services is an essential condition for sustainable development. Access to modern energy contributes to economic development and poverty alleviation as well as to the improvement of living standards (IEA 2014b). Before 1965, the ROK lacked infrastructure and services for electricity access and only 25.5% of households had access to electricity services. Over 60% of the ROK's households were living in rural regions, with only 12% of those households having access to electricity services. This limited access to electricity services, especially in rural areas, became a major barrier constraining economic development. Thus, electrification entered the national policy agenda in 1965. Along with rural development policies, such as Saemaul Movement, the government of the ROK and KEPCO, the state-owned electric power company, extensively implemented electrification projects in both rural and urban areas until the late 1970s (MKE and KEPCO 2012). As a result, the ROK's electricity accessibility increased rapidly and reached over 90% by 1980, with 100% electrification achieved by the mid-2000s.

Since 1981, the ROK's electricity accessibility has slowly increased, reaching 100% in 2012 according to World Bank Indicator,[2] as shown in Figure 5.2. Before 1980, the electrification projects were primarily focused in rural areas with mid- to large-group households for efficient use of the electrification budget (MKE and KEPCO 2012). Since 1980, the ROK has expanded the targets of the electrification project to small-group households in rural areas and distant islands to provide electricity services to all households and thus achieve target 7.1.

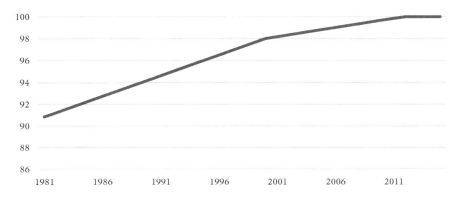

Figure 5.2 Access to electricity (%)
Source: World Development Indicator (October 2016 Vintage) and author's calculation.

Renewable energy

- *Target 7.2: By 2030, increase substantially the share of renewable energy in the global energy mix.*
- *Indicator 7.2.1: Renewable energy share in the total final energy consumption.*

The deployment of renewable energy provides multiple socio-economic benefits, such as new market opportunities, expanding energy access, and carbon emission reductions (IRENA 2017). Though renewable energy was considered as a very expensive energy source, technological development has significantly lowered the cost of generating electricity from renewable energy sources in recent years, leading to significant global renewable power capacity and increased investment. Increasing social demands for curbing climate change further accelerates the deployment of renewable energy globally. Thus, a large number of countries established policy frameworks and targets to accelerate the deployment of renewable energy (Frankfurt School–UNEP Centre/BNEF 2016). The ROK has also recognized the importance of renewable energy in reducing GHG emissions, enhancing energy security, and exploring new market opportunities. Accordingly, the ROK government has established a policy framework and promoted the deployment of renewable energy since the 1980s.

Since the definition of renewable energy varies by institutions, this chapter chose to follow the range of renewable energy widely used in the ROK that classifies hydropower as renewable (Korea Energy Agency Homepage). The data used in this chapter is provided by KEEI (2016), and the share of renewable energy is calculated by dividing the primary energy supply from hydro and renewable energy by the total primary energy supply. Moreover, the renewable energy data collected by KEEI (2016) indicates that the data before 1991 is based on the use of 'firewood.' However, the use of 'firewood' causes environmental pollution and accelerates deforestation, so the use of 'firewood' was significantly lowered in the late 1980s and became minimal in the ROK. Hence, the chapter excluded the use of 'firewood' from the primary energy supply from renewable energy.

As shown in Figure 5.3, the share of renewable energy of the ROK has been increasing since 1980. Because the ROK has been largely dependent on energy imports, diversification of energy supply and reducing dependence on energy imports have been key challenges for the ROK's energy policy (IEA 2012). Recognizing the necessity for renewable energy in terms of energy security, the Alternative Energy Development Promotion Act was enacted in 1987. The purpose of the initial act was to establish the legal basis for providing support for the development and deployment of renewable energy technologies (KMOGL 1987). Since 1987, the ROK has introduced energy policies and relevant legal frameworks for promoting renewable energy.

Figure 5.4 shows how the ROK's energy plan has changed over the last 15 years. In general, the Renewable Energy Basic Plan includes the development and deployment of renewable energy technologies, the national targets for share of renewables, and supportive policy measures that promote renewable energy.

In 2000, the ROK established the first Basic Plan for Dissemination and Development of Alternative Energy Technologies to further develop and disseminate

Goal 7: affordable and clean energy 69

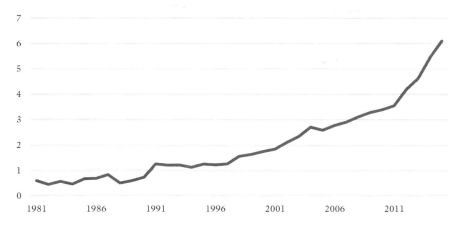

Figure 5.3 Share of renewable energy (%)
Source: Author's calculation; data from Korea Energy Economics Institute (2016).
Note: Renewable sources include hydro power but exclude firewood (traditional renewable source).

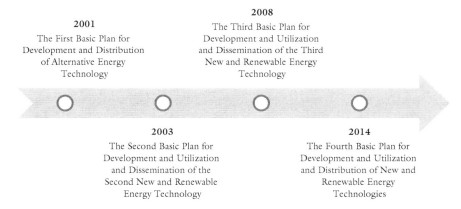

Figure 5.4 Overview of renewable energy basic plan
Source: Boo et al. 2013.

renewable energy technologies. The plan targeted the promotion of establishing infrastructure and technology development and included deployment policies for renewable energy. The plan especially announced the introduction of feed-in-tariff (FiT) to promote the dissemination of renewable energy. Based on this plan, the government established the target of supplying 2% of the primary energy supply from renewable sources by 2003 (MOTIE 2000).

The Second Basic Plan for the Development and Utilization of New Renewable Energy Technology, established in 2003, was the first mid- to long-term plan (with a planned period of ten years or more) to supply 3% of primary energy supply from renewable energy by 2006 and 5% of primary energy supply from renewable energy by 2011. The plan selectively supported three technologies (solar, wind, and fuel cell) with significant potential and indicated the ROK's plan to expand supportive renewable policies such as FiT and tax incentives (MOTIE 2003).

Though the ROK implemented various policies supporting the development and deployment of renewable energy, the ROK failed to achieve the short-term target established in the Second Basic Plan. The Third Basic Plan for the Development and Utilization of the New and Renewable Energy Technology identified the reason for failing to achieve the short-term target as lacking the linkage between the development of renewable energy technologies and the policies for supporting their dissemination. Thus, the Plan suggested both a Technology Road Map and a Product Road Map to facilitate the development and deployment of renewable energy technologies. Moreover, the Plan announced a shift in renewable policy from FiT to Renewable Portfolio Standard (RPS) in 2012. The Third Basic Plan also presented the long-term and comprehensive vision of the ROK's renewable energy towards 2030. Along with the National Energy Basic Plan, the ROK established a target of achieving a share of renewable energy of 6.1% by 2020 and 11.0% by 2030 (MKE 2008).

The Fourth Renewable Energy Basic Plan revised and set the new target for achieving 11% of the share of renewable supply to 2035. In this plan, the government focused on fostering solar and wind power and reducing the share of wasted energy. Moreover, the plan emphasized the importance of and established policies for supporting private investment in renewable energy. Also, the plan extended the target periods of achieving 10% share of renewable energy an additional two years and adjusted the weights of renewable energy certificate (MOTIE 2014b).

The newly elected administration's energy policy is focused on reducing nuclear and coal power generation and expanding the use of renewable energy and natural gas. They decided to curb the construction of new coal and nuclear power plants and to gradually shut down older nuclear power plants. In addition, the government plans to reduce energy demand significantly. The goal of the new energy policy is to raise the utilization rate of LNG power plants and to achieve a 20% share of renewable energy from total electricity generation by 2030. To facilitate the shift towards renewables and natural gas, the government decided to raise the consumption tax for coal and include the environmental costs when deciding to dispatch an order. Moreover, the government's plan includes various supportive policies for small-scale renewable providers, including the expansion of distributed power (MOTIE 2017).

To promote the development and deployment of renewable energy, the ROK initially introduced FiT in 2001 and shifted towards RPS in 2012. In 2001, the ROK introduced FiT to accelerate investments in renewable energy. The typical policy for promoting renewable energy such as FiT is a direct subsidy program providing high and fixed electricity price for a long-term period, supporting the cost recovery of renewable investments (Conture et al. 2010). The funding source to financially support FiT was the Electric Power Industry Foundation Fund. Technology development, other renewable energy policies, and the

Goal 7: affordable and clean energy   71

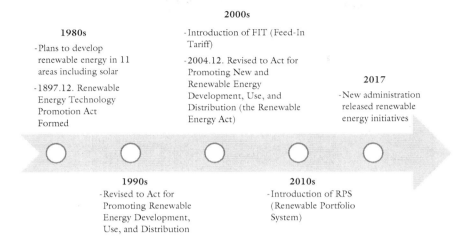

Figure 5.5 Overview of renewable energy-related policies
Source: LAWASIA, South Korea's Renewable Energy Policy under the New Climate Change Framework.

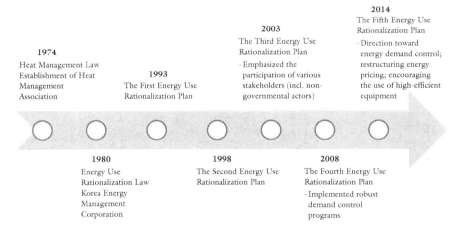

Figure 5.6 Overview of energy conservation and efficiency policies

feed-in-tariff allowed the ROK to further develop renewable sources. The share of renewables has gradually increased since 2002, and it reached 3.5% in 2010 (Figure 5.6). However, further deployment of renewable energy increased the financial burden on the Electric Power Industry Foundation Fund. The funding required to maintain FiT had increased significantly, and the government started to consider the policy shift from FiT to RPS (Yu 2009).

As a result, the ROK transitioned its renewable policy from FiT to RPS in 2012. Renewable Portfolio Standards (RPS) is a mandatory system that requires large electricity providers with 500MW or more capacity to generate a portion of electricity from renewable sources (KEA Homepage). Though RPS, the ROK has established a plan to generate 10% of electricity from renewable sources by 2024. To enhance the effectiveness of RPS, the ROK has implemented a weight system for renewable energy certificates that enables renewable providers to benefit from selling the weighted number of certificates. The introduction of RPS has accelerated the deployment of renewables since 2012 and increased the share of renewables sharply from 3.5% (2011) to 6.1% (2015), as shown in Figure 5.3. Table 5.1 indicates the annual plan of RPS target by 2023.

Energy conservation and efficiency

- *Target 7.3: By 2030, double the global rate of improvement in energy efficiency.*

Improvements in energy efficiency at all stages of the energy stream are a crucial part of achieving SDG 7. According to the IEA, improvements in energy efficiency provide various economic benefits, such as better resource management, higher industrial productivity, and stronger energy security; social benefits, such as improved health and well-being; and environmental benefits, such as reductions in greenhouse gas emissions (IEA 2014a). For instance, investment in energy efficiency creates new markets and employment and contributes to reducing energy consumption without hurting a country's economy. Also, reducing greenhouse gas emissions and air pollutants can improve human health as well as combat climate change. As an effective measure of achieving sustainable development, countries are giving significant attention to energy efficiency investments, reaching USD 231 billion in 2016, globally (IEA 2017). Improving energy conservation and efficiency have been important agendas because the ROK lacks natural energy resources, requiring existing energy sources to be

Table 5.1 RPS targets

Year	'12	'13	'14	'15	'16	'17	'18	'19	'20	'21	'22	'23~
Ratio (%)	2.0	2.5	3.0	3.0	3.5	4.0	5.0	6.0	7.0	8.0	9.0	10.0
Quantity of supply	6,420	9,210	11,577	12,375	15,081	17,043	-	-	-	-	-	-

Source: Korea Energy Agency.

Note: Quantity of supply = total amount of power generation (excluding renewable energy generation) * duty ration obligatory renewable service supply ratio (additional table no.3 of Enforcement Ordinance of the Act on the Promotion of the Deployment, Use and Diffusion of New and Renewable Energy)

used more efficiently. Thus, the country has put extensive efforts into improving energy conservation and efficiency for decades. To measure the progress of energy efficiency, the United Nations has selected energy intensity as an indicator. Primary energy intensity is "obtained by dividing total primary energy supply over gross domestic product" (UNSTATS 2016).

After two oil shocks in the 1970s, the ROK realized that high energy reliance and rapidly increasing energy consumption are major threats to energy security and the economy. Especially since economic growth, led by energy-consuming manufacturing sectors such as petrochemical, steel, and electronics, has rapidly increased the ROK's energy consumption. The government of the ROK realized improvements in energy efficiency and conservation would be beneficial to its national energy security as well as slowing the energy consumption growth rate. Accordingly, the national agenda and institutional framework to improve energy efficiency were established, and measures have been extensively implemented in various sectors, especially in the industrial sector. After the first oil shock, the ROK established the Heat Management Law in 1974, and the Heat Management Association was established in order to manage industrial heat (National Law Information Center 1974). The target of the law promoted the rational use of fuel and heat in the industrial sector. Though the law initially targeted only the industrial sector, it allowed the government of the ROK to begin establishing various energy conservation policies.

After the second oil shock in 1979, the ROK accelerated the introduction of energy efficiency policies. The government established Energy Use Rationalization Law (formerly Heat Management Law) in 1980, and it stipulated the establishment of an energy conservation plan and that the Korea Energy Management Corporation[3] manage the implementation of energy efficiency measures (National Law Information Center 1980). Also, the law introduced target energy intensity and energy efficiency rating policies. As a consequence, the government established the first energy use rationalization plan in 1993 and revises it every five years (Boo et al. 2013).

The objectives of the first energy use rationalization plan, which was established in 1993, were (1) establishing the grounds for transitioning to the energy conserving economy, (2) restraining the energy consumption growth rate below the economic growth rate, and (3) building capacity to reducing CO_2 emission in preparation for strengthening environmental regulations (Boo et al. 2013). The first plan emphasized the technological development for enhancing efficiency of energy equipment, rationalized energy prices, and introduced the incentive system for the rational use of energy (KEEI 2006). However, the first plan failed to achieve the target because of continued low exchange rates and energy prices during the target period, accelerating energy and electricity consumption.

The second energy use rationalization plan was established in 1998 when the ROK was suffering from the Asian Financial Crisis. The plan promoted the reform of the energy industry and energy price regulations, fostering of high-efficiency equipment, furthering the use of Energy Service Companies, and the expansion of demand management investments (Ministry of Commerce Industry and Energy 1991).

As with the prior plans, the third energy use rationalization plan promoted the transition of the ROK economy towards a low energy consuming economy and the rationalization of an energy pricing scheme (KEMCO 2004). Additionally, the third plan emphasized the participation of various stakeholders, such as local governments, non-governmental organization, and households, in energy conservation activities. It raised public awareness of energy conservation and encouraged both local governments and non-governmental organizations to promote the implementation of conservation measures. Moreover, the plan included the development of new and renewable energy technologies and the establishment of the framework for responding to the climate change regime.

When the government established its fourth energy use rationalization plan, the global oil price surged and exceeded $100 per barrel (KOSIS 2017), worsening the national trade balance. Accordingly, the objectives of the fourth plan were to improve national energy efficiency by 11.3% by 2012, to overcome the difficulties from high oil prices, to respond to climate change agreements, and to improve the trade balance. The government continued to provide incentives for research and development of energy efficiency technologies. In particular, the government announced the implementation of robust demand control measures, such as phasing out incandescent light bulbs and the introduction of the top runner program.[4] The initial target of the top runner program was air conditioners on the market, and the product range was expanded to other product segments, including refrigerators. Moreover, the plan introduced dynamic pricing for effective management of energy demand (Prime Minister's Office and the Ministry of Knowledge Economy 2008).

The Fifth Energy Use Rationalization Plan, established in 2014, announced a target of reducing 4.1% of final energy consumption and improving 3.8% of energy intensity compared to business-as-usual by 2017. Also, the second Energy Master Plan announced a shift in direction towards energy demand-control and reduction of final energy consumption by 15% by 2035 through policies such as restructuring energy pricing and encouraging the use of high-efficient appliances and equipment (Ministry of Trade, Industry, and Energy 2014b). The government runs three major energy efficiency management programs: energy efficiency labels and standards program; high-efficiency appliance certification program; and e-standby program. Energy efficiency labels and the standards program require 27 selected products to indicate their energy efficiency grade based on their efficiency level and energy consumption. The manufacturers are not allowed to produce or sell their products if the efficiency is below the minimum energy performance standard (MEPS). The high-efficiency appliance certification program is a voluntary certification that the manufacturers can receive for energy equipment that demonstrate high energy efficiency above the standards set by the government. The e-standby program is a mandatory reporting program for 21 products where manufacturers report the amount of standby energy consumption of products and the government issues warning labels on products below the standby energy standards (Korea Energy Agency, "Energy Efficiency Program").

Goal 7: affordable and clean energy 75

To facilitate the effectiveness of energy efficiency policies, the ROK established the Energy Use Rationalization fund, which is managed and run by Korea Energy Management Corporation, to support the successful financial implementation of energy efficiency measures. The funding comes from a special consumption tax on petroleum products, the endowment of government or non-government agencies, loan, income from fund operation, and income defined in the presidential decree (National Law Information Center 1980). This fund is utilized for energy conservation and efficiency projects, such as R&D, installation of energy-saving equipment, and projects for alternative energy. The multi-decade efforts to establishing institutional frameworks and implementing measures for efficient use of energy directly contributed to improving the ROK's performance in achieving SDG 7.

As identified in target 7.3 and indicator 7.3.1, energy intensity, which is units of energy per unit of GDP, was mainly used to measure the progress of energy efficiency, translated as the amount of energy used to produce a unit of value added. Figure 5.7 shows the trends of the ROK's energy intensity during the periods of 1981–2015.

Figure 5.7 shows a gradual decreasing trend of energy intensity with an extreme spike in the late 1990s. The sudden spike can be explained by the extreme change in exchange rate during the financial crisis. Since the value of the Korean won significantly depreciated, the energy intensity nominated by US dollars worsened. Even excluding this period, however, the improvement of energy intensity has not been impressive since the late 1980s, and it has maintained a higher level than other OECD countries. According to the OECD Factbook 2015–2016, the ROK was ranked 30th out of 34 OECD countries, and the energy intensity was approximately 30% higher than the OECD average (OECD 2016). This

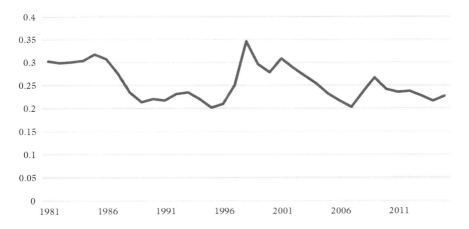

Figure 5.7 Energy intensity (toe per US dollar 2010)

Source: Author's calculation; data from Korea Energy Economics Institute (2016) and World Bank Database (accessed November 17, 2017).

can be explained, in part, by the ROK's industrial structure, which focused on the energy-consuming manufacturing sector, such as petrochemical, electronics, steel. The value added from the manufacturing sector (% of GDP) had increased and reached approximately 30% in 1988, and has not changed significantly since. This indicates that the decades of efforts to enhance energy efficiency improved energy efficiency in various sectors, but the industrial structure is highly focused on energy-consuming industries, limiting further improvements in energy intensity.

Improving energy efficiency has been an important agenda for the ROK. Along with rapid economic development, primary energy consumption has increased rapidly at a rate of 8.41% since 1981. However, the ROK's very limited domestic natural resources required the country to import most of its primary energy from other countries. As a result, the reliance on energy import increased and reached 97.3% in 1996; it had only changed to 94.8% energy dependence as of 2015 (KEEI 2016). High energy dependence requires the ROK to maintain efforts in the efficient use and conservation of energy sources.

International cooperation to promote clean energy technology

- *Target 7.a: By 2030, enhance international cooperation to facilitate access to clean energy research and technology, including renewable energy, energy efficiency and advanced and cleaner fossil-fuel technology, and promote investment in energy infrastructure and clean energy technology.*

In the Paris Agreement of 2015, all parties of the UNFCCC agreed to strengthen collective actions to tackle climate change. To support the efforts of developing countries' climate actions, developed countries pledged to mobilize US$100 billion per year by 2020. The GCF will be a key channel to mobilize financial sources for climate mitigation and adaptation. In addition to the ROK's efforts to low-carbon green growth during the Myung-bak Lee administration, the ROK is host to the secretariat of the GCF and initially committed US$40 million towards "readiness and preparatory support activities." According to GCF, the ROK's contribution to GCF reached approximately $100 million as of December 2017. Since there is no data available for the indicator that is used to evaluate target 7.a, this indicator is excluded from the analysis. Also, the detailed efforts regarding the ROK's climate action will be further discussed in Chapter 8.

Infrastructure and technology for modern and sustainable energy services

- *Target 7.b: By 2030, expand infrastructure and upgrade technology for supplying modern and sustainable energy services for all in developing countries, in particular least developed countries, small island developing States, and landlocked developing countries, in accordance with their respective programmes of support.*

The indicator suggests the use of two measures to evaluate the performance of target 7.b. However, the data for investments in energy efficiency as percentage of GDP is not available for the ROK, so only the amount of foreign direct investment in financial transfer for infrastructure and technology to sustainable development services, provided by Foreign Investment Statistics, Ministry of Trade, Industry, and Energy, was used. Especially among foreign direct investment by sector, investment in the electricity and gas sectors was used as a representative indicator.

Foreign investment in the electricity and gas sectors was highly regulated until the late 1990s. In addition to market reform in the power sector in the late 1990s, preparation for joining the OECD and the 1997 financial crisis allowed the ROK to slowly open its electricity and gas sectors to foreign direct investment (Lee 2007; Song and An 2007; Seo 2008). However, the electricity and gas sectors are classified as restricted sectors for foreign direct investment (Korea Ministry of Government Legislation 2016), and foreigners are allowed to invest a restricted amount stipulated by rules and laws. Figure 5.8. shows the amount of foreign capital invested in the electricity and gas sectors.

Results from factor analysis

In order to establish an index that presents the historical performance of the ROK's efforts in achieving SDG 7, factor analysis was conducted. Briefly, factor analysis is a statistical method used to describe variability among observed, correlated variables in terms of a potentially lower number of unobserved variables called factors.

Though the use of all indicators defined in each target is ideal for examining the ROK's progress in achieving SDG 7, the selected data were used to run factor analysis and create an index due to limited data availability and applicability of specific indicators. The data used are the following: the proportion of the population with access to electricity, renewable energy share of total final

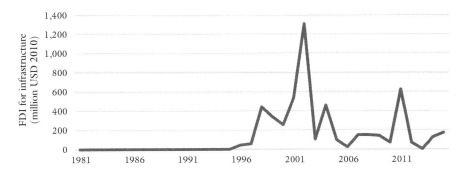

Figure 5.8 Foreign direct investment in electricity and gas sector (million USD 2010)
Source: Data from Ministry of Trade, Industry, and Energy (accessed November 9, 2017).

energy consumption, energy intensity measured in terms of primary energy and GDP, and the amount of foreign direct investment in financial transfer for infrastructure and technology to sustainable development. For the renewable energy share of total final energy consumption, the chapter intends to exclude the use of traditional renewables and reflect modern renewables. Before 1991, firewood, which is a traditional biomass, was classified as renewable and was largely used in power generation, leading the estimated portion of renewables in the 1980s to be higher than today. Due to environmental and health reasons, the use of firewood rapidly declined in the late 1980s. To correct this bias, the chapter excluded the use of firewood before 1991 from our dataset; instead, hydropower generation was included in this analysis. To examine the appropriateness of the factor analysis, KMO and Bartlett's test have been conducted. The results from Bartlett test of sphericity justified the validity of factor analysis with 0.000 of p-value, but the KMO result was 0.474, which was a little less than 0.5.

The key concept of factor analysis is that various observed variables have similar patterns of response because they are all related to a latent variable. In every factor analysis, there are the same factors as variables. Each factor catches a certain amount of the overall variance in the indicated variables, and the factors are enumerated by the amount of variation they explain. The eigenvalue is a measure of how much of the variance of the indicated variable a factor explains. Any factor with an eigenvalue ≥1 explains more variance than a single indicated variable (Reyment 1997).

The weight of each indicator has been calculated as shown in Table 5.2. The weights of four indicators are as follows: access to electricity (37.92%); share of renewables (32.93%); FDI on utility (17.16%); and energy intensity (11.99%). The results imply that two major indicators – access to electricity and share of renewables – can explain more than 70% of variances in the sample. However, the other two variables – FDI on utility and energy intensity – only explain 29% of the variance. This can be explained, in part, by the fact that FDI on utility does not have a clear trend with irregular spikes, and the gradual decreasing trend of energy intensity has stagnated since the late 1990s.

The index created by factor analysis shown in Figure 5.9 presents a clear upward trend. This result indicates that the ROK's SDG 7 has continuously improved since 1980. The positive movements of all indicators, except FDI on utility, led the improvement of SDG 7 index in the 1980s. Increasing access to electricity and the improvement in energy intensity in particular led the improvement of

Table 5.2 Factor loadings and index weights for SDG 7

Variable	Factor 1	Factor 2	Weight
Access to electricity	0.9347	0.0909	37.92%
FDI on utility	0.3030	0.6287	17.16%
Renewable	0.8710	−0.0524	32.93%
Energy intensity	−0.4043	0.5256	11.99%

Goal 7: affordable and clean energy 79

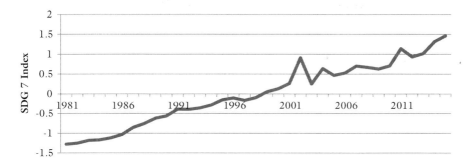

Figure 5.9 Index for SDG 7

the SDG 7 index. In the late 1990s, the progress of access to electricity, which already reached more than 95% in 1995, was slowed down, and the worsening of energy intensity, caused by the extreme depreciation in exchange rate during the financial crisis, slowed down the pace of increasing the SDG 7 index. The restricted allowance to foreign direct investment in electricity and gas sector in the late 1990s, however, and the introduction of renewable policies, such as feed-in-tariff, allowed further progress in achieving SDG 7 in the 2000s. The introduction of Renewable Portfolio Standard in 2012 accelerated the share of renewables, which is an important explanatory variable, leading to the continuing increase of SDG 7 index.

Conclusion

Over the last 50 years, the ROK has significantly developed its economy and progressed in achieving sustainable development. However, the achievement of sustainable energy has always been a major challenge for the ROK since the country is endowed with limited energy resources and its economy is driven heavily by energy-consuming industries, such as petrochemical, steel, and electronics. Accordingly, the ROK has implemented various measures, including energy conservation and efficiency policies and renewable supportive policies, to overcome the challenges faced in the energy sector.

This chapter reviewed the performance of the ROK's progress towards achieving SDG 7 affordable and clean energy over the last 35 years through factor analysis. Due to the limited availability of indicators, four variables were selected and analyzed in the analysis. The results from the analysis show that the ROK has been improving its performance in affordable and clean energy over the last 35 years. However, the main drivers for the improvement of the index have changed over time. In the earlier stage, the progress of access to electricity and energy intensity led to the improvement of the index. Along with the rural development movement in the 1970s (Saemaul Movement), the ROK had implemented extensive investments in enhancing electrification in rural areas. This led the country to achieve over 90% national electrification rate before 1980. In the late 1990s, after access to electricity reached a very high level and its progress stagnated and energy intensity worsened, the progress of the index was relatively slowed down. However, after the significant increase of energy intensity in the late 1990s, presumed to be caused by the extreme fluctuation of exchange rate, the energy intensity has gradually decreased over time. The conditional opening of the electricity and gas sector to foreign direct investment and the introduction of renewable policies, such as feed-in-tariff, accelerated the improvement of the index in the 2000s. In the late 1990s, the ROK was preparing to join the OECD and faced the financial crisis. This led the country to reform its financial sector, including conditional opening of FDI in the utility sector. Accordingly, FDI in electricity and gas sector spiked in the early 2000s and contributed to improving the index. Moreover, the shift of renewable policy towards RPS in 2012 accelerated the further penetration of renewables in final energy consumption, and this has been a major driver for the improvement of the index in recent years. Though the analysis excluded international cooperation to promote clean energy technology from the index, the ROK continues to contribute to international cooperation in enhancing global efforts in achieving SDG 7. For instance, the ROK is host to the secretariat of GCF and contributed approximately $100 million as of December 2017.

The results from the factor analysis show that access to electricity and the share of renewables are the most important factors, explaining over 70% of the variance in the sample. Access to electricity, however, reached 100% in 2012 according to the World Bank Indicator,[5] which suggests that access to electricity cannot be improved upon further. Also, the law and rules for foreign direct investment limit the amount of foreign direct investment in the electricity and gas sectors. Unless the ROK government further deregulates and opens the electricity and gas markets, foreign direct investment in the electricity and gas sectors cannot be significantly increased. Moreover, despite decades of efforts in enhancing energy conservation and efficiency, the ROK's energy intensity has been slow to progress because industrial structure, which is focused on high energy-consuming sectors, has not significantly changed over the decades. These circumstances suggest that the ROK should encourage the further penetration of renewables as well as the improvement of energy intensity in order to improve the progress in achieving SDG 7 in the future. Continued progress in meeting the RPS requirements in particular, which can significantly increase the renewable energy share, will be critical. The success of the national energy plan to restrain energy demand will be important to improve the ROK's energy intensity.

Notes

1 RISE is a program launched by SE4ALL and the World Bank. The program monitors the "progress towards establishing the necessary policy and regulatory frameworks for sustainable energy."

Goal 7: affordable and clean energy 81

2 The analysis used the World Bank Development Indicator (October 2016 vintage). The World Bank Indicator provides "access to electricity (%)" every five years. From 1981 to 2000, the chapter assumes that the access to electricity increases annually with the average percentage change of the "access to electricity (%)" between 1990 and 2000. From 2000 to 2010, the chapter assumes that the access to electricity increases annually with the average percentage change between 2000 and 2010.
3 Formerly, its name was Heat Management Association, and it was changed to the Korea Energy Management Corporation. Recently, it changed its name to the Korea Energy Agency in 2015.
4 The top runner program set the target efficiency standard as the best technology available on the market or the model with the highest energy efficiency, and the program requires the average efficiency of all models that the manufacturer produces on the market to exceed the target efficiency standard within the predetermined target years (Prime Minister's Office and the Ministry of Knowledge Economy 2008).
5 Though the SE4ALL project (SE4ALL 2017) indicates that Korea has reached the access to electricity of 100% in 1995, the data used the World Bank Indicator (October 2016), which provided access to electricity data for every 5 years.

Reference

Boo, K, J. Ryu, H. Kim, and J. Park. 2013. *2012 Modularization of Korea's Development Experience: Energy Policies.* Sejong: Ministry of Strategy and Finance, Republic of Korea.
Conture, T. D., K. Kreycik, and E. Williams. 2010. "A Policymaker's Guide to Feed-in-Tariff Policy Design." *NREL/TP-6A2–44849.* Accessed November 11, 2017. www.nrel.gov/docs/fy10osti/44849.pdf
Frankfurt School–UNEP Centre and Bloomberg New Energy Finance. 2016. *Global Trends in Renewable Energy Investment 2016.* Frankfurt am Main: Frankfurt School of Finance & Management gGmbH. Accessed November 24, 2017. http://fs-unep-centre.org/sites/default/files/publications/globaltrendsinrenewableenergyinvestment2016lowres_0.pdf
Intergovernmental Panel on Climate Change (IPCC). *Climate Change 2014: Mitigation of Climate Change.* New York: Cambridge University Press. Accessed November 11, 2017. www.ipcc.ch/pdf/assessment-report/ar5/wg3/ipcc_wg3_ar5_full.pdf
International Energy Agency. 2012. *Energy Policies of IEA Countries: The Republic of Korea 2012.* Paris: OECD/IEA. Accessed November 13, 2017. www.iea.org/publications/freepublications/publication/Korea2012_free.pdf
International Energy Agency (IEA). 2014a. *Capturing the Multiple Benefits of Energy Efficiency.* Paris: OECD/IEA. www.iea.org/publications/freepublications/publication/Captur_the_MultiplBenef_ofEnergyEficiency.pdf
International Energy Agency (IEA). 2014b. *World Energy Outlook 2014.* Paris: OECD/IEA (International Energy Agency).
International Energy Agency. 2017. *Energy Efficiency Market Report.* Paris: OECD/IEA.
International Renewable Energy Agency. 2017. *Renewable Energy Benefits: Understanding the Socio-economics.* Abu Dhabi: IRENA.
Korea Energy Agency Official Site. "Energy Efficiency Program." Accessed November 4, 2017. http://eep.energy.or.kr/main/main.aspx

Korea Energy Agency Official Site. "Renewable Portfolio Standards (RPS)." Accessed November 12, 2017. www.energy.or.kr/renew_eng/new/standards.aspx/

Korea Energy Economics Institute. 2006. *The History of Energy Policy*. [In Korean]. Ulsan: KEEI. www.keei.re.kr/keei/download/HEP20.pdfs

Korea Energy Economics Institute. 2016. *Yearbook of Energy Statistics*. Ulsan: KEEI.

Korea Ministry of Government Legislation. 1987. "Alternative Energy Development Promotion Act." [In Korean]. Accessed December 2, 2017. www.law.go.kr/lsInfoP.do?lsiSeq=166&ancYd=19871204&ancNo=03990&efYd=19880101&nwJoYnInfo=N&efGubun=Y&chrClsCd=010202#0000

Korea Ministry of Government Legislation. 2016. "Rules for Foreign Direct Investment." [In Korean]. Accessed November 23, 2017. www.law.go.kr/admRulLsInfoP.do?admRulSeq=2100000059689

KOSIS. "International Oil Price [data]." Accessed November 17, 2017. http://kosis.kr/statHtml/statHtml.do?orgId=392&tblId=DT_AA124

LAWASIA. 2017. "South Korea's Renewable Energy Policy Under the New Climate Change Framework." 30th LAWASIA Conference, Tokyo, Japan.

Lee, Y. 2007. "Foreign Direct Investment." National Archives of Korea. Accessed November 10, 2017. www.archives.go.kr/next/search/listSubjectDescription.do?id=006698

Ministry of Commerce Industry and Energy. 1991. "The Second Energy Use Rationalization Plan." MOCIE Press release. [In Korean]. Accessed November 12, 2017. www.kdi.re.kr/policy/ep_view.jsp?idx=28310

Ministry of Commerce Industry and Energy. 2004. "The Third Energy Use Rationalization Plan." [In Korean]. Accessed November 12, 2017. www.kemco.or.kr/nd_upload/pds/040824%203%EC%B0%A8%ED%95%A9%EB%A6%AC%ED%99%94%EA%B8%B0%EB%B3%B8%EA%B3%84%ED%9A%8D(%EC%B5%9C%EC%A2%85).pdf]

Ministry of Knowledge Economy. 2008. *The Third Basic Plan for the Development and Utilization of the New and Renewable Energy Technology*. [In Korean]. Accessed November 10, 2017. www.aurum.re.kr/Legal/PlanFileDownLoad.aspx?num=181

Ministry of Knowledge Economy and Korea Electric Power Corporation. 2012. *2011 Economic Development Experience Modularization Project: For Spreading Power Supply Rural Telephone Business*. [In Korean]. Accessed November 11, 2017. www.kdi.re.kr/common/report_download.jsp?list_no=12856&member_pub=2&type=pub&cacheclear=59

Ministry of Trade, Industry, and Energy. 2000. *Basic Plan for Dissemination and Development of Alternative Energy Technologies*. [In Korean]. Accessed October 25, 2017. www.knrec.or.kr/dfile/policy_support/1.%20%EB%8C%80%EC%B2%B4%EC%97%90%EB%84%88%EC%A7%80%20%EA%B8%B0%EC%88%A0%EA%B0%9C%EB%B0%9C%EB%B3%B4%EA%B8%89%20%EA%B8%B0%EB%B3%B8%EA%B3%84-%ED%9A%8D.pdf

Ministry of Trade, Industry, and Energy. 2003. *The Second Basic Plan for the Development and Utilization of the New Renewable Energy Technology*. [In Korean]. Accessed October 25, 2017. www.knrec.or.kr/dfile/policy_support/2.%20%EC%A0%9C2%EC%B0%A8%20%EC%8B%A0%EC%9E%AC%EC%83%9D%EC%97%90%EB%84%88%EC%A7%80%20%EA%B8%B0%EC%88%A0%EA%B0%9C%EB%B0%9C%20%EB%B0%8F%20%EC%9D%B4%EC%9A%A9%EB%B3%B4%EA%B8%89%20%EA%B8%B0%EB%B3%B8%EA%B3%84%ED%9A%8D.pdf

Ministry of Trade, Industry, and Energy. 2014a. *The 4th Basic Plan for Development and Utilization and Distribution of New and Renewable Energy Technologies.* [In Korean]. Accessed October 25, 2017. www.knrec.or.kr/dfile/policy_support/4.%20%EC%A0%9C4%EC%B0%A8%20%EC%8B%A0%EC%9E%AC%EC%83%9D%EC%97%90%EB%84%88%EC%A7%80%20%EA%B8%B0%EC%88%A0%EA%B0%9C%EB%B0%9C%20%EB%B0%8F%20%EC%9D%B4%EC%9A%A9%EB%B3-%B4%EA%B8%89%20%EA%B8%B0%EB%B3%B8%EA%B3%84%ED%9A%8D.pdf

Ministry of Trade, Industry, and Energy. 2014b. *The Second Energy Master Plan.* [In Korean]. Accessed October 26, 2017. www.motie.go.kr/common/download.do?fid=bbs&bbs_cd_n=16&bbs_seq_n=78654&file_seq_n=3

Ministry of Trade, Industry, and Energy. 2017. "The 8th Plan of Electricity Supply and Demand." [In Korean]. www.motie.go.kr/common/download.do?fid=bbs&bbs_cd_n=81&bbs_seq_n=159970&file_seq_n=3

National Law Information Center. 1974. *Heat Management Law.* [In Korean].. Accessed November 4, 2017. www.law.go.kr/lsEfInfoP.do?lsiSeq=169#

National Law Information Center. 1980. *Energy Use Rationalization Law.* [In Korean]. Accessed November 4, 2017. http://law.go.kr/lsInfoP.do?lsiSeq=7880&ancYd=19791228&ancNo=03181&efYd=19800629&nwJoYnInfo=N&efGubun=Y&chrClsCd=010202#0000

OECD. 2016. "Energy and Transport." In *OECD Factbook 2015–2016.* Paris: OECD.

Prime Minister's Office and the Ministry of Knowledge Economy. 2008. "Improve of Energy Efficiency by 11.3% by 2012." Prime Minister's Office and Ministry of Knowledge Economy press release. [In Korean]. Accessed November 25, 2017. www.motie.go.kr/motie/ne/presse/press2/bbs/bbsView.do?bbs_seq_n=45314&bbs_cd_n=81

Regulatory Indicators for Sustainable Energy (RISE) Homepage. "Overall Scores." Accessed December 20, 2017. http://rise.worldbank.org/scores

Reyment, A. R. 1997. "Multiple Group Principal Component Analysis." *Mathematical Geology*, 29.1: 1–16.

SE4ALL. 2012. "A Global Action Agenda, Pathways for Concerted Action Toward Sustainable Energy for All." Accessed December 10, 2017. www.un.org/wcm/webdav/site/sustainableenergyforall/shared/Documents/SEFA-Action%20Agenda-Final.pdf

SE4ALL. 2017. *Global Tracking Framework.* New York: Sustainable Energy for All Initiative. Accessed December 10, 2017. www.se4all.org/global-tracking-framework.

Seo, C. 2008. "Analysis of Korean Legal System on Foreign Direct Investment in Energy Industry." *Korea International Trade Law Association*, 17.2.

Song, Y., and Jun An. 2007. "The Effectiveness of Foreign Capital Regulation in Korea as a Defensive Mechanism of Hostile M&A." *KIEP Policy References 07–08.* [In Korean].

UN General Assembly. 2015. "Resolution Adopted by the General Assembly on 25 September 2015." Accessed October 27, 2017. http://unctad.org/meetings/en/SessionalDocuments/ares70d1_en.pdf

UNSTATS. 2016. "Goal 7. Ensure Access to Affordable, Reliable, Sustainable and Modern Energy for All." Accessed October 10, 2017. https://unstats.un.org/sdgs/files/metadata-compilation/Metadata-Goal-7.pdf

World Bank Database. "GDP (Current US$) [data]." Accessed November 17, 2017. https://data.worldbank.org/indicator/NY.GDP.MKTP.CD?end=2016&locations=KR&start=1960&view=chart

World Wide Fund (WWF). 2014. "Will Developing Countries Lead the Renewable Energy Race?" Accessed December 10, 2017. http://climate-energy.blogs.panda.org/2014/10/16/meet-developing-countries-leading-renewables-race/

Yu, J. 2009. *Analysis on the Issues of the Introduction of RPS*. Seoul: National Assembly Research Service. [In Korean]. Accessed December 7, 2017. http://drm.nars.go.kr:7003/sd/imageviewer?ViewerYn=Y&type=H&doc_id=42582&fileName=KO2YhOyViOuztOqzoOyEnDAyM%2B2YuC0yMDA5MDQwMSnsi6Dsnqzsg53sl5DrhIjsp4Ag7J2Y66y07ZWg64u57KCcIOuPhOyeheq0gOugqCDsn4HsoJDrtoTshJ0ucGRm

6 Goal 8: decent network and economic growth

Sung Jin Kang, Sun Lee, and Seo Kyung Lim

Introduction

SDG 8 aims to promote sustainable economic growth and productive employment, like macroeconomic policies that are generally focused on growth with employment. However, the ROK is currently experiencing economic growth but with a lower employment rate than before. It is necessary to establish policies to stabilize the economy based on the interrelationship of growth and employment, which is essential for sustainable development.

The UN SDSN Report released an index of SDG 8 in the ROK: (1) Adjusted GDP Growth (−7.2%); (2) Percentage of children 5–14 years old involved in child labor (0%); (3) Adults (15 years and older) with an account at a bank or other financial institution or with a mobile-money-service provider (95.7%); (4) Employment-to-population ratio (66.1%); (5) Youth not in employment, education, or training (NEET, 18). The index score of SDG 8 is 78.6; however, since many other indicators of SDG 8 are excluded, additional analysis in accordance to national features are necessary (Sachs et al. 2017, 110–111). Furthermore, the UN SDSN follows an arbitrary classification to determine the degree of achievement of each SDG even though many indicator variables are excluded from the index.

This study estimates the economic sustainability for SDG 8. Applying factor analysis, this study analyzes and captures the change of the nation's economic sustainability over time for SDG 8 with 12 sub-goals from 1990 to 2015. Based on the statistical data, the SDG 8 index has fluctuated over time, but showed an overall increasing trend. The indicators related to economic growth in particular display a great influence on the index, while the sustainability level of 1998 was the lowest.

This chapter begins with an introduction to the policies of the Korean government related to the SDG 8. Following this, the economic trend of Korea based upon the indicators of SDG 8 is presented, showing the limitations of the data. The penultimate section suggests the direction of future sustainability policy based on the SDG 8 index. Finally, the chapter concludes with policy implications.

Relevant policy overview

Since the beginning of the 1990s, the ROK government has been making efforts to reorganize and reestablish the Five-Year Plan of the Seventh Economic Social Development, i.e. the Five-Year Plan of the New Economy, which is to enhance industrial superiority, improve social equity, and seek overall balanced development with a perspective of mid- to long-term application. In addition, the government has continued its endeavor with sustainable economic development plans that focus on economic reformation, extension of welfare policy, achievement of a higher growth rate, and job creation.

The government has established sustainable development strategies and policies at the national level for the implementation of SDG 8. The national plans include the Basic Plans for Sustainable Development, National Sustainable Development, the Five-Year Plan for Green Growth, the Industrial Technology Innovation Promotion Act, and Creative Economy Action Plan.[1] Figure 6.1 presents an overview of the important national plans for sustainable development.

First, the Third Basic Plan for Sustainable Development (2016~2035) addresses problems such as economic recession, slowing productivity, the labor shortage due to the low birth rate, and the aging trend. By solving these problems, the government intends to promote the sustainability of economic growth and transformation of the industrial structure. It includes four implementation plans: the creation of a resource-recycling economic society, the establishment of a sustainable economic base, efficient energy use, and human resource development and job creation.

Second, the National Sustainable Development and the Five-Year Plan for Green Growth facilitate the implementation of the National Strategy for Green

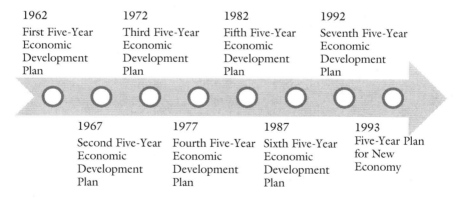

Figure 6.1 National policies relevant to SDG 8

Source: Joint Work of Relevant Ministries (2013, 2014b); Sustainable Development Portal, "Basic Plan for National Sustainable Strategy." Accessed May 8, 2017. http://ncsd.go.kr/app/sub03/22_tab3.do; Green Growth Korea, "Five-Year Plan." Accessed May 8, 2017. www.greengrowth.go.kr/menu001/sub002/GRG_001_202.do.

Growth. The major achievements for SDG 8 by Policy Directions of the Second Green Growth Plan in 2014 are as follows: the selection of 27 major green technologies (2009); improving the level of green technology through expansion of R&D investment and the establishment of the Basic Plan for Resource Circulation (2011); the establishment of targets for resource productivity and circulation; the construction of eight eco-industrial complexes (EIP); the continuous expansion of investment in high value-added services and advanced convergence technologies; and, lastly, an increase in production.

However, since the development of the main green technologies is not enough to promote market creation and industrial growth, these positive effects do not spread sufficiently to small and medium enterprises (SME). In addition, a higher proportion of the manufacturing sector made it difficult to transform the existing industrial structure. In 2014, the ROK government, recognizing the need for a strategy to complement such problems, proposed key tasks for creating an ecosystem for the green creative industry, which includes the development of high-tech convergence green technology, development of green creative industries, establishment of a resource cycling economic structure, rationalization of regulations, and cultivation of human resource in green sectors, along with key performance indicators and target levels.

Finally, the Creative Economy in Action Plan 2013 is an economic strategy for creating jobs through new industries that combine scientific technology and ICT, market creation, and strengthening existing industries. They are closely related to SDG 8, suggesting strategies for cultivating industries that focus on growth engines and capacity building.

In addition, along with the policy strategy described above, each ministry has published policies for SDG 8, which can be largely categorized into policies for industry and employment. Figure 6.2 shows detailed policies that are related to SDG 8. Poverty and job creation, as well as the formation of the environmental system in industries, are the foundation of these policies. It also suits the purpose of SDG 8 with regard to the establishment of mid- to long-term plans.

The Sixth Industrial Technology Innovation Plan, published in 2014, enhances creativity and productivity of the R&D industry as the industrial mechanism changes and proposes a leap forward in industrial power by creating a virtuous circle in industrial technology.[2] Among the strategies, the development of technologies, nurturing of local industries, and fostering of human resources are closely related to SDG 8. Related indicators include global market share, export, industrial employment, level of technology compared with advanced countries, local employment, industrial human resources development, and job creation.

The policy for employment is the basic plan for labor welfare promotion, which is to support overall worker-related life and environment. In other words, improving the work environment of workers and the social safety net functions performed by the government. As concerns about employment grew, policies to achieve job security were also announced. In addition, the government has established mid- to long-term plans and implemented policies for job stability.

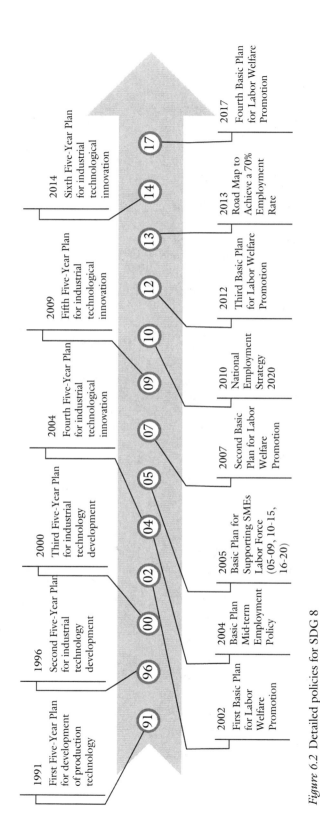

Figure 6.2 Detailed policies for SDG 8

Source: Lim et al. (2016, 76–80); MOTIE (2013); Ministry of Employment and Labor (2017).

Unlike previous policies, the focus is on the interaction between the environment and the economy, and efforts to establish sustainable policies from the perspective of the green economy through a virtuous cycle can be seen. This implies that the strategies of SDGs should be implemented in harmony rather than separately. Therefore, this study intends to utilize the empirical analysis results of SDG 8 to suggest policy directions.

Data for economic growth trend

Definition of variables and data source

Table 6.1 introduces the list of variables that encompass SDG 8. The goal is divided into 12 sub-goals with corresponding indicators. They include economic growth, employment, material footprint, gender wage gap, unemployment rate, child labor rate, frequency and severity rate, tourism expenditure, bank-related factors, and ODA amounts. However, since not all variables have an equal length of time, only variables with similar timespans are used. For example, indicators for the child labor rate and the level of national compliance of labor rights are excluded due to the lack of available data. Also, unlike the UN SDSN index, which uses static data, this study constructs an index using indicators with at least 19 years of available data to consider the trends of SDG indicators.

Analysis on the performance in Goal 8 by target

Sub-goals 8.1 and 8.2 represent the overall trends of the economic growth rates where GDP per capita represents the standard of living of a country. First, sub-goal 8.1 aims to maintain a steady economic growth rate for each country. In the case of the least developed countries (LDC), a standard of minimum annual growth rate of 7% is used to measure sustainable economic growth (sub-goal 8.1). Since the ROK is not an LDC, the annual growth rate of real GDP per capita is used as the measurement of sustainable economic growth. Second, sub-goal 8.2 indicates the growth rate of economic productivity. This is based on the annual growth rate of real GDP per worker. In this study, the data for annual growth rate of GDP per employed person from the World Development Indicator (WDI) is used. As it can be seen in Figure 6.3, the indicators for sub-goals 8.1 and 8.2 show a similar trend over time. The growth rates decline during the two economic crises: the Korean financial crisis in 1997; and the global financial crisis in 2008.

Sub-goal 8.3 represents the share of informal employment of the non-agriculture sector. The International Labor Organization (ILO) explains that the informal economy accounts for three-quarters of all non-agricultural employment in developing countries. Even though it is difficult to generalize the quality of informal employment, it mostly means that low employment conditions are correlated with an increase of poverty.[3] However, for the ROK, statistics of informal employment for the non-agriculture sector is limited, and only the total

Table 6.1 Variables and year coverage used in SDG 8 index

Goal	Indicator	Variables	Year	Source	Effect	Included in analysis
8.1	8.1.1	GDP per capita growth (annual %, constant 2010)	1991–2015	WDI	(+)	Yes
8.2	8.2.1	GDP per employed person growth (annual %, constant 2011)	1992–2015	WDI	(+)	Yes
8.3	8.3.1	Informal employment (non-agriculture)	–	–	(–)	No
8.4	8.4.1	Material footprint (total, per GDP, per capita)	2000–2010	UN data	(–)	No
	8.4.2	DMC (million tons)	1991–2012	Kim et al.	(–)	Yes
	8.4.2	DMC per GDP (tons per USD)	1991–2012	(2010), OECD	(–)	Yes
	8.4.2	DMC per capita (tons per person)	1991–2012		(–)	Yes
8.5	8.5.1	Gender wage gap (%)	2000–2015	OECD	(–)	Yes
	8.5.2	Unemployment 15+ (%)	1991–2015	ILO	(–)	Yes
	8.5.2	rate by sex in 15–24 (%)	1991–2015		(–)	Yes
	8.5.2	age group 15–64 (%)	1981–1989 2000–2015		(–)	Yes
	8.5.2	24+ (%)	1991–2015		(–)	Yes
8.6	8.6.1	NEET percentage in age group	2008–2013	OECD	(–)	No
8.7	8.7.1	Child labor rate (%)	–	–	(–)	No
8.8	8.8.1	Frequency rate	1991–2015	KOSIS	(–)	Yes
	8.8.1	Severity rate	1991–2015	MOEL	(–)	Yes
	8.8.2	Level of national compliance of labor rights	–	–	(+)	No
8.9	8.9.1	Tourism real GDP (billion USD)	1995–2015	WTTC	(+)	Yes
	8.9.1	Tourism percentage of GDP	1995–2015		(+)	Yes
	8.9.2	Tourism % share of total employment	1995–2015		(+)	Yes
8.10	8.10.1	Bank branches (BOK)	1999–2015	BOK	(+)	Yes
	8.10.1	ATMs (BOK)	1992–2015		(+)	Yes
	8.10.2	Electronic finance services (BOK)	1991–2015		(+)	Yes
8.a	8.a.1	ODA commitments (LCDs, million USD, constant 2015)	1991–1993 1995–2015	OECD	(+)	Yes
		ODA disbursements (LCDs, million USD, constant 2015)	1991–2015		(+)	Yes
8.b	8.b.1	Public expenditure (%)	1991–2015	KOSIS	(+)	Yes

Source: The detailed sources of the data are listed in references.

Note:

1) See Appendix for detailed explanation.
2) MOEL is Ministry of Employment and Labor.

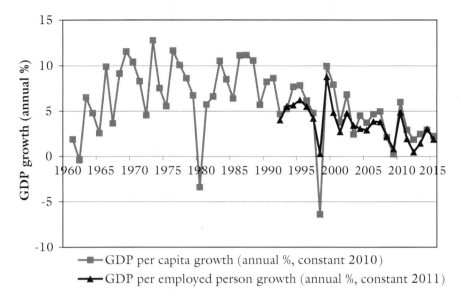

Figure 6.3 Growth rates of GDP per capita and GDP per employed person (annual %)

Source: The World Bank, World Development Indicators. "GDP Per Capita Growth (Annual %) and GDP Per Person Employed (Constant 2011 PPP $)." Accessed May 8, 2017. https://data.worldbank.org.

number of informal workers in the total industry is available. Therefore, for sub-goal 8.3, only the trend of informal workers in the total industry (including the non-agricultural sector) and non-agriculture sector is examined.

Figure 6.4 shows the share of informal workers in the non-agriculture sector and total industry by gender. The share of informal workers to total workers in the total industry shows a decreasing trend, and the share of female informal workers is higher than their male counterparts. Also, to examine sub-goal 8.3, the share of informal workers in the non-agriculture sector is examined. The result shows that in 2009, the shares of informal male and female workers in the non-agriculture sector were 15.01% and 9.60%, respectively. By 2015, the share had decreased to 13.54% and 8.24% for male and female informal workers, respectively. However, a caveat is that the data is only available for six years (2009–2013, and 2015). Therefore, this indicator is excluded from the factor analysis.

Sub-goal 8.4 examines economic growth with low environmental degradation by measuring the improved efficiency in consumption and production of resources. The indicators are material footprint (MF) and domestic material consumption (DMC). Since MF is not available over the whole period, only DMC is used to represent the indicator of sub-goal 8.4. Like sub-goal 8.3, the trend of MF is examined, which represents the quantity of raw materials as a property

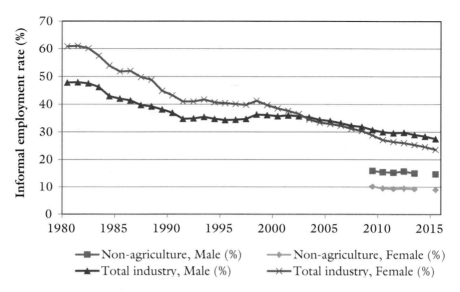

Figure 6.4 Informal employment rate by non-agricultural industry and gender (%)
Source: KOSIS. "Total and Non-agriculture Informal Employed Worker." Accessed September 10, 2017. http://kosis.kr/; ILO. "Informal Economy." Accessed May 8, 2017. www.ilo.org/global/topics/employment-promotion/informal-economy/lang–en/index.htm.

of a global material extraction of a country's domestic final demand. Table 6.2 shows the trend of Korea's MF per GDP (2000–2010), which tends to fall over the years.

DMC implies how efficiently resources are being used in the country. DMC measures the total amount of materials directly used by an economy and is defined as the annual quantity of raw materials extracted from domestic territory, plus all physical imports, minus all physical exports.[4] Figure 6.5 represents three variables: DMC; ratio of DMC to GDP; and DMC per capita. DMC is shown to have decreased two times in 1998 and 2009, which are the years after the financial crises. This suggests that the consumption of domestic materials tends to decrease as the economic activity of the economic entities is reduced. In terms of percentage, the increase in GDP is greater than the increase in DMC, meaning that there is an overall dematerialization trend in the ROK. However, in 1998 and 2008–2009, the percentage increase in DMC was greater than the increase in GDP, showing that the consumption of material is relatively low compared to the value-added from economic activities. On the other hand, the per capita consumption of materials increased from 9.64 in 1991 to 14.18 in 2012. This shows that DMC per capita is increasing faster than the increase in population, and it shows that consumption of material is increasing for economic entities such as households and businesses.

Table 6.2 Material footprint

(unit: million tons, tons per constant 2010 USD, tons per person)

	MF	2000	2001	2002	2003	2004	2005	2006	2007	2008	2009	2010
ROK	Total	1,014	1,020	1,071	1,164	1,175	1,088	1,090	1,140	1,156	1,078	1,125
	per GDP	1.4	1.4	1.3	1.4	1.4	1.2	1.2	1.1	1.1	1.0	1.0
	per capita	21.6	21.5	22.5	24.3	24.4	22.6	22.5	23.4	23.6	21.9	22.7
WOR	Total	48,479	49,369	50,004	52,778	55,770	58,673	61,561	64,863	65,511	65,731	69,329
	per GDP	1.2	1.2	1.2	1.2	1.2	1.3	1.3	1.3	1.3	1.3	1.3
	per capita	8.0	8.0	8.1	8.4	8.8	9.1	9.4	9.8	9.8	9.7	10.1

Source: The United Nations Statistics Division. "Material Footprint, Material Footprint Per Capita and Material Footprint Per Unit of GDP." Accessed June 19, 2017. http://data.un.org; The World Bank, World Development Indicators. "GDP Per Capita (Constant 2010) and Population." Accessed June 19, 2017. https://data.worldbank.org.

Note:

1) Material footprint (MF) is the attribution of global material extraction to domestic final demand of a country. It is calculated as raw material equivalent of imports (RMEIM) plus domestic extraction (DE) minus raw material equivalents of exports (RMEEX).

2) MF per GDP and MF per capita figures are calculated by the author.

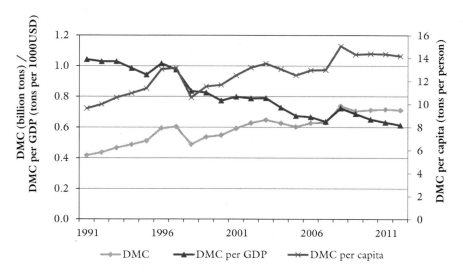

Figure 6.5 Domestic material consumption per GDP and capita

Source: Kim et al. (2010, 16); OECD.Stat. "Material Resources." Accessed September 10, 2017. http://stats.oecd.org/Index.aspx?DataSetCode=material_resources#; The World Bank, World Development Indicators. "GDP Per Capita (Constant 2010) and Population." Accessed May 8, 2017. https://data.worldbank.org.

Note:

(1) DMC per GDP and DMC per capita figures are calculated by the author.

(2) GDP unit is constant 2010 USD.

For sub-goal 8.5, the indicators of the labor market situation, which are represented by gender wage gap and age-specific or gender-specific unemployment rates, are used. According to Okun's law, there is a negative correlation between the output of a country and unemployment (Okun 1962), so efforts to create sustainable jobs are also a part of economic growth. In this study, we used the gender wage gap by the OECD and the unemployment statistics provided by the ILO to examine the current wage gap situation in the ROK. The gender wage gap has gradually decreased since 2000, with the exception of the manufacturing sector (see Figure 6.6). This indicator was extrapolated with manufacturing sector statistics due to the lack of statistics before 2000. Figure 6.7 and Figure 6.8 show various unemployment rates in Korea. The unemployment rate by total, male, and female age groups showed similar trends, and the highest level was recorded around 1998.

Sub-goal 8.6 indicates the percentage of 15–24 years old who are not in education, employment, or training (NEET). Table 6.3 shows the trend of NEET by age groups. From 2008 to 2013, the average for all age groups for the ROK is at a minimum of 15.92 and a maximum of 17.08, which is greater than the OECD average. Sub-goal 8.7, on the other hand, is a measure of the proportion of child labor, which does not fit the ROK situation.

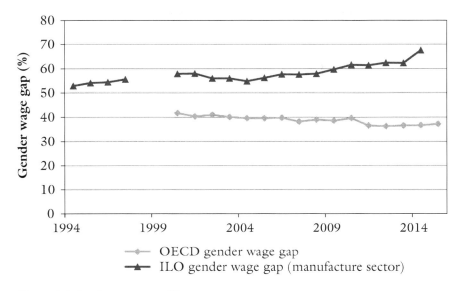

Figure 6.6 Gender wage gap (%)

Source: OECD (2017a); ILO STAT. "Average Hourly Earnings of Female and Male Employees." Accessed July 20, 2017. www.ilo.org/ilostat.

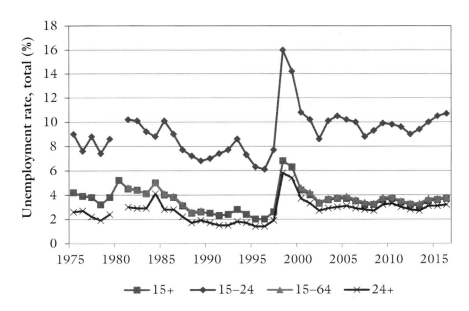

Figure 6.7 Unemployment rate by age group (%)

Source: ILOSTAT. "Unemployment Rate by Sex and Age." Accessed July 20, 2017. www.ilo.org/ilostat.

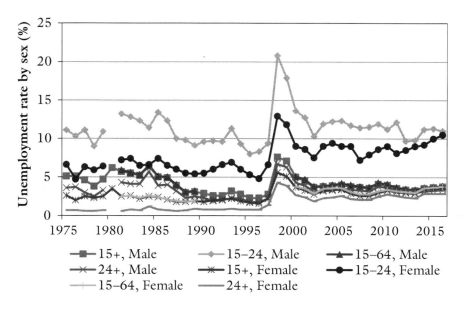

Figure 6.8 Unemployment rate by male and female (%)

Source: ILOSTAT. "Unemployment Rate by Sex and Age." Accessed July 20, 2017. www.ilo.org/ilostat.

Table 6.3 Youth not in employment, education or training (NEET) % by age group

(unit: %)

Age groups	Country	2008	2009	2010	2011	2012	2013
15–19	Korea	7.04	6.95	8.47	8.72	8.55	7.75
	OECD	7.06	8.43	7.90	7.99	6.85	7.06
20–24	Korea	22.20	23.01	23.51	23.29	22.52	22.16
	OECD	15.46	18.32	18.71	18.33	17.56	18.20
15–29	Korea	18.51	19.00	19.25	18.79	18.47	18.05
	OECD	13.59	15.72	15.85	15.75	15.01	15.58
Average	ROK	15.92	16.32	17.08	16.93	16.51	15.98
	OECD	12.04	14.16	14.15	14.02	13.14	13.61

Source: OECD (2017b). "Youth Not in Employment, Education or Training (NEET) (indicator)." Accessed September 4, 2017. doi: 10.1787/72d1033a-en.

Note: OECD is average of OECD countries.

In addition, frequency rate, intensity, and severity rate are used as proxies of qualitative sustainability of work, which are assumed to be indicators of sub-goal 8.8 (see Figure 6.9). The frequency rate is the measure of accidents, which occurred in relation to the working time or the number of workers, and the

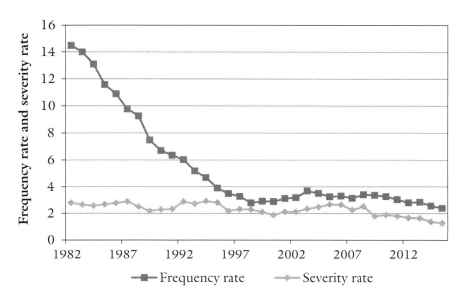

Figure 6.9 Sustainability of work indicators
Source: KOSIS. "Work Frequency Rate and Severity Rate." Accessed September 10, 2017. http://kosis.kr/; Laborstat from MOEL. "Industrial Disaster." Accessed June 28, 2017. http://laborstat.moel.go.kr/.

severity rate is the value expressed in terms of the number of working days lost in relation to total working hours. In addition, the variables tend to show a decreasing trend, indicating that the safety of labor due to industrial accidents is increasingly guaranteed, but it is also suggested that continuous efforts for a high-quality work environment are needed in the future.

Indicators of sustainable tourism promotion (sub-goal 8.9) are value-added in tourism as a proportion of total GDP, employment in tourism, and total value-added in tourism. These indicators are provided by the World Travel & Tourism Council (WTTC). In the ROK, tourism-related indicators fell after the financial crisis, but the trend is gradually increasing. Figure 6.10 shows the indicator trends of sub-goal 8.9 for the tourism industry. The value-added by tourism has been shown to be increasing, while the proportion of tourism in GDP is decreasing. In addition, the ratio of job creation in the tourism industry tends to increase steadily. OECD (2016) suggested that the tourism industry plays an important role in stimulating economic activity, continuous tourism promotion for employment and exportation are necessities for sustainable growth in the ROK.

Sub-goal 8.10, as the last indicator of SDG 8, represents the capacity of financial institutions. This is based on the number of ATMs and the percentage

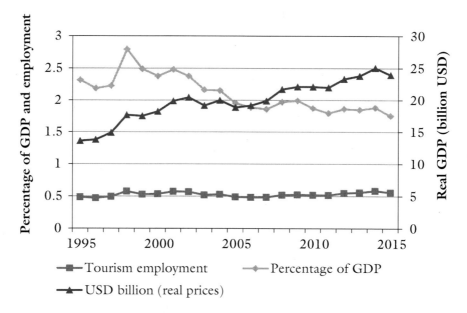

Figure 6.10 Share of tourism contribution to GDP and employment

Source: WTTC. "Direct Contribution to Employment and GDP." Accessed September 28, 2017. www.wttc.org/datagateway.

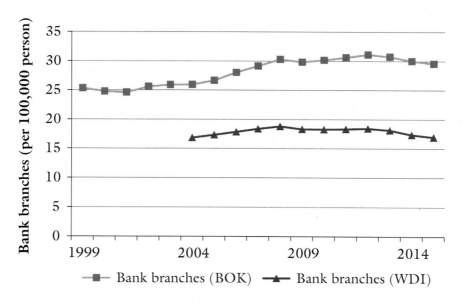

Figure 6.11 Number of commercial bank branches

Source: Bank of Korea Database. "Bank Branches." Accessed September 8, 2017. https://ecos.bok.or.kr; The World Bank, Global Financial Development. "Bank Branches." Accessed September 8, 2017. https://data.worldbank.org.

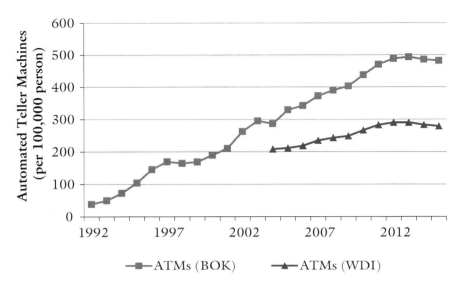

Figure 6.12 Number of automated teller machines

Source: Bank of Korea Database. "Number of Automated Teller Machines." Accessed September 8, 2017. https://ecos.bok.or.kr; The World Bank, Global Financial Development. "Number of Automated Teller Machines (Per 100,000 Person)." Accessed September 8, 2017. https://data.worldbank.org.

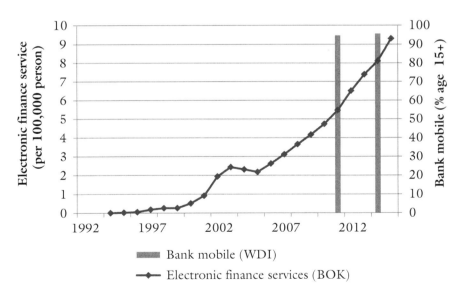

Figure 6.13 Proportion of adults (15 years and older) with electronic finance services

Source: Bank of Korea Database. "Electronic Finance Services." Accessed September 8, 2017. https://ecos.bok.or.kr; The World Bank, Global Financial Development. "Bank Mobile (% Age 15+)." Accessed September 8, 2017. https://data.worldbank.org.

of adults using accounts or other financial services (see Figures 6.11 to 6.13). The indicators are provided by both the WDI and Bank of Korea (BOK). However, since the WDI data does not cover the whole period under examination, the BOK data is used in this chapter. Even though the indicators by the BOK are shown to be higher than those by the WDI, both datasets show a consistent trend over the years. Furthermore, the increasing trend of financial variables implies the strong capability of financial institutions in the ROK.

SDG 8 provides sub-goals for trade transactions, payment assistance, social security, and employment programs. The OECD Aid for Trade commitments,[5] disbursements, and public expenditure are used as indicators. Figure 6.14 represents the trend of Aid for Trade commitment and disbursement. The ROK has shown a significant increase in Aid for Trade commitment to LDCs since 2000, and the inclination of disbursement has been relatively gradual since the 1990s.

Public expenditure is composed of public welfare in accordance with demographics data (see Figure 6.15). Public expenditure includes all financial flows of public institutions for social purposes. In this respect, this sub-goal can confirm if the function of the social safety net is working well. According to the OECD Social Expenditure DB, public expenditure of the ROK increased from 2.7% in 1990 to 9.3% in 2013. The compounded annual growth rate (CAGR) of public expenditure for the ROK (5.3%) is higher than the US (1.5%), Japanese (3.1%), and OECD average (0.9%). Annual public expenditure of the ROK is relatively lower than other countries, but it shows an overall increasing trend.

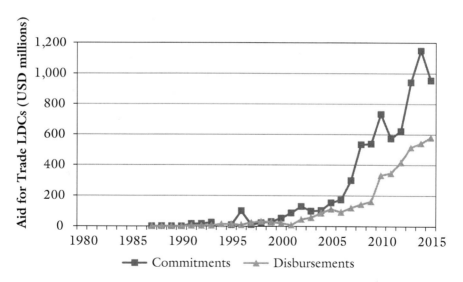

Figure 6.14 The OECD aid for trade commitments and disbursements (LDCs)

Source: OECD.Stat. "Aid for Trade." Accessed July 9, 2017. www.oecd.org/dac/aft/aid-for-tradestatisticalqueries.htm.

Goal 8: decent network and economic growth 101

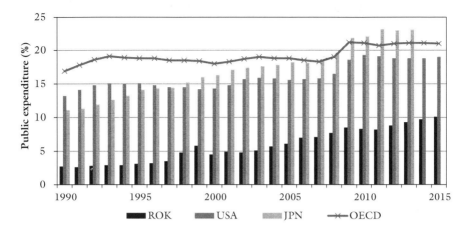

Figure 6.15 The OECD public expenditure (%)
Source: OECD. "Social Expenditure Database." Accessed November 1, 2017. www.oecd.org/social/expenditure.htm.
Note:
1) Figures for 2014–2016 are preliminary.
2) OECD is Average of OECD countries.

Empirical results

Results from factor analysis

$$Goal\ 8\ Index = \sum_{i=1}^{9} w_i \left(sub\_goal\right)_i \qquad (1)$$

where i is the sub-goals (8.1, 8.2, 8.4, 8.5, 8.8, 8.9, 8,10, 8.a, and 8.b), w_i is the weight of $sub\text{-}goal_i$ from factor analysis, and $(sub\text{-}goal)_i$ is a simple average of standardized indicators which belong to $(sub\text{-}goal)_i$.

SDG 8 indicators can be related to each other in that it is essential to understand the structure of the correlation between variables. The SDG 8 index is expressed in equation (1), where the weight of the sub-goals is extracted based on the factor analysis results. To derive the final index, this section divides the structure of the index into two parts. First, regression: inter- and extrapolation of missing value are used to estimate the missing values of the indicators. Second, all sub-goals are standardized before proceeding to factor analysis. Afterwards, factor analysis is performed to calculate the weight of each indicator.[6]

The number of components extracted is equal to the number of observed variables in the analysis. The cumulative value represents the explanatory power of the factors used to examine the distribution of each variable. As shown in Table 6.4, there are three factors that influence the variables. These three factors

Table 6.4 First factor extraction statistics

Factor	Eigenvalue	Difference	Proportion	Cumulative
Factor 1	4.9132	3.0594	0.5459	0.5459
Factor 2	1.8538	0.7892	0.2060	0.7519
Factor 3	1.0646	0.5770	0.1183	0.8702
Factor 4	0.4875	0.0944	0.0542	0.9243
Factor 5	0.3931	0.2256	0.0437	0.9680
Factor 6	0.1676	0.0726	0.0186	0.9866
Factor 7	0.0950	0.0800	0.0106	0.9972
Factor 8	0.0150	0.0048	0.0017	0.9989
Factor 9	0.0102	.	0.0011	1.0000

Source: Author's own.

Note:

1) LR test: independent vs. saturated: chi2(36) = 260.46, Prob.>chi2 = 0.0000

2) Principal-component factors instead of principal factors

combined have an explanatory power of about 87.02% for the selected variables. The factors' cumulative values were as high as 3.06 and as low as 1.06. As the SDG 8 index consists of nine variables, the factors of the variables were categorized into related groups. Afterwards, orthogonal varimax rotation method was used to perform the factor analysis, which emphasized the mutual independence among the factors.

The factors with eigenvalue above 1.0 are presented in Table 6.5. Factor rotation has been used to redistribute the factors to show significant patterns, which allows meaningful interpretation of the results.

A second weighting of the index was derived by using the factor loadings of the indicators. Factors with common components were categorized into factor 1, factor 2, and factor 3. Then sub-goals were selected based on the factors with a high value of factor loadings. Afterwards, the SDG 8 index weight was calculated using the technique explained in Chapter 2 (see Table 6.6). From the highest factor loadings and using explained variation, the final weight of SGD 8 index was obtained. According to the calculated weights, GDP per growth rate (%) is the most important factor affecting the index. The weight of sub-goal 8.8, indicating industrial accidents (8.50%), was the smallest.

Results from trend

Figures 6.16 to 6.18 show the trends of sub-goals from 1991 to 2015 based on factor loading values. The trends of sub-goals 8.1 and 8.2 show the level of living and productivity in the ROK. From this result, the level of sustainability is shown to be low during the financial crises in 1997 and 2008. In addition, the level of economic growth is becoming increasingly flat, and government policies need to be prepared for this.

The transition of sub-goals belonging to factor 1 is as follows. First, we can see that the variation is relatively large for sub-goal 8.4, which is an indicator

Table 6.5 Orthogonal varimax rotation factors

Factor	Variance	Difference	Proportion	Cumulative
Factor 1	3.8996	1.9069	0.4333	0.4333
Factor 2	1.9927	0.0534	0.2214	0.6547
Factor 3	1.9393	.	0.2155	0.8702

Source: Author's own.

Note: LR test: independent vs. saturated: chi2(36) = 260.46, Prob.>chi2 = 0.0000

Table 6.6 Factor loadings and index weights for SDG 8

Sub index	Factor 1	Factor 2	Factor 3	Weight
Goal 8.1	−0.1312	0.9413	−0.2344	12.84
Goal 8.2	−0.3776	0.8971	−0.1015	11.66
Goal 8.4	0.7987	−0.1327	−0.2302	9.24
Goal 8.5	0.0161	0.1512	−0.9191	12.24
Goal 8.8	0.7659	−0.1162	0.4905	8.50
Goal 8.9	0.1846	−0.2586	0.8136	9.59
Goal 8.10	0.9115	−0.2690	−0.0370	12.04
Goal 8.a	0.9263	−0.1989	0.0782	12.43
Goal 8.b	0.8900	−0.2625	0.2577	11.47

Source: Author's own.

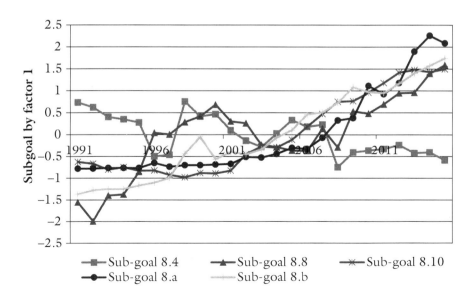

Figure 6.16 Sub-goal trend by factor 1

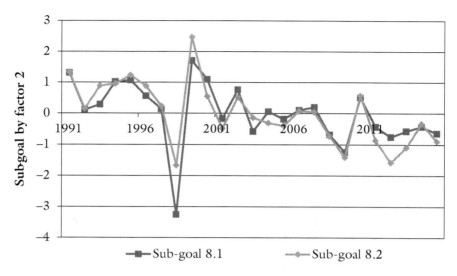

Figure 6.17 Sub-goal trend by factor 2

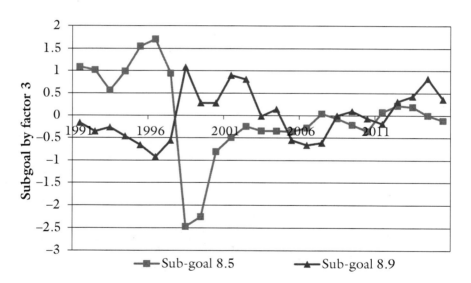

Figure 6.18 Sub-goal trend by factor 3

of resource consumption. This implies that the ROK should implement a strategy that considers both economic growth and the environment simultaneously. For sub-goal 8.10, access to financial services is expanding, confirming that the capacity of domestic financial institutions is strengthened. Moreover, the results of sub-goal 8.a from the assistance of the poorest countries show a gradual increase. The strategy should be set up towards mass-production and to develop the domestic industry through various aid, not simply aid for international relations. Sub-goal 8.b shows the expenditure of the government that represents social security, which represents the gradually improving level of social security through government spending in the ROK.

Sub-goal 8.5 is an indicator of the level of equality of jobs, and is an index composed of gender wage gap and unemployment rate. Since it is observed that the graph plunges during the financial crisis, it can be said that the indicator changes according to the economic situation. In addition, sub-goal 8.8 is an indicator of job quality, industrial accidents, and workday loss. The results show that the degree of sustainability has been steadily increasing since 1990. Indicators related to tourism also show a similar pattern, and it is necessary to consider ways to distribute the strategy focused on manufacturing industry to the service industry.

Figure 6.19 shows the trends of the preceding indicators along with the weighting, which is the last result of this chapter. As seen from the graph, the SDG 8 index in the ROK is lowest after the financial crisis in 1998 (about –0.972), but it shows a gradually increasing trend afterwards. However, even if the index itself shows an increasing pattern, it is necessary to establish governmental policy to cope with the changing social, economic, and environmental situation of the world.

Conclusion and implications

The economy in the ROK rapidly grew from the 1960s to 1970s by having manufacturing industries at its center, which led to USD 20 thousand of GNI

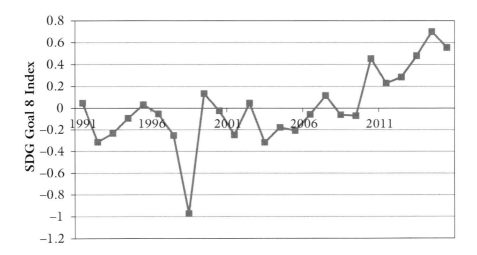

Figure 6.19 Index for SDG 8

per capita by 2006. Although it has been developing rapidly, the GNI per capita has yet to reach USD 30 thousand. This is due to a rapid decrease in economic growth rate, which requires further strategies to prepare for job creation and sustainable economy.

According to the research on national competitiveness from WEF (2017), Korean GCI (Global Competitiveness Index) has ranked 26th out of 137 nations for four consecutive years (2014–2017). However, the ranks were previously higher: 11th in 2007; 19th in 2009; 22nd in 2010; and 24th in 2011. In the case of the four standard basic factors, the ranks have improved from the previous year: policy (63rd to 58th); infrastructure (10th to 8th); macroeconomic (3rd to 2nd); and, health and fundamental education (29th to 28th). On the other hand, in the efficiency enhancement indicator, the sub-indicators showed improvements for 2015 to 2017, but are still low-ranked: the labor market efficiency (77th to 73rd); and the financial market maturity (80th to 74th). This is reflected in higher values of SDG 8, but each of the sub-goals still requires detailed planning for improvement.

To enhance national competitiveness, it is necessary to establish a strategy based on sustainable macroeconomic policies. In other words, as we have seen in this chapter, economic growth has been declining since the 1990s with no significant increase. In addition, as shown in the SDG 8 index, the effect of the economic growth rate indicator is larger than the other sub-goals, and other turbulence, such as global financial crises, has a great influence on the index. Nevertheless, it is unclear whether strategies to account for these situations are being established. In terms of the employment indicator, the employment and unemployment rates have been stagnant since the 2000s. Furthermore, the aging population and the low fertility rate will lead to a decline in productivity in the future, which will hinder the ROK's economic growth.

In the past, the government has pursued policies to stabilize the economy and to increase productivity, while also focusing on employment policies that take social welfare into consideration. Since 1992, efforts have been made to disseminate the concept of sustainable development, and establish governmental organizations to plan and implement sustainable development strategies. However, the lack of flexibility in the policies makes it difficult to say that the concept of sustainable development is fully implemented in the ROK. The three dimensions of sustainable development (economy, social, and environment) and institutions are fundamental to society, and it is necessary to design strategies that can harmonize these elements.

Therefore, a policy should be designed that considers not only the economic indicators measured for SDG 8, but also other SDGs examined throughout this book. To examine the sustainability of an economy, the employment rate is an important indicator, but other indicators, such as income distribution and quality of life, are equally important. In other words, the key goal of a sustainable development strategy is to improve all aspects of human society, including the environment, social development, and eradication of poverty.

This chapter examined the current situation of the ROK economy based on SDG 8 from 1991 to 2015 and provided direction for sustainable development policies. However, there are limitations for international comparison as the indicators do not have continuous data, and only the domestic conditions of the ROK are considered. Furthermore, as the units of each indicator differ, the factor analysis method was used to make the indicators comparable; however, as the results represents the minimum and maximum points of the indicators, only the overall trend of the indicators could be examined. Thus, it is difficult to suggest that the sustainable development goals have been achieved. Therefore, in future research, it will be necessary to standardize the indicators based on certain sustainable targets and make the indicators comparable between countries.

Notes

1 Kang et al. (2015) suggest government policies for transitioning to the green economy in response to SDGs and refer to three national plans (the Five-Year Plan for Green Growth, the Industrial Technology Innovation Promotion Act, and Creative Economy Action Plan) as key for achieving SDG 8. They also present the overlapping strategies with tables, considering that domestic policies cover the SDG.
2 The goal of achieving the vision is to achieve $100 million in exports, increase the number of globally specialized companies, increase the share of private companies in R&D expenses of universities and research institutes, improve the world ranking of Triadic Patents Families per million researchers, increase the industrial technology level relative to advanced countries, and increase the world market share and proportion of high-tech industry exports (Joint Work of Relevant Ministries 2016, 15).
3 International Labor Organization (ILO). "Informal Economy." Accessed May 8, 2017. www.ilo.org/global/topics/employment-promotion/informal-economy/lang-en/index.htm
4 Eurostat. "Domestic Material Consumption." Accessed November 11, 2017. http://ec.europa.eu/eurostat/statistics-explained/index.php/Glossary:Domestic_material_consumption_(DMC)
5 Aid for Trade commitments are registered from the date on which the loan or grant agreement is signed or the obligation is otherwise made known to the recipient (e.g. in the case of budgetary allocations to overseas territories, the final vote of the budget should be taken as the date of commitment). For certain special expenditures (e.g. emergency aid), the date of disbursement may be taken as the date of commitment and on a disbursement basis (i.e. actual expenditures).
6 For more information, see Chapter 2 in this book.

References

Bank of Korea Database. "Bank Branches, Number of Automated Teller Machines and Electronic Finance Services." Accessed September 8, 2017. https://ecos.bok.or.kr.

Eurostat. "Domestic Material Consumption." Accessed November 11, 2017. http://ec.europa.eu/eurostat/statistics-explained/index.php/Glossary:Domestic_material_consumption_(DMC)

Green Growth Korea. "Five-Year Plan." Accessed May 8, 2017. www.greengrowth.go.kr/menu001/sub002/GRG_001_202.do

International Labour Organization (ILO). "Informal Economy." Accessed May 8, 2017. www.ilo.org/global/topics/employment-promotion/informal-economy/lang–en/index.htm

International Labour Organization (ILO) STAT. "Average Hourly Earnings of Female and Male Employees, Unemployment Rate by Sex and Age." Accessed July 20, 2017. www.ilo.org/ilostat

Joint Work of Relevant Ministries. 2013. "Creative Economy Action Plans." [In Korean]. Accessed May 20, 2017. http://msip.go.kr/web/msipContents/contentsView.do?cateId=mssw311&artId=1212332

Joint Work of Relevant Ministries. 2014a. "Second Five-Year Plan for Green Growth." [In Korean]. Accessed May 20, 2017. www.greengrowth.go.kr/download/140603-2full.pdf

Joint Work of Relevant Ministries. 2014b. "Three-Year Plan for Economic Innovation." [In Korean]. Accessed May 20, 2017. http://mosf.go.kr/com/bbs/detailComtPolbbsView.do;jsessionid=U8dpoaq+OeACp4rR1da315yH.node10?searchBbsId1=MOSFBBS_000000000039&searchNttId1=OLD_4019852&menuNo=5020200

Joint Work of Relevant Ministries. 2016. "Third National Strategy for Sustainable Development: 2016–2035." [In Korean]. Accessed May 20, 2017. http://ncsd.go.kr/app/board/infoResearchReport/view.do?bbsSeq=7177

Kang, S. I., H. W. Lee, J. M. Chu, J. H. Kim, and C. K. Kim. 2015. *The Green Economy Implementation Strategies of Korea in Response to Post 2015-SDGs* [in Korean], Korea Environment Institute. Sejong: KEI.

Kim, G. I., J. H. Kim, and G. J. Lee. 2010. *Trends of Resource Circulation Indicator in Korea*. Korea Environment Institute. Sejong: KEI. [In Korean].

Korean Statistical Information Service (KOSIS). "Total and Non-Agriculture Informal Employed Worker, Frequency Rate and Severity Rate." Accessed September 10, 2017. http://kosis.kr/

Laborstat from MOEL. "Industrial Disaster." Accessed June 28, 2017. http://laborstat.moel.go.kr/

Lim, S. Y., S. G. Kim, and J. H. Kim. 2016. *A Study for the Effective Domestic Implementation of the Economic and Industrial Aspects of the Sustainable Development Goals (SDGs) Korea*. Sejong: Krishna Institute of Engineering and Technology. [In Korean].

Ministry of Employment and Labor (MOEL). 2017. "4th Basic Plan for Labor Welfare Promotion." [In Korean]. Accessed May 20, 2017. www.moel.go.kr/policy/policydata/view.do?bbs_seq=1489107213172

Ministry of Trade, Industry and Energy (MOTIE). 2013. "6th Five Plan for Technological Innovation." [In Korean]. Accessed May 20, 2017. www.motie.go.kr/motie/py/td/majorpolicy/bbs/bbsView.do?bbs_seq_n=84&bbs_cd_n=22

Okun, A. M. 1962. "Potential GNP, Its Measurement and Significance." In *Proceedings of the Business and Economic Statistics Section of the American Statistical Association*, 89–104. Alexandria, VA: American Statistical Association.

Organisation for Economic Co-operation and Development (OECD). 2016. "OECD Tourism Trends and Policies 2016." Paris: OECD Publications. Accessed September 28, 2017. http://dx.doi.org/10.1787/tour-2016-en

Organisation for Economic Co-operation and Development (OECD). 2017a. "Gender Wage Gap (indicator)." Accessed November 12, 2017. doi:10.1787/7cee77aa-en

Organisation for Economic Co-operation and Development (OECD). 2017b. "Youth Not in Employment, Education or Training (NEET) (indicator)." Accessed September 4, 2017. doi:10.1787/72d1033a-en

Organisation for Economic Co-operation and Development (OECD). "Social Expenditure Database." Accessed November 1, 2017. www.oecd.org/social/expenditure.htm

Organisation for Economic Co-operation and Development (OECD). Stat. "Material Resources." Accessed September 10, 2017. http://stats.oecd.org/Index.aspx?DataSetCode=material_resources#

Organisation for Economic Co-operation and Development (OECD). "Aid for Trade." Accessed July 9, 2017. www.oecd.org/dac/aft/aid-for-tradestatisticalqueries.htm

Sachs, J., Schmidt-Traub, G., Kroll, C., Durand-Delacre, D., and Teksoz, K. 2017. "SDG Index and Dashboards Report 2017." New York: Bertelsmann Stiftung and Sustainable Development Solutions Network (SDSN). Accessed July 16, 2017. http://unsdsn.org/resources/publications/sdg-index-and-dashboards-report-2017/

Sustainable Development Portal. "Basic Plan for National Sustainable Strategy." Accessed May 8, 2017. http://ncsd.go.kr/app/sub03/22_tab3.do

World Bank, Global Financial Development. "Bank Branches (per 100,000 person), Number of Automated Teller Machines (per 100,000 person) and Bank Mobile (% age 15+)." Accessed September 8, 2017. https://data.worldbank.org

World Bank, World Development Indicators. "GDP Per Capita Growth (Annual %), GDP Per Person Employed (Constant 2011 PPP $), GDP Per Capita (Constant 2010) and Population." Accessed May 8, 2017. https://data.worldbank.org

World Economic Forum (WEF). 2017. *The Global Competitiveness Report 2017–2018*. Geneva: World Economic Forum.

World Travels & Tourism Council (WTTC). "Direct Contribution to Employment and GDP." Accessed September 28, 2017. www.wttc.org/datagateway

7 Goal 11: sustainable city and communities

Jaemin Song and Eun Woo Lee

Introduction

The world is experiencing an unprecedented growth in urban population. The year 2007 marked the turning point when the majority of the global population lived in urban areas for the first time in history, as shown in Figure 7.1. The UN (2016) estimates that 60% of the global population will live in urban areas by 2030, accelerated by population and economic growth, especially in developing countries. Cities account for approximately 80% of global GDP as a locus of economic activity and wealth creation (World Bank 2010). The concentration of population and economic activity in cities, however, has inevitably brought about a variety of urban challenges, including the provision of adequate housings, environmental degradation, inequality, and high energy consumption. Thus, failing to properly manage such urban issues significantly threatens sustainable development of the globe. The role of cities in sustainable development efforts is indeed key to achieving sustainable development at the national and global level (UN 1992).

Acknowledging the importance of cities, the UN endorsed Goal 11, known as "urban SDG," as a stand-alone goal out of 17 SDGs, dedicated to the sustainable development of cities. Goal 11, titled as "make cities and human settlements inclusive, safe, resilient and sustainable," consists of seven action targets and three means of implementation (MOI) with 15 indicators, covering diverse urban issues from housing, transport, environment, urban planning, and disaster management to the provision of public spaces. Goal 11 will help policy makers develop proper policies focusing on specific targets to achieve the sustainable development of cities.

In the case of the ROK, the country has experienced an unprecedentedly rapid increase in the urban population. Over the last 60 years, since the end of the Korean War in 1953, the urbanization rate exploded from 39.41% in 1960 to 90% in 2015. During the process of rapid urbanization and industrialization in the 1970s and 1980s, government policies prioritized on economic development, resulting in the degradation of environmental quality. However, recognizing the limitations and problems of the development-oriented policy, the

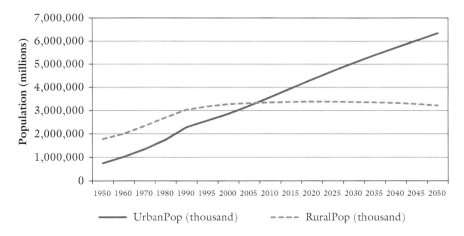

Figure 7.1 Urban and rural population
Source: UN (2014b), author edited.

government started putting greater emphasis on balanced development, with sustainable development becoming a key national agenda in the late 1990s (Lee et al. 2011).

However, there has been no rigorous quantitative evaluation on the implementation of sustainable development efforts of cities in the ROK. There is no doubt that the ROK has achieved miraculous economic development over the last century, transforming from a recipient of international aid to a donor country. However, whether the process of urbanization, including the current pathway, has been sustainable or not has not been fully tested in a comprehensive way; previous research has focused on specific sectors, including housing (Park 1998; Ha 1994; Kim and Park 2016), transportation (Hwang 2012; Lee 2013), environment (Chu 2007; Ministry of Environment 2014), and growth management (Yoo 2001; UN-Habitat 2014) in their evaluation of sustainable development of the country. Against this backdrop, this chapter aims to assess the urban sustainability of the ROK using the framework of SDG 11 from 1980 to 2015 by analyzing relevant indicators, drawing lessons for the ROK to move forward, and providing implications for other countries.

Relevant policy overview

In response to the introduction of Agenda 21 by the international community in 1992, the Korean government developed its national plans in 1996 to implement Agenda 21 and established the Presidential National Commission on Sustainable Development in 2000 (Yoon 2002). In addition, the central government developed and disseminated a Guideline for Local Agenda 21 (LA21) in April 1997, with the aim of assisting local governments to prepare their own LA21 in conjunction with the national action plan. Each local government established its own LA21 taking into consideration their economic, environmental, and social circumstances (Yoon 2002). The introduction of Agenda 21 as well as LA21 was the major transitional point for Korea in improving its awareness in the importance and necessity of sustainable development at both the national and local level (Moon 2002). By 2006, almost 90% (222 out of 248) of the local administrative districts nationwide were either planning or already implementing LA21 (Ministry of Environment 2006).

To promote LA21, the Korean Council for LA21 (KCLA 21) was established in 2000, the name was later changed to the Local Sustainability Alliance of Korea (LSAK) in 2006. Its main role is to support the preparation and promotion of projects under LA21 by promoting knowledge exchange among local governments and providing education and training(Park et al. 2009).

Another important driver for local sustainability was the introduction of green growth policies in 2010. The ROK has been at the forefront of the green growth movements, with comprehensive policy frameworks in the National Strategy for Green Growth (2009~2050) and the Five-Year Plan (2009~2013). Green growth policy sets a development model for energy, environment, and economic policies (OECD 2013). According to the national policy, all local municipalities are required to establish their own green growth action plans (OECD 2012). For instance, Seoul, the capital city, established a five-year green growth plan that includes the introduction of a smart grid network, increasing energy efficiency, promoting green technologies, and the reinforcement of the climate change monitoring system (OECD 2012).

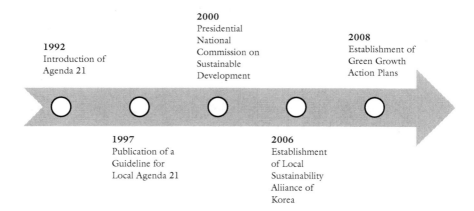

Figure 7.2 Overview of local sustainable development policies

Data

Definition of indicators and data source

The Inter-Agency and Expert Group on SDG Indicators (IAEG–SDGs) has developed and proposed indicators for each target to evaluate the level of its achievement, which were agreed upon at the 48th session of the United Nations Statistical Commission in March 2017. The use of common indicators for evaluation is desirable and important for a consistent and comparable assessment both in analyzing sustainable development within a country over a long period of time and for comparing across countries. Thus, it would be ideal for each country as well as local governments to be equipped with a database depository system in the future to measure and track the indicators. However, the current database system in many countries, including the ROK, does not include all of the indicators to be collected due to various reasons, such as different national contexts and technical and financial issues. Thus, the most appropriate data available was selected for each indicator for this study, as shown in Table 7.1. More details on each indicator are provided in the following section.

Results

Analysis on the performance of the ROK in Goal 11 by target

Target 11.1: housing

- *Target 11.1: By 2030, ensure access for all to adequate, safe and affordable housing and basic services and upgrade slums*
- *Indicator 11.1.1: Proportion of urban population living in shanty houses and vinyl greenhouses*

Target 11.1 aims to ensure the provision of adequate, safe, and affordable housing and basic services. Until the mid-1980s, the shortage of housing was a major issue in the ROK due to fast-growing demand. Since the government tended to put a relatively lower priority on the housing sector, compared to infrastructure or the manufacturing sector, the strong policy focus on economic development resulted in insufficient investment in housing. However, since the 1980s, the Korean government has made continuous efforts in supplying a large number of housing units to cope with the sharp increase in housing prices caused by housing shortages, especially in metropolitan areas. Large-scale housing projects were made in line with new town development by providing large-scale developable land to the National Housing Corporation and the Land Development Corporation (Kim and Park 2016). As a result, the housing supply rate has improved significantly, from 86% in 1995 to 102.3% in 2015.

Table 7.1 Variables used for SDG 11 index

Indicator by UN	Modified indicator in the study	
	Indicator	Data source
11.1.1 Proportion of urban population living in slums, informal settlements or inadequate housing	- Proportion of shanty houses and vinyl greenhouses	KOSIS, "Population Census" (1970–2015, 5 years)
11.2.1 Proportion of population that has convenient access to public transport, by sex, age and persons with disabilities	- Modal share of public transportation	KOSIS, "Type of the Household Use Commuting by the Means of Transportation'" (1990–2010, every 5 years)
11.3.1 Ratio of land consumption rate to population growth rate	- Ratio of growth rate of urban area to growth rate of population	UPIS (1970–2015) KOSIS (1960–2015)
11.3.2 Proportion of cities with a direct participation structure of civil society in urban planning and management that operate regularly and democratically	- Number of counties and cities with Master Plan	UPIS (1983–2015)
11.4.1 Total expenditure (public and private) per capita spent on the preservation, protection and conservation of all cultural and natural heritage, by type of heritage (cultural, natural, mixed and World Heritage Centre designation), level of government (national, regional and local/municipal), type of expenditure (operating expenditure/investment) and type of private funding (donations in kind, private non-profit sector and sponsorship)	- Annual budget on cultural heritage	KOSIS, "Budget of Cultural Assets Management Compared to Government Budget" (2000–2015)
11.5.1 Number of deaths, missing persons and persons affected by disaster per 100,000 people	- Number of deaths (with missing people) and people affected by disaster	Ministry of Public Safety and Security, "Disaster Annual Report" (1916–2015)
11.5.2 Direct disaster economic loss in relation to global GDP, including disaster damage to critical infrastructure and disruption of basic services	- Total economic loss due to natural disaster	World Bank, GDP

11.6.1 Proportion of urban solid waste regularly collected and with adequate final discharge out of total urban solid waste generated, by cities	- Waste generation per capita per day - Recycling rate	KOSIS, "Generation of Waste per Resident per Day" (1985–2015) KOSIS, "Recycling Rate" (1985–2015)
11.6.2 Annual mean levels of fine particulate matter (e.g. PM2.5 and PM10) in cities (population weighted)	- Concentration of PM10 in cities (population weighted)	Ministry of Environment (1995–2015)
11.7.1 Average share of the built-up area of cities that is open space for public use for all, by sex, age and persons with disabilities	- Size of public space including stream, park, and road surface	Ministry of Land, Infrastructure, and Transport, "Administrative District" (1978–2013)
11.7.2 Proportion of persons victim of physical or sexual harassment, by sex, age, disability status and place of occurrence, in the previous 12 months	- Victim rate Victim [women, children (under 6), elderly (over 60)]	KOSIS "Crime Victim Age, Sex" (1994–2015)

Table 7.2 Housing welfare road map

Income deciles	Characteristics	Assistance
1 (bottom)	Unable to pay market rents	Small public rental units Housing benefit
2–4	Unable to purchase homes	Small or medium-sized public rental units Concessional loans for *chonsei* deposits
5–6	Able to purchase homes with some assistance	Small or medium-sized houses at subsidized prices F Concessional mortgage loans
7 and above	Able to purchase homes with own means	Tax benefits

Source: Ministry of Construction and Transportation (2003).

In addition to the provision of new housing, various measures have been introduced to ensure adequate quality and affordability of housing. The government introduced a housing welfare road map in 2003, shown in Table 7.2, to enhance housing for vulnerable groups by providing one million public rental units over ten years (Kim and Park 2016).

The housing quality has steadily improved since the 1980s. The major key indicators for housing quality, such as average number of rooms per household, average floor area per person, and share of dwellings with adequate urban service, have also significantly improved, as shown in Table 7.3.

The trend in the proportion of the population living in slums, the indicator for target 11.1, is based on a housing census report published by Ministry of Land, Infrastructure and Transport and clearly demonstrates the improvement in housing quality, as shown in Figure 7.3.

In 1980, inappropriate housing accounted for approximately 40% of total housing. However, its ratio has fallen significantly to approximately 5% as of 2015. The ratio of the population living in inadequate housing has fallen to only 0.12% in Seoul. This impressive achievement is the result of a combination of policies and projects, including the Act on the Maintenance and Improvement of Urban Areas and Dwelling Condition for Residents adopted in 2003, the Special Act on the Promotion of Urban Renewal adopted in 2005, and the Special Act for Promotion and Support of Urban Regeneration in 2013. The residential environment improvement project under the Act on the Maintenance and Improvement of Urban Areas and Dwelling Condition for Residents has contributed to the expansion of necessary infrastructure and common facilities for low-income residents. Compared to the average percentage of the population living in slums (UN 2014a) in developing region, as shown in Figure 7.3, the ROK is in much better condition.

Goal 11: sustainable cities and communities

Table 7.3 Key housing quality indicator

	1980	1990	2000	2010
Average number of rooms per household	2.2	2.5	3.4	3.7
Average floor area per person (square meters)	10.1	14.3	20.2	25.0
Average floor area per household (square meters)	45.8	51.0	63.1	67.4
Dwellings per 1,000 inhabitants	142	170	249	364
Share of dwellings with piped water (%)	56.1	74.0	85.0	97.9
Share of dwellings with modern toilets (%)	18.4	51.3	86.9	97.0
Share of dwellings with bathroom (%)	22.1	44.1	89.1	98.4
Share of dwellings with hot water (%)	9.9	34.1	87.4	96.9

Source: Statistics ROK, http://kostat.go.kr.

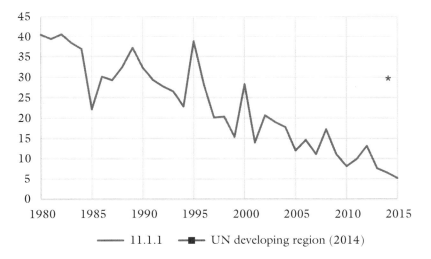

Figure 7.3 Population living in slums (%)
Source: KOSIS. "Population Census (1970–2015, 5 Years)."

Target 11.2: transport

- Target 11.2: By 2030, provide access to safe, affordable, accessible and sustainable transport systems for all, improving road safety, notably by expanding public

transport, with special attention to the needs of those in vulnerable situations, women, children, persons with disabilities and older persons
- *Indicator 11.2.1: Modal share of public transportation*

Target 11.2 emphasizes the importance of public transportation to secure mobility of vulnerable groups, including women, children, persons with disabilities, and the elderly. The primary mode of public transportation in the ROK changed from tram to bus in the 1970s and 1980s, and then to urban railway in the 1990s. Since the 2000s, high-speed rail, aviation, and inter-city buses have been playing an important role in long distance travel between cities or regions (Lee and Lim 2013).

Rapid urbanization coupled with economic growth led to a significant increase in the number of cars, exacerbating traffic conditions in the 1980s. Thus, the government needed a new mode of urban public transportation complementing buses in large cities, including Seoul. Against this backdrop, a national plan to construct urban railways was introduced and the first urban railway in the country, Seoul Subway Line 1, was finally built in the 1970s. Its introduction opened an era of urban rail-centered mass transit systems in metropolitan cities in the ROK. In the meantime, the demand for bus service declined until the 2000s due to increased use of private vehicles, worsening the financial conditions of bus companies (Hwang 2012). The government carried out public transportation system reform through the introduction of a quasi-public operation system, restructuring bus routes and building the Bus Rapid Transit (BRT) system and median bus lanes. As of 2015, the number of bus riders was around 4 million, 1.8 times greater than urban railway users.

In analyzing sub-goal 11.2, an average modal share of public transportation was used to evaluate the current status of sub-goal 11.2 in the ROK. The modal share was calculated as the percentage of travelers using the train, subway, or bus.

Figure 7.4 shows the trend in the modal share of public transportation over time. The data shows an upward trend in the modal share of public transportation, starting from around 25% in the early 1980s and increasing to around 45%. However, there are significant discrepancies in the level of modal share of public transportation by city. Large cities such as Seoul, Busan, and Incheon display a much higher modal share of public transportation than small and medium-sized cities. In Seoul, public transportation modes account for around 65% of total transportation. Due to economies of scale, cities with a larger population are likely to have better public transportation with a higher percentage of public transportation usage.

Target 11.3: sustainable urban management

- *Target 11.3: By 2030, enhance inclusive and sustainable urbanization and capacity for participatory, integrated and sustainable human settlement planning and management in all countries*
- *Indicator 11.3.1: Ratio of land consumption rate to population growth rate*
- *Indicator 11.3.2: Number of cities with official master plans*

Goal 11: sustainable cities and communities 119

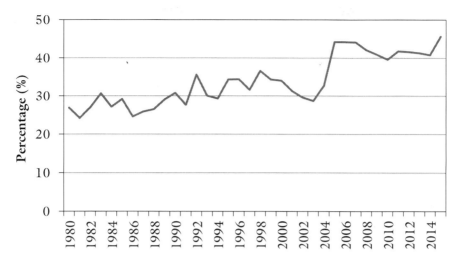

Figure 7.4 Share of public transportation (%)
Source: KOSIS. "Type of the Household Use Commuting by the Means of Transportation (1990–2010 Every 5 Years)."

Indicator 11.3.1 measures the ratio of land consumption rate to the population growth rate to ensure an efficient use of land for urban growth. The Korean government has been implementing proactive measures for growth management. The restrictive zone for urban growth in the ROK, the so-called greenbelt, is a good example of such a policy. In the 1970s and 1980s, the increase in population density in Seoul was much greater than the national average. To manage its growth, the government introduced the greenbelt system in 1971. The size of the greenbelt in the Seoul Metropolitan Area is quite large, consisting of a band averaging about 10 km wide that begins about 15 km from Seoul's central business district, as shown in Figure 7.5. There are different evaluations on the effectiveness of the green belt system. Given the fact that many of those living outside the green belt area commute to Seoul, it does not seem to be a powerful tool for growth management. However, it has significantly contributed to the preservation of agricultural land and green space (Bengston and Youn 2004).

Figure 7.6 shows the historical trend in the ratio of land consumption rate to population growth rate, measuring whether an efficient use of land for urban growth has been realized in the ROK in relation to target 11.3. Annual data of land use change would not capture the general trend of the physical expansion over time; thus, the analysis of changes in land use as well as the population has been conducted with a decadal period. For values of the ratio greater than one, it implies physical expansion of the built-up area growing faster than the population growth, which could be referred to as urban sprawl. The figure shows the phenomena of urban sprawl was most severe in the 1990s and 2000s. This can be explained by the large-scale urban development projects during those periods,

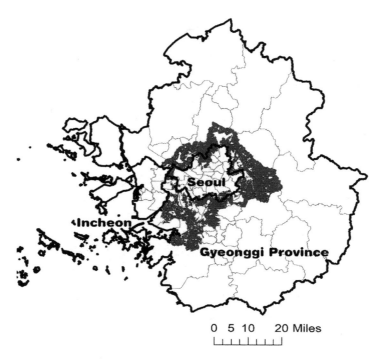

Figure 7.5 Map of greenbelt in Seoul metropolitan area

Source: Korea national spatial data infrastructure portal, adjusted from Korea National Spatial Data Infrastructure Portal.

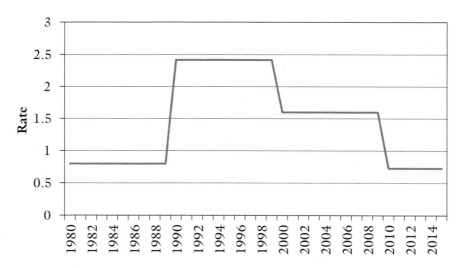

Figure 7.6 Decadal trend in land consumption rate to population growth rate
Source: UPIS, KOSIS.

especially in the Seoul metropolitan area including Gyeonggi Province. To stabilize housing prices and address housing shortages, the government started new town projects in the Seoul metropolitan area. The first new town project was implemented from 1989 to 1996, while the second was from 2001 to 2015 (Ministry of Land, Infrastructure and Transportation 2015). The development of new towns in the neighboring province and Seoul was the major driver for spatial expansion, facilitated by improvements in mobility by using private vehicles and public transportation.

Indicator 11.3.2 measures the level of civic participation in urban planning and management. In the past, the opinions of residents were not well heard in urban planning and management in the ROK. Experts and government officials led urban planning and development through a top-down approach. The main structure of public participation was merely through public inspection and public hearing, as expressed in the National Land Planning and Utilization Act, which provided only a passive way of participating in the decision-making process (Yoon et al. 2014). Recently, the system and process of civic participation have improved significantly. Active civic participation has been practiced in developing Cheongju City Master Plan, Seoul City Master Plan, Suwon City Master Plan, and Gyeonggi Province General Plan. Special efforts are being made to encourage civic participation in the various stages of urban planning and management from the brainstorming stage up to the decision-making process.

For the analysis, the accumulated number of cities and counties that developed official master plans was used as a proxy for practicing sustainable urban planning and management. Figure 7.7 demonstrates the increasing number of cities and counties equipped with contemporary urban planning practices. However, it

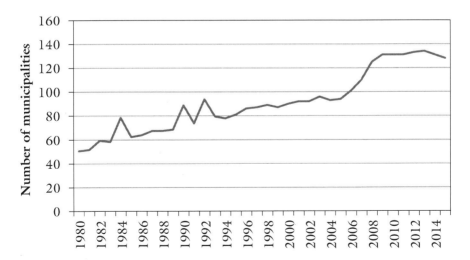

Figure 7.7 Number of municipalities with urban planning
Source: UPIS (1983–2015).

should be kept in mind that more efforts should be made to institutionalize civic participation in urban planning and management.

Target 11.4: cultural and natural heritage

- *Target 11.4.1: Strengthen efforts to protect and safeguard the world's cultural and natural heritage*
- *Indicator 11.4.1: Total budget on heritage management*

Target 11.4 aims to ensure that sufficient efforts and expenditures are made to protect and safeguard cultural and natural heritage. Recognizing the importance of safeguarding cultural and natural heritage, the Korean government inaugurated the Bureau of Cultural Property Organization as a specialized administrative unit in 1961. The Cultural Properties Protection Law developed in 1962 was the first step in the safeguarding system for cultural heritage (Kim et al. 2011). Since then, a variety of legislation and policies have been introduced. The best policies include the Qualification System for the Restoration Engineer of Cultural Properties, the Transmission System for Intangible Cultural Property, and the One Heritage One Keeper campaign. As of 2013, the ROK had designated 411 national treasures, 2,317 treasures, 485 historic sites, and 104 scenic sites. At the local level, each city or province has their own department in charge of cultural heritage. In addition, the government continues to make efforts to raise public awareness of its value through campaigns and events.

In this analysis, the total budget for heritage management by the Cultural Heritage Administration was used as a proxy for indicator 11.4.1. As shown in Figure 7.8, the budget for cultural heritage has steadily increased over time. However, the cultural heritage budget per person at the city level shows a wide range, with a few cities allocating no budget at all for cultural heritage. In fact,

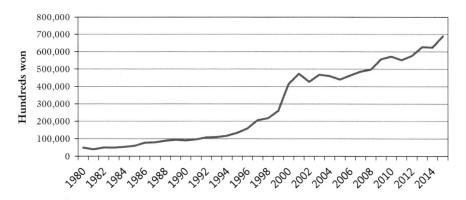

Figure 7.8 Heritage management budget

Source: KOSIS. "Budget of Cultural Assets Management Compared to Government Budget (2000–2015)."

Goal 11: sustainable cities and communities   123

older cities with a large number of historical heritages tend to have relatively higher expenditure on their preservation and conservation. In addition, it should be noted that the heritage management budget accounts for only 1.24% of the total government budget, despite the steady increase in the budget over time.

Target 11.5: natural disaster

- *Target 11.5: By 2030, significantly reduce the number of deaths and the number of people affected and substantially decrease the direct economic losses relative to global gross domestic product caused by disasters, including water-related disasters, with a focus on protecting the poor and people in vulnerable situations*
- *Indicator 11.5.1: Number of persons affected by disaster per 100,000 people*
- *Indicator 11.5.2: Property loss in relation to GDP due to disaster*

Target 11.5 aims to reduce both human and property loss caused by natural disasters. In general, the number of affected humans as well as the scale of economic loss caused by disasters do not show a clear trend but are rather affected by the scale and strength of natural disasters on an irregular basis, as shown in Figures 7.9 and 7.10. Though there exist some positive correlations between the two indicators, human and property loss, sensitivity to natural disasters is not homogeneous. Since 1991, the number of deaths due to natural disasters has significantly reduced, but Figure 7.10 still shows cases with significant amounts of property loss until a decade ago, especially in 2002 and 2003. The large damages were the results of Typhoon Rusa and Typhoon Maemi, which drew strong public attention to the need for more comprehensive natural disaster management.

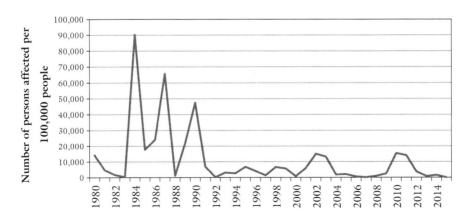

Figure 7.9 Number of persons affected per 100,000 people by disaster
Source: Ministry of Public Safety and Security. Disaster Annual Report (1916–2015).

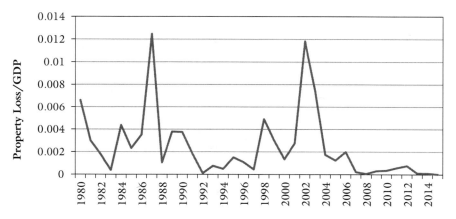

Figure 7.10 Property loss per GDP due to disaster
Source: Ministry of Public Safety and Security. Disaster Annual Report (1916–2015).

Figure 7.11 illustrates the disaster management system of the ROK. The system works at three spatial levels – central, provincial, and local government. The central government oversees establishing and implementing the agenda for basic policies for natural disaster and safety, while provincial governments coordinate implementation of policies dealing with a large-scale disaster with the central government and assist local governments. Local governments are responsible for developing and implementing a local plan on the ground (Yoon 2014). In general, disaster management in the ROK has improved, reforming the relevant institutions and governance structure and putting more emphasis on pre-disaster mitigation. However, there is still room for further improvements in coordination and communication between and within relevant organizations.

Target 11.6: environment

- *Target 11.6: By 2030, reduce the adverse per capita environmental impact of cities, including by paying special attention to air quality and municipal and other waste management*
- *Indicator 11.6.1: Waste generation per capita and recycling ratio*
- *Indicator 11.6.2: Annual mean levels of PM10 in cities (population weighted)*

The Korean government has made great strides in sustainable waste management through the introduction of several effective policy measures. The policy shift from waste treatment to demand-side management has significantly reduced waste and remarkably increased recycling. Now, the country aims to become a zero-waste society by moving towards a circular economy.

Until the 1970s, the primary governmental task related to waste management simply involved the collection, transfer, and open dumping of waste. However,

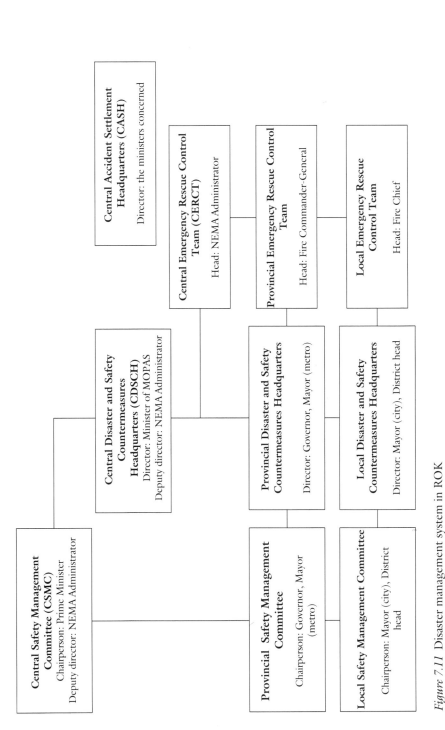

Figure 7.11 Disaster management system in ROK
Source: Yoon (2014), author edited.

with the rapid increase of waste, the waste sector became a critical social concern in the 1980s due to its serious environmental, social, and health consequences. Since then, an integrated approach has been introduced with a heavy focus on demand-side management for waste reduction at the source, including waste minimization and improved recycling. In addition, waste treatment responsibility has become shared between consumers and producers. Since the early 1990s, producers of waste that is difficult to recycle have had to bear some costs as well, which has affected the total product life-cycle by promoting environmentally friendly design and manufacturing.

Two major indictors for the performance of sustainable waste management – the per capita waste generation and the recycling ratio – clearly reflect the successful waste management practices in the ROK, as shown in Figures 7.12 and 7.13. The per capita waste generation, as shown in Figure 7.12, steadily increased with continuous economic development up to the early 1990s; however, it subsequently dropped significantly from 2.1kg/day in 1991 to 1kg/day in 2014. This reduction occurred primarily in the early 1990s, with the level remaining relatively constant over the last two decades. The current level was much lower than the OECD average of 1.42kg/day/capita as of 2015(OECD 2015).

More importantly, Figure 7.13 clearly demonstrates that the amount of recycled waste has grown enormously. Accordingly, the amount of waste land-filled or incinerated has drastically diminished, extending the service life of existing landfills. The level of recycling has reached 60%, which is much higher than the average for European countries (European Environment Agency 2013).

The Korean government has made significant endeavors to improve air quality. In the 1980s, the major pollutants targeted for air quality control included sulfur dioxide gas (SO_2), carbon monoxide, nitrogen dioxide, total suspended particles (TSP), ozone, and hydrocarbons. However, with economic and

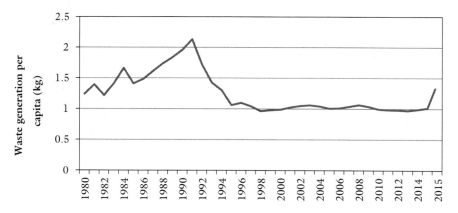

Figure 7.12 Waste generation per capita

Source: KOSIS. "Generation of Waste Per Resident Per Day" (1985–2015).

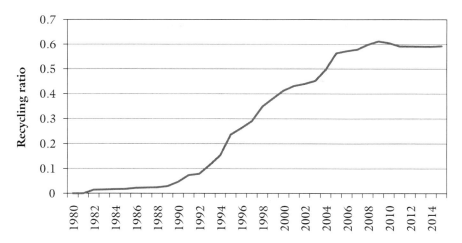

Figure 7.13 Recycling ratio
Source: KOSIS. "Recycling Rate" (1985–2015).

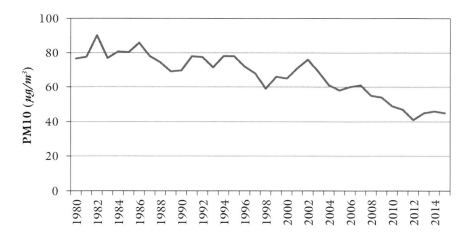

Figure 7.14 Mean values of PM10 in cities (population weighted)
Source: Ministry of Environment (1995–2015).

Table 7.4 Comparisons of PM10 concentration of Seoul with other cities

$\mu g/m^3$	2009	2010	2011	2012	2013	2014
Seoul	54	49	47	41	45	46
Los Angeles	32	27	29	30	29	30
Tokyo	31	21	21	20	21	–
Paris	28	27	27	26	26	22
London	19	18	23	19	18	20

Source: Ministry of Environment (2015).

technical development, additional pollutants were added. Standards for PM10 were first introduced in 1995, which led to continuous improvements in the level of PM10 concentration over time, as shown in Figure 7.14. Increased supply of clean fuels such as low sulfur oil, LNG, lead-free gasoline, and tighter emissions regulations (Ministry of Environment 2016) are some of the measures the government has introduced for air quality control. On the other hand, standards for PM2.5 were only recently introduced in 2015. There is no long-time series data on PM 2.5, so the concentration of PM10 was used for the analysis of indicator 11.6.2. Despite significant improvements in PM10 levels over the last decade, the current level is still twice the recommended level by WHO (2016), calling for continuous efforts in lowering particulate matters in the atmosphere.

In fact, comparisons of PM10 concentrations with cities in other countries demonstrate that the air quality of Seoul is far below comparable cities, as shown in Table 7.4. The PM10 levels in Paris, Tokyo, and London are merely half that of Seoul. Thus, more stringent and effective policy needs to be developed and implemented to further improve air quality.

Target 11.7: public space

- *Target 11.7: By 2030, provide universal access to safe, inclusive and accessible, green and public spaces, in particular for women and children, older persons and persons with disabilities*
- *Indicator 11.7.1: Size of public space*
- *Indicator 11.7.2: Proportion of persons victim of physical or sexual harassment, by sex, age, disability status and place of occurrence, in the previous 12 months*

Green and open spaces provide multiple benefits, including improving the environment of neighborhoods, increasing the property value of the area, and building stronger social networks by encouraging social interactions. Thus, providing safe, inclusive, and accessible green and open spaces is one of the key interests of urban planners and policymakers. In the study, the amount of public space has been introduced as an indicator to evaluate the achievement of target 11.7, which included squares, parks, green spaces, amusement parks, and public open space as public space.

In the past, housing supply was the priority interest of the government to cope with the fast-growing population in urban areas, while urban green space did not receive much attention. However, there has been an increasing demand for green and open space recently. As a result, the total size of public space has expanded in the ROK, as shown in Figure 7.15. Here, public space includes road surfaces, parks, and streams.

Despite the steady increase in the size of public space, when compared to the status of urban green space of other cities, it is not satisfactory. OECD (2014) found that the ROK does not make good use of 1.1 million hectares of its urban forest, with only 7.76m^2/person of accessible green space, failing to meet the

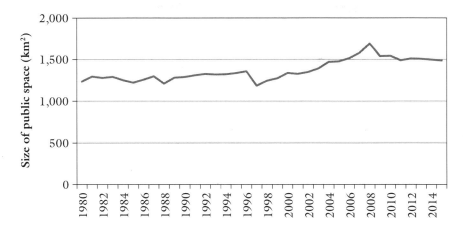

Figure 7.15 Size of public space
Source: Ministry of Land, Infrastructure, and Transport, Administrative District (1978–2013).

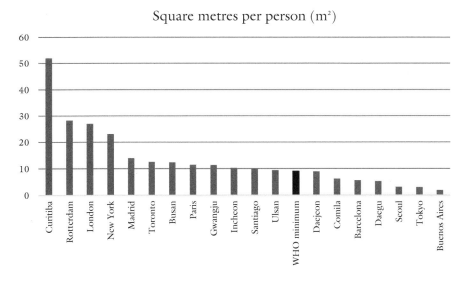

Figure 7.16 Green space per person in selected cities
Source: OECD (2014), author edited.

international standard. Figure 7.16 compares green space per capita in major Korean cities with international cities.

The next important indicator for target 11.7 is related to safety. The role of government in the intervention, prevention, and punishment of violence is vital. Since the 1990s, a series of laws concerning sexual and domestic violence has been introduced by the Korean government. In 2010, the Act on the Prevention of Sexual Assault and Protection was enacted, aiming to strengthen support for victims of sexual assault(Park 2015). However, the number of victims and cases related to sexual assault is rapidly rising, as shown in Figure 7.17. Similarly, the number of victims, who are either women, children under 6, or elderly above 60, has sharply increased over time, as shown in Figure 7.18. Thus, it is urgent that the government introduce and implement effective measures to mitigate against violence. In fact, the ROK has been making efforts to reduce crime by introducing and revising relevant policies and laws. The rapid increase in the number of crimes could be partly explained

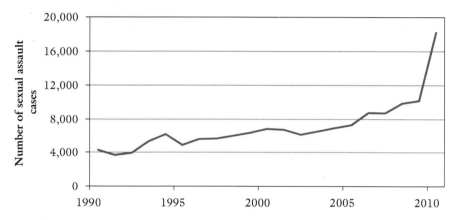

Figure 7.17 Number of sexual assault cases (National Police Agency 2013)
Source: KOSIS, Crime Victim Age, Sex (1994–2015).

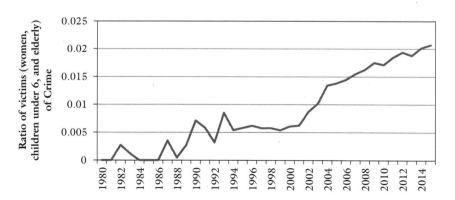

Figure 7.18 Ratio of victims of crime
Source: KOSIS, Crime Victim Age, Sex (1994–2015).

by the increase in the reporting of crimes. Changing social attitudes towards victims have led victims to actively and publicly seek justice by reporting their cases, while in the past victims tried to hide the facts out of fear of social stigmatization (Kwack 2015).

Analysis on the performance of the ROK in Goal 11 by the integrated index

Calculation of the integrated index score using factor analysis

To calculate the integrated index score for Goal 11, factor analysis was performed to determine weights for each indicator as follows.

First, KMO and Bartlett's test were conducted to verify the appropriateness of the factor analysis. The results from both test statistics justify the validity of factor analysis, with 0.8 for the KMO test and 0.000 of significance for Bartlett's test.

In this study, eigenvalues were used as a guideline to identify major factors. Factors with an eigenvalue higher than 1 have been taken into consideration. Accordingly, two components have been identified as shown in Table 7.5. Next, the varimax method was used to rotate factors and classify targets into the proper factors. Table 7.5 shows that factor 1 includes targets 11.1, 11.2, 11.4, and 11.5, while factor 2 includes targets 11.3, 11.6, and 11.7.

Next, the weight of each indicator was calculated as shown in Table 7.5. The target of disaster management (target 11.5) had the lowest weight of 0.06, while weights of the other targets were relatively similar, falling within the range of 0.13 and 0.18. The results imply that the indicator for disaster management did not have strong explanatory power compared to other indicators. This is understandable given that the disaster-related indicator does not have a clear trend over time with irregular peaks on the occurrence of severe natural disasters. The weighted index can now be calculated using weights in Table 7.5.

Table 7.5 Factor loadings and index weights for SDG 11

Target	Factor 1	Factor 2	Weight
Target11.1	−0.905	−0.039	16.2%
Target11.2	0.929	−0.028	17.0%
Target11.3	0.422	0.782	15.6%
Target11.4	0.936	−0.001	17.3%
Target11.5	−0.526	0.209	6.3%
Target11.6	−0.555	0.637	14.1%
Target11.7	−0.196	0.806	13.6%

Extraction Method: Principal Component Analysis.
Rotation Method: Varimax with Kaiser Normalization.
Rotation converged in 3 iterations.

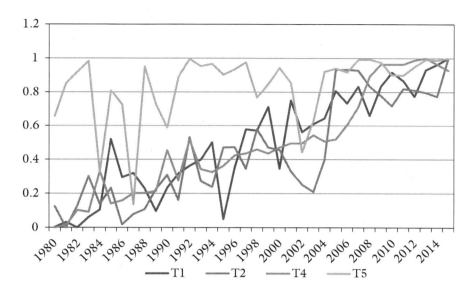

Figure 7.19 Trend of targets by factor 1

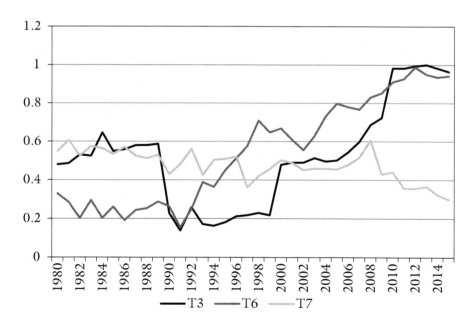

Figure 7.20 Trend of targets by factor 2

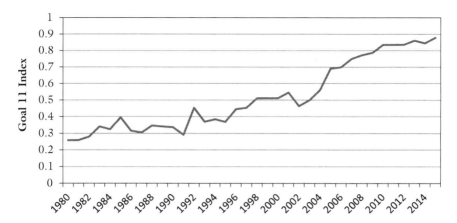

Figure 7.21 Index for SDG 11

Changes in the integrated index score over time

Figure 7.21 illustrates changes in the integrated index for Goal 11 over the last 35 years. It demonstrates that the ROK has made steady improvements in urban SDGs over the last 35 years, with a rising trend. But the speed of the improvement has not been homogenous over time. The improvement in the integrated index was slow until the early 1990s, while there has been significant progress since the early 2000s. The major drivers for improvement include improvement in housing (target 11.1), protection of cultural heritage (target 11.4), and improvement in environmental quality (target 11.6).

Conclusions and implications

Conclusions

This chapter reviewed the performance of the ROK in urban sustainability based on the framework of Goal 11 under the SDGs over the past 35 years, using a thorough quantitative analysis of relevant indicators. The results from the analysis of the integrated index for Goal 11 clearly demonstrate that the ROK has been making steady improvements in urban sustainability over time. The decade of the 2000s was the period in which the most advancements were recorded. As discussed in the introduction, the diverse urban problems, including housing shortages and quality issues, environmental degradation, and congestion caused by the rapid economic development and urbanization in the 1970s and 1980s, called for serious attention to the need for a paradigm shift in policy direction. The 1990s was the period in which sustainable development became one of the critical components to be considered in national and local policy. Thus, the efforts of the government in sustainable development, coupled with the paradigm shift in policy direction in the 1990s, are likely to have been a major driver for the significant improvements in urban sustainability measured by the integrated index for Goal 11 in the 2000s.

However, the analysis of each target in this study also illustrates that there are discrepancies in the level of the improvements over time across sectors. In general, the ROK has made remarkable progress in the housing sector, urban growth management, and preservation of cultural heritage and environmental areas, while minor improvements are observed in the sectors of public transportation, participatory planning, and expansion of public space. However, this study found that the ROK is currently facing significant challenges in building safe cities, with a sharp rise in the number of sexual assault cases and the ratio of vulnerable group victims of crime. More specifically, the following have been observed in each sector.

- *Inappropriate housing has been reduced from 40% to 5% over the past 35 years, due to the introduction of effective policies and legislation.*
- *The data shows a gradually increasing trend in the modal share of public transportation. Currently, the central government and local governments are making efforts to promote the use of public transportation, from both demand and supply sides.*
- *In urban growth management, the major indicator – the ratio of land consumption rate to population rate, which is a good measure of urban sprawl – has been improved in the ROK since large-scale new town projects were completed in the 1990s and 2000s.*
- *Participatory planning has yet to be fully in place in the ROK, though a few cities and provinces recently developed their master plans with active involvement of citizens. Such practices are expected to be expanded to other local governments in the near future.*
- *The analysis on waste generation, recycling ratio, and concentration of PM10 signify remarkable improvements in environmental quality. Despite the positive trend, comparisons with international cities in terms of air quality show that there is still much room for improvement.*
- *The disaster management system in the ROK has strengthened, with increasing occurrences of extreme weather events due to climate change. Although fatalities seem to be mitigated, the scale of property loss is on rise.*
- *The number of sexual assaults and the number of victims of crime, who are either women, children under 6, or elderly above 60, are growing at a fast rate, calling for the introduction and implementation of effective policies and measures.*

Implications

This study attempted to quantify and evaluate the progress in urban sustainability over the past 35 years in the ROK. Based on the analysis, several policy implications can be drawn. First, despite the improvements of the integrated index for Goal 11 over time, the analysis of each indicator revealed which areas are winners and which losers, showing big discrepancies in the level of progress across different areas. Thus, those areas with poor performance, for example the crime issue, should be given more attention by the ROK in moving forward. Another important noteworthy point is the fact that although one area has made great advancement during the studied time period, it does not necessarily mean that the ROK is doing well in that specific area, because the current performance level might not be sufficient when compared with other countries, as discussed in the analysis of public space in the previous section. Thus, cross-checking with other countries is useful and beneficial for better understanding the status of a country in implementing and achieving SDGs. In this regard, the study will enable other countries to conduct a comparative study with the ROK using the same methodologies and indicators.

Second, though interactions between the targets were not the main focus of this study, it was found that pursuing one target could conflict with the implementation of another target. For example, the rapid physical expansion of built-up areas observed under target 11.3 is likely to have a close linkage with the provision of good public transportation under target 11.2. In the case of the Seoul metropolitan area, the success of the new towns in the neighboring cities of Seoul was possible thanks to good inter-city public transportation, including subways and buses, generating a large volume of long-distance commuting and eventually contributing to the fast expansion of built-up areas. Indeed, effective urban growth management can be realized only with a carefully designed public transportation infrastructure. Thus, in pursuing targets under the SDG, policy makers should consider the potential interactions between different targets and try to minimize expected side effects.

Lastly, the national statistics system needs to be improved and modified to fully support the current global SDG indicators. This study faced difficulties in accessing disaggregated data, for example, indicators 11.2.1, 11.5.1, and 11.7.1. As discussed, comparative study at both the national and local level is useful and necessary for a country or a city to move towards sustainable development. The use of common indicators is key for a comparative study. Though there are still many criticisms and controversies over the selected SDG indicators (Simon et al. 2016), the government needs to try to keep up with international trends by establishing an appropriate database system or developing its proxy indicators given the country context.

References

Bengston, D. and Y.C. Youn. 2004. "Seoul's Greenbelt: An Experiment in Urban Containment." In *Policies for Managing Urban Growth and Landscape Change: A Key to Conservation in the 21st Century*. 27–34. St. Paul, MN: U.S. Department of Agriculture.

Chu, J. 2007. "Policies on Promoting Environmental industries and international cooperation." *Korea Environmental Policy Bulletin*, 3.5.

European Environment Agency. 2013. "Managing Municipal Solid Waste – A Review of Achievements in 32 European Countries." EEA Report No 2/2013, European Environment Agency.
Ha, S. 1994. "Low-Income Housing Policies in the Republic of Korea." *Cities*, 11.2: 107–114.
Hwang, S. K. 2012. *Korea's Best Practices in the Transport: Lessons from Transition in Urban Transport Policy*. Gyeonggi-do: KOTI Knowledge Sharing Report.
Kim, C., J. H. Choe, and Y. G. Jeong. 2011. "A Safeguarding System for Cultural Heritage in Korea: Focused on the Activities of Restoration, Transmission, and Protection of Designated Cultural Properties." Modularization of Korea's Development Experience. Ministry of Strategy and Finance.
Kim, K. H., and M. Park. 2016. "Housing Policy in the Republic of Korea." ADBI Working Paper 570. Tokyo: Asian Development Bank Institute.
Kwack. 2015. "Sexual Crime Is About 27 Thousands Case, It's More Than 26% More Than a Year Ago(Comprehensive)." *Yonhapnews*, March 19.
Lee, S. 2013. "Valuing Convenience in Public Transport in the Korean Context." *OECD Discussion Paper*, No. 2013-17.
Lee, S. M., and J. S. Lim. 2013. "Best Experiences from Public Transport Reform." KOTI Knowledge Sharing Report Issue 9. Gyeonggi-do: The Korea Transport Institute.
Lee, S. H., M. S. Moon, Y. B. Jang, I. S. Park, M. J. Chai, and S. Y. Choi. 2011. "Comparative Study of Urbanization Process in Korea and China." *Policy Studies*, 28: 1–114.
Local Sustainability Alliance of Korea. 2014. "Local Sustainable Development Movement in Korea." LSAK&KICSD Brochure.
Ministry of Construction and Transportation. *Housing Welfare Assistance Plan for Low-Income Households in Korea*. Seoul: Ministry of Construction and Transportation.
Ministry of Environment. 2006. *Choice for Sustainable Development: LA21 in Korea*. New Delhi: Ministry of Environment.
Ministry of Environment. 2014. *Annual Report of Ambient Air Quality in Korea*. Incheon: Ministry of Environment.
Ministry of Environment. 2015. *Environmental Statistics Yearbook*. Sejoing: Ministry of Environment.
Ministry of Environment. 2016. Atmospheric Environment Annual Report. Accessed October 21, 2017. http://webbook.me.go.kr/DLi-File/NIER/09/5618423.pdf
Ministry of Land, Infrastructure and Transportation. 2015. "New Town Policy of Korea." Ministry of Land, Infrastructure and Transportation.
Moon, K. 2002. "Status and Evaluation of LA21." *Journal of Local Government and Administration*, 179–198.
National Police Agency. 2013. Crime Statistics 2013. Accessed September 15, 2017. www.police.go.kr/portal/main/contents.do?menuNo=200559
OECD. 2012. "The Korean Green Growth Strategy and its Implementation in Urban Areas." In *OECD Urban Policy Reviews*. Korea: OECD Publishing.
OECD. 2013. *Green Growth in Cities. OECD Green Growth Studies*. Paris: OECD Publishing.
OECD. 2014. *Compact City Policies: Korea: Towards Sustainable and Inclusive Growth*. Paris: OECD Green Growth Studies.
OECD. 2015. "Environmental at a Glance." OECD* Indicator. Paris: OECD Publishing.

Park, B. 1998. "Where Do Tigers Sleep at Night? The State's Role in Housing Policy in South Korea and Singapore." *Economic Geography*, 74.3: 272–288.

Park, D. S. 2015. "Study on the Welfare Support for Sexual Crime Victims." *Journal of Welfare for the Correction*, 36: 45–65.

Park, S., and P. Han. 2009. *Estimation of Regional Economic Development Effects and Maximization Plan of Low Carbon Green Growth.* Wonju: Korea Research Institute for Local Administration.

Simon, D. et al. 2016. "Developing and Testing the Urban Sustainable Development Goals Targets and Indicators – A Five-City Study." *Environment and Urbanization*, 28.1: 49–63.

UN. 1992. "Agenda 21." Accessed September 2, 2017. https://sustainabledevelopment.un.org/content/documents/Agenda21.pdf

UN. 2014a. "Proportion of Urban Population Living in Slums." Accessed November 14, 2017. http://data.un.org/Data.aspx?d=SDGs&f=series%3aEN_LND_SLUM

UN. 2014b. "World Urbanization Prospects: The 2014 Revision." Accessed November 14, 2017. https://esa.un.org/unpd/wup/publications/files/wup2014-highlights.pdf

UN. 2016. "The World's Cities in 2016." Accessed October 8, 2017. www.un.org/en/development/desa/population/publications/pdf/urbanization/the_worlds_cities_in_2016_data_booklet.pdf

UN-Habitat. 2014. *National Report for Habitat III: Republic of Korea.* Nairobi, Kenya: UN-Habitat.

WHO. 2016. "Ambient (outdoor) Air Quality and Health." Accessed November 23, 2017. www.who.int/mediacentre/factsheets/fs313/en/

World Bank. 2010. "Cities and Climate Change: An Urgent Agenda." *Urban Development Series Knowledge Papers*, No. 10. Washington, DC: World Bank.

Yoo, B. 2001. "Metropolitan Growth Management and Green Belt in Korea." *Environmental Publications*, 39: 115–126.

Yoon, J., J. Choi., D. Kim, S. Kim and J. Seo. 2014. *National Report for Habitat III.* Sejong: Ministry of Land, Infrastructure and Transport.

Yoon, D. 2014. "Disaster Policies and Emergency Management in Korea." In *Disaster and Development*, edited by N. Kapucu and K. Liou, 149–164. Envrionmental Hazards.

Yoon, S. 2002. "The Local Agenda21, the First Step of Sustainable Development." Ministry of Environment.

8 Goal 13: climate action

Tae Yong Jung, Hanbee Lee, and Dohyun Park

Introduction

SDG 13 aims at taking urgent action to combat climate change and its adverse effects. The UNFCCC defines climate change as a change in climate induced by human activities either directly or indirectly that alters the composition of the global atmosphere and occurs for a sufficient period of time in addition to natural climate variability. Therefore, this goal is about the actions that should be taken to minimize the adverse impacts of climate change on ecosystems and its effects on human activities.

This chapter covers the ROK's progress towards achieving SDG 13, which has not yet been quantitatively analyzed, since the indicators of SDG 13 are qualitatively described and evaluated based on policies. In addition, according to the IAEG–SDGs, the indicators are Tier 2 and 3, meaning that indicators are either conceptually clear, have an internationally established methodology, and standards are available but data are not regularly produced by countries (Tier 2); or no internationally established methodology or standards are yet available for the indicator, but methodology and standards are being (or will be) developed or tested (Tier 3). This chapter is organized as follows; the introduction of SDG 13 will be illustrated in the context of the UNFCCC and the recent Paris Agreement at COP21 in 2015. Each indicator will be examined by using global trends and, more specifically, the ROK's actions regarding each indicator.

Definition of the goal and the indicators

Since the beginning of the Industrial Revolution, anthropogenic factors have changed the climate system, largely due to the emissions of GHG, which include chlorofluorocarbons (CFCs), methane, and CO_2, which have increased by almost 50% in the years following 1990. The large quantity of anthropogenic GHG results in global warming, causing the temperature of the planet to rise. SDG 13 is about the actions that should be urgently taken to minimize the adverse effects of climate change through both GHG mitigation and climate adaptation measures. Addressing SDG 13 is crucial to strengthen the resilience of all countries affected by climate change, but especially those in developing and vulnerable areas.

SDG 13 is subdivided into five detailed targets and seven indicators. In general, detailed targets are to enhance national level capacity for implementing climate change mitigation to minimize the effects of climate change (13.1 and 13.2), educate and empower (13.3 and 13.b), and to provide finance (13.a). Goal 13 incorporates extensive policies and measures covering all aspects of everyday life. The development and results of these policies and measures will be instrumental in determining whether the ROK is ready to tackle, and is capable of tackling, climate change. Thus, evaluating climate policy becomes a process that requires special prudence and preciseness. Considering that climate policy is a comparatively new area of public policy, this chapter reviews precedent studies on climate policy evaluation, and follows with the most relevant model for the ROK case.

SDG 13 and UNFCCC

Climate change and sustainable development are inextricably linked. Climate change presents the single biggest threat to development, and its unprecedented widespread effects disproportionately burden the poorest and most vulnerable. SDG 13 expressly acknowledges that the "UNFCCC is the primary international, intergovernmental forum for negotiating the global response to climate change," while the UNFCCC's SBSTA acknowledges the "importance and inter-linkages" of climate and the sustainable development agenda, recognizing that they are two separate but parallel processes (United Nations 2017). In fact, most countries reporting on their NDCs under the UNFCCC Paris Agreement are also working towards the 17 SDGs agreed upon by the UN.

The Paris Agreement is the product of years of work under the UNFCCC, signed in April 2016 by 175 member states. It attempts to mitigate GHG emissions while accelerating and intensifying actions and investments needed for a sustainable, low-carbon future. It builds on the experience of the Kyoto Protocol, although its design is vastly different: it is based on a "bottom-up" approach where each country sets its own emissions reduction target through INDC to reduce GHG emissions beyond 2020 and keep the global temperature rise within 2 degrees, aiming for 1.5 degrees above pre-industrial levels. As of April 4, 2016, 189 of the 197 Parties to the UNFCCC have submitted 161 INDCs (the European Commission submitted one joint INDC). Of these, 137 included climate adaptation components. This is an important milestone for vulnerable countries, as it establishes a global priority on a long-term goal for climate adaptation on par with GHG mitigation. Parties reference nearly every sector and area of the economy in the climate adaptation component of their INDCs. The top three priority areas are water, agriculture, and health, which coincide with the top climate hazards that Parties identified – floods, drought, and increasing temperatures.

By appropriately identifying the linkages between NDCs and SDGs, policymakers can effectively and efficiently take actions to achieve both SDGs and NDCs. For example, initiating renewable energy programs under SDG 13.2 achieves lowered GHG emission levels declared under NDC. According to the WRI's analysis of the linkage between climate change governance and the SDGs, the strongest areas of alignment between the NDCs and SDG 13 targets converged around "poverty alleviation, energy, agriculture and land use, forestry, infrastructure and cities and human settlements" (Northrop et al. 2016).

Then Secretary-General of the UN, Ki-moon Ban spoke to the participants at the annual World Economic Forum in 2016 about the 2030 SDGs and the Paris Climate Agreement (COP21), saying, "The only agenda greater than our promises is to deliver and implement these two important agreements." He also mentioned that the 17 SDGs and climate change are indivisible because climate change undermines development gains and that a holistic approach is now possible, pointing to the critical nexus between development and climate change. "The SDGs move us towards development models that are more sustainable."

Trends in achieving Goal 13 in ROK

In terms of national policies on climate change adaptation and mitigation, the ROK has established a wide array of legal institutions and policy frameworks for the past few decades as demonstrated in Figure 8.1. In the following section, the ROK's recent attempts to combat climate change will be scrutinized according to the sub-goals of SDG 13.

Goal 13.1: strengthen resilience and adaptive capacity to climate-related hazards and natural disasters in all countries

The ROK is located in the temperate zone of the mid-latitude and shows a variety of seasonal changes along with regional diversity. The winter season is cold and dry while the summer season is affected by monsoons. Besides the variability of the winter and summer seasons, the autumn and spring seasons are short and mild. The ROK's natural disasters are commonly caused by torrential rain

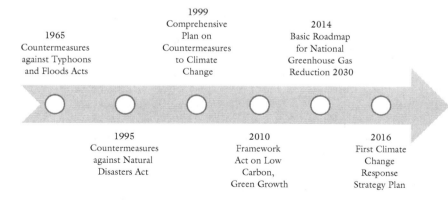

Figure 8.1 Flow of natural disaster and climate change countermeasures
Source: Author's own.

and typhoons. Between 2006 and 2015, natural disasters have annually cost on average 22 lives, as shown in Figure 8.2. Torrential rains accounted for 81.9% of deaths caused by natural disasters, while typhoons brought significant loss particularly in 2007 and 2012. However, in general, the trends in the number of deaths caused by natural disasters have been decreasing.

Climate change has caused increased climate instability such as erratic precipitation and rising sea levels. In the past 97 years (from 1912 to 2008), the average amount of annual precipitation has increased. However, the number of precipitation days has decreased, while the frequency of torrential rain has increased. Meanwhile, the sea level of the Korean peninsula's southern coasts of Busan rose 7.8cm (approximately 2.2mm per year between 1973 and 2006), while Jeju Island's coast rose 21.9cm between 1964 and 2006. Furthermore, the ROK has increasingly become subtropical, where the northern and southern coasts are clearly getting warmer every year (Ministry of Public Safety and Security 2015).

With the aim of reducing underlying disaster risk factors, countries have begun considering and implementing a variety of different mechanisms, including climate change adaptation projects and programs, environmental impact assessments, integrated planning, payments for ecosystem services, and legislation for the protection of environmentally sensitive areas. According to UNSTATS, 95 countries voluntarily agreed to a self-assessment on the inclusion of legislative and/or regulatory provisions for managing disaster risk. Among them, 83 countries, including the ROK, have such provisions in place.

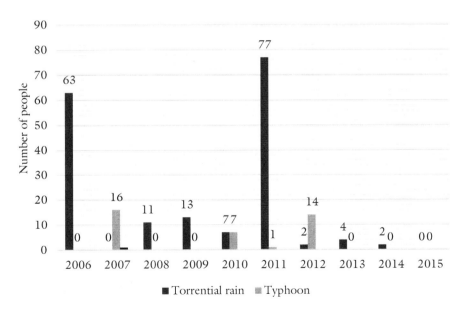

Figure 8.2 Deaths caused by natural disasters (2006–2015)
Source: Ministry of Public Safety and Security (2015).

Prior to 1995, the Countermeasures against Typhoons and Floods Act defined the laws and regulations for protecting lives and property from natural disasters. It was revised and named as the Countermeasures against Natural Disasters Act in 1995. Since then, the Countermeasures have reflected the growing concern of Korean society regarding aggravated natural disasters. Table 8.1 summarizes the scope, action plans, and amendments of the natural disaster acts across the years.

As Table 8.1 demonstrates, the scope of natural disasters recognized by the Korean legal system has extended and the focus of the action plans has shifted from *ex post facto* response to prevention. In the meantime, the Countermeasures have devoted a significant part of their text to defining the responsibilities for disaster management systems on national agencies. The central government is to establish and implement a comprehensive plan for the prevention and preparation of natural disasters. The Chief of the agency responsible for disaster management shall conduct consultation for natural disaster mitigation, improve the conditions of areas exposed to threats, and provide information on disaster and emergency assistance. However, the ROK does not yet fully differentiate natural disasters caused by climate change and other extreme weather events in terms of legal frameworks and compensation structures. A comprehensive framework to tackle natural disaster in both ex-ante and ex-post is required to respond to climate change in a timely manner.

Goal 13.2: integrate climate change measures into national policies, strategies and planning

During the industrialization period from the 1970s to the 1990s, the ROK relied heavily on coal-fired power generation to supply cheap and stable energy. The cost of achieving remarkable economic growth was rapid environmental degradation. Even now, ROK's contribution of GHG emissions has not diminished, despite growing public awareness of the impacts on climate change.

As implied by Figure 8.3, total GHG emissions have grown at an average annual rate of 5.29% since 1990. In 2014, the national GHG emissions amounted to 691 million tons, of which 589 million tons resulted from fuel combustion. Energy and industrial processes made up 94.7% of total emissions. Despite being the seventh largest emitter globally, ROK has established and implemented comprehensive measures to fight climate changes several times in the past. Starting in 2009, climate change was integrated into the national Green Growth Plan, and in December 2016, the First Climate Change Response Strategy Plan was released.

The First Climate Change Response Strategy Plan released in 2016 is the first comprehensive plan that covers the ROK's medium- and long-term climate change strategies and specific action plans in preparation for the post-2020 era. It includes all relevant policies and measures, such as GHG reduction, adaptation to climate change, and international cooperation. Table 8.2 summarizes the major targets, tasks, respective jurisdictions, and institutional progress.

The focus of the countermeasures against climate change has shifted from a reduction-centered paradigm towards market and technology-based

Table 8.1 Countermeasures against Natural Disasters Act

	Scope	Action plans	Amendments
Countermeasures against Typhoons and Floods Act (1967)	Floods, torrential rain, heavy snow, typhoons, tsunami, and any other disaster caused by natural phenomena corresponding thereto	- Establishment of fundamental infrastructure for natural disaster prevention and forecast	
Countermeasures against Natural Disasters Act (2005)	Typhoon, flood, heavy rain, strong wind, wind wave, tidal wave, tidal water, heavy snowfall, drought, earthquake, yellow sand, and corresponding thereto	- Prior consultations about examination of disaster impact - Designation of area vulnerable to natural disaster - Development of central emergency support system - Development and publication of plan to undertake disaster restoration projects	- Provided legal and institutional framework for prevention and restoration of natural disasters - Shifted the focus from response to prevention
Countermeasures against Natural Disasters Act (2012)	Typhoon, flood, downpour, strong wind, wind and waves, tidal wave, heavy snowfall, lightning, drought, earthquake, sandy dust, red tide, and other natural phenomena equivalent thereto	- Cultivation of prevention technology and industry - Promotion of cooperation among local governments - Establishment of targets on local natural disaster prevention	- Defined specific responsibilities for disaster management on the national agencies - Recognized the intensity of climate change
Countermeasures against Natural Disasters Act (2016)	Typhoon, flood, downpour, strong wind, wind and waves, tidal wave, heavy snowfall, lightning, drought, earthquake, sandy dust, algae outbreaks, ebb and flow, volcanic activity, collision of space objects, and other natural phenomena equivalent thereto	- Revision of prior consultations on re-examinations of factors influencing disasters	- Alleviated the person in charge of natural disaster prevention and response from deputy director to minister

Source: Adapted from National Law Information Center (2017).

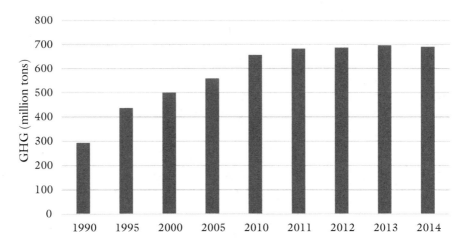

Figure 8.3 Total GHG emissions (excluding LULUCF), selected years
Source: OECD (2017).

climate-integration. The Plan aims for a happy society safe from climate change, to strengthen the role of the private sector, and to enhance the harmonization of the economy, society, and environment so that they can effectively accept and implement the relevant policies. The main objectives include expanding the renewable energy supply and use of clean fuel, improving energy efficiency, and utilizing the carbon market. In addition, to advance climate change monitoring and forecasting, scientific risk management systems, such as climate change satellites, will be introduced. The government also plans to encourage citizens to participate in emissions reduction.

If national climate actions are effectively implemented and accumulated, it would help the ROK a leading country in the global response to climate change. At the same time, it is also expected to strengthen national capacity to prevent natural disasters and disasters caused by climate change, thereby securing the safety of its people.

The Basic Roadmap for National Greenhouse Gas Reduction 2030 declared a systematic implementation plan to achieve a target of 37% (of BAU) reduction in GHG emission as declared in the ROK's NDC at the Paris Agreement.

The Roadmap serves as the barometer for emissions reduction before the post-2020 climate regime. According to the Roadmap, 219 million tons (25.7% of BAU) of the 315 million ton target will be reduced in eight sectors, including power generation, industry, building, etc. The plan was drawn from multiple consultations among line ministries, associated organizations, and the private sector.

The power generation sector is responsible for the largest amount of reductions, 64.5 million tons (19.4% of BAU), followed by the industrial sector with 56.4 million tons (11.7%) (Greenhouse Gas Inventory and Research Center 2016). In

Table 8.2 Evaluation of the First Climate Change Response Strategy Plan

	Target	Task	Jurisdiction	Policy and legislation progress
1. Transition to low carbon energy policy	Reduce through clean energy replacement and efficient energy use	Expand renewable energy use, reinforcing low carbon power mix, improving energy efficiency, etc.	Ministry of Trade, Industry and Energy (MOTIE)	- Fourth Renewable Energy Strategic Plan (February 2017) - Proposed exit on nuclear power (June 2017)
2. Cost-effective reduction through carbon market utilization	Reduce through the establishment of the domestic carbon market and linkage with the international carbon market	Activate emissions trading system, utilizing the international market mechanism (IMM)	Ministry and Strategy and Finance (MOSF), Office for Government Policy Coordination	- Second Plan for Emission Trading Scheme (2018~)
3. Foster new industries to cope with climate change and expanding investment in new technology and research	Simultaneously achieve new energy market, job creation, and greenhouse gas reduction	Support the creation of new industries in the private sector, investing in new technologies, etc.	MOTIE, Ministry of Environment (MOE), Ministry of Future Creation and Science (MFCS), Ministry of Oceans and Fisheries (MOF)	- Subsidy guideline for clean energy vehicles (January 2017~)
4. Establish a society safe from abnormal climate changes	Reduce and minimizing risk and damage caused by climate change	Analyze and manage scientific impacts of climate change, constructing a society that is safe from climate change, etc.	Ministry of Environment (MOE), Korea Meteorological Administration (KMA), etc.	- Creation of Disaster and Safety Management Department (July 2017~)
5. Enhance carbon absorption and circulation functions	Mitigate and offset reduction burden through contributing to forest greenhouse gas reduction	Enhance the function of carbon sinks, promote transition to resource recycling society	MOE, MOF, etc.	
6. Strengthen international cooperation to respond to the post-2020	Raise international recognition of Korea's efforts to respond to climate change	Strengthen the negotiation ability of the Korean government and the inspection ability of reduction goal implementation	Ministry of Foreign Affairs (MOFA), MOE, Office for Government Policy Coordination	- Participation in international climate action highlighted in Moon administration's 5-year plan
7. Establish the foundation for the practice and participation for the citizens	Activate national climate change response network	Establish climate change governance, forming a national consensus to climate change	MOE, MOTIE, Office for Government Policy Coordination	- (highlighted in the following section on climate change education)

Source: Author's own.

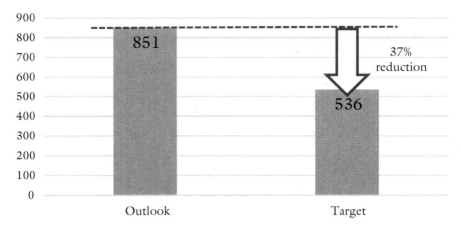

Figure 8.4 GHG emissions reduction target for 2030 (million tons)
Source: Government of Republic of Korea (2016).

particular, 96 million tons of GHG is supposed to be reduced through the IMM. However, overseas reduction of GHG emissions requires certain preconditions to be satisfied, such as international agreements detailing reduction goals, expansion of the global emission trading market, and preparation of financing plans. Thus, the ROK government plans to map a more detailed plan to meet the conditions of the IMM. The government has clearly stated that plans would continuously revise and supplement the roadmap, reflecting international trends and domestic conditions. Making a strong connection between the GHG reduction roadmap and the national energy roadmap continues to be a demanding challenge for achieving integrated national goals for the ROK in the energy sector and climate policy.

Goal 13.3: *improve education, awareness-raising and human and institutional capacity on climate change mitigation, adaptation, impact reduction and early warning*

A quick and accurate early warning system is essential to reduce the negative impacts of natural disasters. It incorporates not only forecasting of natural disasters but also concerns the location of shelters and providing action plans for victims. The Cell Broadcasting Service (CBS)-based Phone Disaster Notification Broadcasting System sends alerts via text message to mobile users through the base stations of domestic telecommunication companies. To reach the largest number of residents with as much information as possible in a limited amount of time, other measures engage in operating early warning, including: Automatic Verbal (Text) Notification System, Automatic Rainfall Warning System, Disaster Notification Board System, TV Disaster Warning Broadcasting System, and Radio Disaster Warning Broadcasting System (Oh and Park 2009).

Nevertheless, the ROK's early warning system was severely criticized after an earthquake of 5.8 magnitude in Gyeongju, Kyungbuk Province on September 12, 2016. The text alerts were sent out ten minutes after the earthquake and in the meantime the whole nation feared for their safety (Ock 2016). As a result, the Korea Meteorological Administration was entrusted with full control over an early warning system and has been pursuing improvements in speed through technological advances.

Capacity building on climate action can be defined as improving various measures to understand and initiate action to combat climate change. Education is an important resource in mitigating current impacts while preparing future generations to sustainably adapt against further propagation of climate change (Mermer 2010). In the case of the ROK, 'environmental conservation' and 'energy saving' education programs have been in place since the early 1990s, though without climate change related content. In 2008, under the overall curriculum revision plan, these two programs have gone under review to include climate change education.

In Cho et al. (2013), an analysis of ROK's climate change education across primary, middle, and high school was conducted to evaluate the depth and coverage of the content. The authors found that the education program was mostly concerned with climate mitigation and very little on climate adaptation. In the curriculum the causes of climate change were slightly referred to and the causes mentioned included only anthropogenic effects. Furthermore, climate change's natural phenomenon and the systematic causes were not presented in the curriculum. The ROK's "cause and solution" approach to climate change education limits the understanding of climate change as a problem that can be fixed with solutions rather than teaching a holistic picture of the concept and multi-sectoral impacts. Table 8.3 indicates the number and the degree of coverage (filled circle) for each climate change topic by school level.

In addition to the critique on the content of the education itself, climate change education in the ROK has yet to be approached in a holistic manner in which the issue is dealt as a separate unit or section rather than dispersed across various subjects and education levels. Currently, climate change is covered in selected sections of environmental and science education and is dealt with at the school and teacher's discretion. In addition, the training and education for

Table 8.3 Climate change contents included in scholastic curriculum

School level	Causes			Phenomenon				Impacts				Response	
	C1	C2	C3	P1	P2	P3	P4	I1	I2	I3	I4	R1	R2
Primary		•OO		O	O			O	O	O		••OO	
Middle	•O	•••	O		OO		O	•	•O	•O	OO	••OO	
High	OOO	•			•				OO	OO		OOOOO	

Source: Adapted from Cho et al. (2013).

teachers remains weak and limited. The ROK's primary to high school education is undergoing a curriculum revision as of 2017 and from an unofficial interview with the Ministry of Education, the revised curriculum on climate change has involved various academic experts and the Ministry of Environment in order to incorporate a more holistic and up to date program. Beyond the classroom, education on climate change has been initiated in the private sector, local municipalities, and research foundations by developing and promoting education programs and even designated centers.

Climate change education and experience centers are mostly local initiatives, where various cities and provinces have built centers to conduct education programs and exhibitions for the local community to participate in. These centers are targeted for all ages, which limits the level of the information to be accessible to all. More focused education with targeted populations such as executive education programs are also available from organizations such as the Climate Change Center, a non-profit organization currently led by the former prime minister Han Duck-Soo with the mission of creating a low-carbon society with citizens across the globe through education and policy making.

The importance of educational policies and curricula that expose countermeasures against climate change in terms of GHG mitigation and climate adaptation while promoting knowledge and understanding of the causes and impacts of climate change has been well recognized and proven by studies on the predictors of public climate change awareness and risk perception across 119 countries (Lee et al. 2015). Lee et al. (2015) have found that educational attainment is the single strongest predictor of climate change awareness among various sociodemographic characteristics, geography, and perceived well-being.

Even though climate change is visibly proceeding and public concern about climate change is increasing both nationally and internationally, teenagers' and students' perception of climate change is relatively low in the ROK. The annual survey on "environmental perception" conducted by the Ministry of Environment includes a section on the public's awareness of climate change. In the 2015 survey, 97.5% of Koreans (aged 13 years or older) had heard about climate change, but only 4.7% answered that they knew the details and 27.1% had only heard about it, with little awareness. Though this metric is singular and has yet to include information on whether or not the current education on climate change has changed awareness and perception of climate change, it serves as a measure for instigating more action to further build the capacity of the ROK's public on climate action.

Goal 13.a: improve education, awareness-raising and human and institutional capacity on climate change mitigation, adaptation, impact reduction and early warning

Climate finance refers to investments in GHG mitigation, such as renewable energy technologies or climate adaptation activities, which seek to reduce the vulnerability to climate change effects. Although a clear internally agreed definition has yet to be commonly used, research institutes such as the Climate Policy Initiative (CPI) define and track global climate finance flows, which in 2015 amassed t$437 billion. Public funds accounted for $138 billion, with $299 billion from private investment; the recipients were split almost evenly between developed and developing countries (Buchner et al. 2017). Under SDG 13, indicator 13.a states that developed country parties to the UNFCCC are to "implement" their commitment to jointly mobilize USD 100 billion annually by 2020. Meanwhile in the UNFCCC, the inclusion of the figure "USD 100 billion per year" in the Paris Agreement was heavily contested, and ultimately not included, by parties who were against any quantified target on the scale of resources. Instead, it was included in the "Decision" text, which addresses how the agreement will be initiated through shorter-term actions (United Nations Framework Convention on Climate Change 2016). Accordingly, the financial commitment of the Paris Agreement remains the most sensitive aspect due to the disparity and ambiguity left for interpretation in the two texts of the agreement.

However, measures to ensure adequate climate financing exist beyond legal and policy agreements, such as the GCF. The establishment of the fund was agreed at COP 16 to operate as the financial mechanism of the UNFCCC and has become a symbol for the radical shift in climate investment flows, empowering poorer nations to access fast and effective funding. Joint mobilization of USD 100 billion per year by 2020 will be transferred to the management of the GCF from a variety of sources to address the pressing mitigation and adaptation needs of developing countries. Governments also agreed that a major share of "new and additional" multilateral, multi-billion-dollar funding for climate mitigation and adaptation should be channeled through the GCF. At the G7 Summit in June 2015, leaders emphasized GCF's role as a key financial channel for global climate finance (Green Climate Fund 2017). Many developing countries also explicitly expressed their expectations to the Fund in their NDCs. GCF's initial resource mobilization period lasts from 2015 to 2018, and the Fund accepts new pledges on an ongoing basis. As of May 2017, the GCF has raised USD 10.3 billion equivalent in pledges from 43 state governments. The objective is for all pledges to be converted into contribution agreements within one year from the time at which they are made (Buchner et al. 2017).

The ROK, during the Myung-bak Lee from 2008 to 2012, made an aggressive push for low-carbon green growth, a national development strategy aiming to reduce GHG emissions while achieving economic growth through investments in clean-energy technology. In 2009, his administration announced a voluntary GHG reduction target of 30% below 2020 expected levels. Also, the GGGI was launched in 2010 with a mandate of spreading the green growth development paradigm and supporting developing countries. In 2012 at the Rio+20 Summit in Brazil, GGGI became an international organization based on international treaty. In October 2012, four months before the end of Lee's term, the ROK hosted the secretariat of the GCF. As such, the ROK's interest in mobilizing finance to address climate change was fully internalized during the political leadership of former President Lee. Yet, with the subsequent administrations, little to no progress has been initiated, and thus the importance of international actions and agreements on climate finance has risen to make up for the ROK's diminished efforts to mobilize climate finance.

The $10 billion pledged to the GCF includes the ROK's contribution amount of approximately $100 million in the form of grant contribution. In 2013, as soon as the GCF Secretariat was established in Incheon, the ROK government initially announced that $40 million would be granted for capacity building for developing countries. After less than a year, during the UN Climate Summit held in New York in 2014, former Geun-hye Park pledged to expand ROK's contribution to the fund by up to $100 million. Despite having the status of a developing country under the UNFCCC, the ROK's anticipative commitment to the GCF influenced developed countries' participation for the initial fund-raising. At the same time, the ROK government expressed its ambition to play a bridging role between developed and developing countries in regard to the global climate change agenda.

One of the most important aspects about climate finance is catalyzing private-sector investment into mitigation and adaptation. The goal of mobilizing $100 billion per year from 2020 in new and additional funds seems impractical without strong private-sector participation. According to the World Bank Group, to achieve the 2030 Agenda, "financing needs to move from 'billions' in unofficial development assistance to 'trillions' in development investments of all kinds." Public and private financing cooperation is needed to succeed. Persuading the private sector to join and operate domestically and internationally under the principles of the 2030 Agenda is a fundamental task (World Bank 2015). The leadership of the ROK as the host of GCF Secretariat and the mobilized efforts from the international community will be crucial for the sustainability and effectiveness of the GCF and its trickle-down effects for scaled up climate finance (Bradford et al. 2015).

In addition to financial contribution to the GCF, the KDB was approved to be an accredited entity in 2016, the role of which entails identifying projects in developing countries to respond to climate change and proposing them to the fund. KDB was founded as a national entity with the purpose of supplying and managing major industrial capital to help develop the country's economy. Yet, KDB's work now extends beyond the national boundary, helping developing countries promote industries, expand social infrastructure, stabilize financial markets, and facilitate sustainable growth. Furthermore, KDB has made climate change and socially responsible investing priority policy issues, which qualifies the bank to successfully pitch projects for GCF funding.

In addition, KOICA is in the process of getting accreditation from the fund to be the second accredited entity of the ROK. Considering that the organization's mission is supporting socio-economic development of developing countries with grant aid, KOICA is expected to play a bridging role between partner countries and the fund and to provide additional contribution to the fund by co-financing on projects (Kim et al. 2015).

The Paris agreement discussions and SDG 13 efforts should establish principles for the allocation of various types of climate finance, particularly about the use of aid-related climate finance. With innovative solutions and spearheading initiatives mobilizing climate financing for developing countries, the GCF and related organizations should be something that the ROK and the international community get behind.

Goal 13.b: improve education, awareness-raising and human and institutional capacity on climate change mitigation, adaptation, impact reduction and early warning

The typical mechanism for providing financial aid to developing countries is bilateral and multilateral ODA. The OECD monitors such financial flows closely and since the momentum of actions towards mitigating climate change has snowballed since the 2010s, OECD has been collecting statistics on climate ODA as a portion of total ODA.

Statistically, the Rio Marker helps to track climate-related ODA flows with four categories: climate change mitigation; climate change adaptation; biodiversity; and desertification. According to the Rio Marker, Korean climate-related ODA accounted for 19.6% of total ODA in 2015. Although there is some statistical miss due to the fact that many ODA implementing bodies are not yet familiar with the statistical tool, OECD data shows an average of 16.2% of the total Korean ODA went towards climate-related purposes and has slightly increased during 2012–2015 (OECD, 2017).

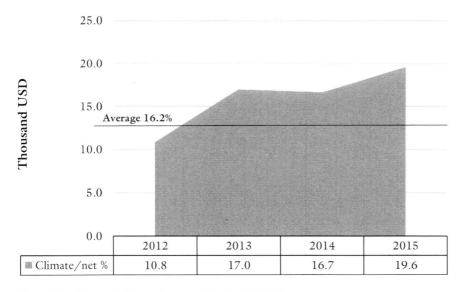

Figure 8.5 Share of climate finance of total ODA (%)

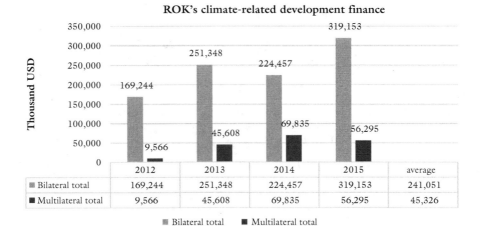

Figure 8.6 Climate-related development finance
Source: Adapted from OECD (2017).

In addition to the ROK's budgeted contribution to the GCF, an additional USD 181 million in climate-related finance, an average of USD 45 million per year, was provided in the form of multilateral development cooperation from 2012 to 2015. This contribution went to various institutions, including multilateral development banks (MDBs), financial intermediary funds (FIFs), and international organizations to finance climate actions.

The ROK's multilateral contributions are managed by the Ministry of Strategy and Finance and the Ministry of Foreign Affairs under the guidelines of the Strategic Plan for International Development Cooperation (Strategic Plan) developed in 2010. The Strategic Plan includes a comprehensive multilateral partnership plan, detailing scopes and focus sectors, scaled-up funding, and methods of bilateral and multilateral assistance. The ROK maintains a bilateral to multilateral ODA ratio of 70:30, where funding through MDBs accounts for approximately 70% of multilateral ODA every year.

A representative multilateral climate-related contribution is the KGGTF to the World Bank. The fund is a partnership focusing on the World Bank's green growth objectives, which support developing countries' sustainable growth strategies and climate-smart investments. The ROK government provided USD 40 million to the fund from 2012 to 2015 and an additional USD 48 million is planned for the 2016–2019 period.

In regard to the ROK's financial support to bilateral climate grants and loans, the ROK has been supporting climate change response and capacity building for developing countries. Many Ministries and government institutions provide small-scale bilateral ODA, but the EDCF managed by the K-EXIM Bank and

KOICA account for the considerable amount of total ODA. The two Korean ODA implementing agencies cover approximately 95% of total climate-related ODA in terms of budget. Generally, grant and loan ratio of Korean bilateral ODA maintains approximately 40:60; the ratio also applies to climate-related ODA.

According to the recent K-EXIM's EDCF Mid-term Strategy for 2018–2020, climate change is one of the core sectors to focus its fund allocation. Traditionally, the fund's climate-related support focused on the climate adaptation side, especially in infrastructure development for water supply and sanitation. Only a few mitigation projects are implemented in renewable energy and transportation sectors.

KOICA's climate change-related grant ODA activities relatively vary in sectors and keep a balance between mitigation and adaptation. The largest amount of budget allocation of KOICA also went to the development of water supply systems due to the demand of recipient countries; however, a considerable number of mitigation assistances were delivered at the same time. On the mitigation side, renewable energy accounts for the largest part, followed by energy efficiency improvement (KOICA 2017).

Delivering not only climate-related supporting projects, both the EDCF and KOICA also recently established the Environmental and Social Safeguard (ESS) to mainstream climate and social impact consideration into their general operation process according to the recommendations from the OECD DAC peer review in 2015. The advent of SDGs and the Paris Agreement also gave positive effects to both organizations to develop mid-term strategies and incorporate climate change as a core strategy. Now, the strategies and guidelines push forward the organizations to increase the number of activities supporting climate change mitigation and adaptation, and to mainstream climate impact consideration into their general activities.

Although there are large amounts of money flowing into climate change mitigation efforts via ODA, it would be a misunderstanding to interpret such numbers as additional or "new" money supporting climate efforts. According to analysis by Homi Kharas at the Brooking Institute (2015), measuring climate finance has statistical issues including double-counting when being reported to the UNFCCC. From 2010 to 2012, developed countries reported about $35 billion in FSF to the UNFCCC. A significant fraction of climate finance is in the form of ODA – an estimated 80% for the fast start financing period of 2010–2012.

According to ODA records, there was an increase in climate-related ODA in the 2010–2012 period, with the largest donors more than doubling their contributions compared to 2009. However, the aggregate volume of aid, including finance-related, did not rise; ODA commitments from DAC donors peaked in 2009 and modestly declined until 2012. Further, a very large increase in climate-related aid was recorded for 2010, the first year of the fast-start financing commitment. Since then, flows have stabilized or declined. Taken together, these data suggest that little of the FSF was actually additional. Rather, it appears to be associated with a labeling of many development projects as climate-related. In fact, climate-related aid accounted for 20% of total country programmable aid in 2013, compared to 9% in 2009 (Kharas 2015).

Such analysis provides a caution for settling with the efforts made and finance mobilized so far towards climate change. ODA and climate finance are not necessarily in conflict with each other. ODA is necessary to aid poor countries in achieving a low-carbon development path, while other sources will be necessary for the specific needs of middle-income developing countries. The issue will ultimately be about forging a consensus between ODA allocations and climate finance that allows for "additionality" to occur.

Climate impacts have the potential to slow, and even reverse, progress on the SDGs. Addressing climate change with a "development focused" perspective as introduced in the 2030 Agenda, including a stand-alone SDG on climate change (SDG 13) was welcomed by member states during the UN Sustainable Development Summit in 2015. This is the first time climate change has been fully incorporated in the development policy framework. Except for the annual resolution on climate change in the Second Committee, there has been little connection between policy making on sustainable development and the UNFCCC (Independent Commission on Multilateralism 2016). SDG 13 has significant implications on the extent to which a number of non-climate-focused SDGs can be achieved, especially those linked to poverty, food security, gender equality, water and sanitation, energy access, reduced inequalities, sustainable cities, and sustainable land use and ecosystems. Among the indicators, 13.b is most relevant to the "development agenda" overarching the SDGs as it specifically notes the assistance needed for LDCs, SIDS, and local and marginalized communities with a focus on women and children.

Within the UNFCCC and Paris Agreement context, integrating development aid in climate finance is highlighted in Article 9(4):

> The provision of scaled-up financial resources should aim to achieve a balance between adaptation and mitigation, taking into account country-driven strategies, and the priorities and needs of developing country Parties, especially those that are particularly vulnerable to the adverse effects of climate change and have significant capacity constraints, such as the least developed countries and small island developing States, considering the need for public and grant-based resources for adaptation.

This article is in parallel to SDG 13.b in that only LDCs and SIDS are mentioned as the most vulnerable category of countries to climate change.

According to Miren Gutierrez, Will McFarland, and Lano Fonua in their ODI working paper, the impact of climate change expands to various aspects of human development from individual to economy-wide scales. The direct impacts of climate change could exacerbate underlying and existing societal issues that further create or exacerbate existing poverty levels. Starting with declining agricultural yields, water availability, and changing disease patterns, for example, households and countries could face growth in unemployment, increasing gender gaps, and flaring of existing political tensions and conflicts. (Gutierrez et al. 2014) Such impacts could result in the collapse of education and health systems, exacerbate unemployment and discrimination issues, and make poverty reduction a more challenging task. The interlinkages of climate change and aspects of social development leading to or out of poverty attest to the importance of mitigating climate change; channeling the necessary resources, financial and non-financial, is at its urgency.

Conclusion

The ROK belongs to the developing countries group by definition of the UNFCCC. In that sense, the country's climate-related policies may be highly appreciated considering they are voluntary and proactive efforts. The emission reduction target to cut 2030 GHG emissions by 37% from BAU levels is also ambitious and higher than its earlier plan for a 15–30% cut. Also, governance and legal framework for climate change in the ROK has relatively enhanced the sustainable structure. During the last decade, several key strategic policies about climate change, including the Climate Change Response Strategic Plan and the Green Growth Strategic Plan, were developed and took effect. In general, the country's contributions to the global climate change cooperation are meaningful in that the country has played a bridging role between developed and developing country groups.

In addition, it is worth praising the country's support of global climate finance by providing a considerable amount of financial and in-kind support through ODA. According to Rio Markers, the ROK's climate-related ODA was almost 20% of the total as of 2015. However, reflecting the practical fact that the ROK has been an OECD DAC member country since 2009, more efforts are needed to play a leading role in global climate change cooperation. It is positive that the representative ODA implementing agencies, the EDCF and KOICA, recognize the importance of climate change issues and have increased relevant supporting activities. They also recently developed their own Environmental and Social Safeguards (ESS) to minimize negative impacts caused while implementing their projects.

However, policy fluctuations according to political regimes clearly hindered sustainable policy enforcement. After the Myung-bak Lee political willingness and support for climate change policy has dramatically weakened and the country's GHG emissions have continuously increased. As a result, the following Geun-hye Park could not meet the former emission reduction pledge to the international society, weakening the nation's voice and responsibility on global climate-related or sustainable development issues.

Although it is too early to evaluate the climate change policy of the current regime, the current government is expected to implement relatively active climate policies. The Jae-in Moon presidency launched in 2017 seems to be highly interested in energy and atmosphere agendas due to severe fine dust and policies to phase out nuclear and coal power. As a result, the government pledged to encourage renewable energy up to 20% until 2030, which is quite an ambitious target because currently renewable energy accounts for less than 5% of the total.

Besides the national climate change action plan, bottom-up implementations from local-level actions are highly expected. Seoul and Incheon are good examples, as they have established their own climate change action plans and declared they will actively respond to the impacts of climate change. For example, Seoul Metropolitan Government declared the Seoul Sustainable Energy Plan, which aims for energy self-sufficiency and emission reduction of up to 10 million tons of CO_2 equivalent by 2020. As a part of the energy initiative, Seoul also pushed ahead with the One Less Nuclear Power Plant initiative, which promotes energy-saving lifestyles at the individual level. As the host city of the GCF secretariat, Incheon Metropolitan City also carries out aggressive climate-related policies. The city government declared the year of 2016 as the peak year for GHG emissions, setting an emission reduction target of 15.2% against BAU by 2020 and 25.9% by 2030. To meet the targets, the city developed various action plans, including initiatives such as Car-free Commuting Day, Green Sharing Market, and the Cutting 1 Ton of GHGs Per Person Campaign (Incheon Metropolitan City 2017).

On the other hand, enhanced civil society activities and increased public awareness brought action-oriented programs such as Ecomom Korea, which brings environmental education through life and environmental activities and eco-life campaigns to mothers and children (Ecomom Korea 2017). Achieving SDG 13 is a long path, and the ROK has just taken the first few steps. Accompanied actions among the government, private sector, and civil society make the ROK's future climate change-related policy implementation promising and sustainable.

References

Bradford, C. I., B. M. Howe, J. K. O'Donnell, A. O'Neil, and S. Snyder. 2015. "South Korea's Role as Host of the Green Climate Fund: Implications for ROK Contributions to Green Growth." In *Middle – Power Korea: Contributions to the Global Agenda*. New York: Council on Foreign Relations.

Buchner, B., P. Oliver, X. Wang, C. Carswell, C. Meattle, and F. Mazza. 2017. "Global Landscape of Climate Finance 2017." Climate Policy Initiative.

Cho, S., C. Kim, S. Hwang, and N. Park. 2013. "Analysis of Climate Change Contents in 2009 Revised Curriculum." In *Proceedings of Korean Society for Environment Education Conference 2013*, 121–124. Cheongju: Korean Society for Environment Education. [In Korean].

Ecomom Korea. [In Korean]. Accessed November 30, 2017. http://ecomomkorea.org/

Government of Republic of Korea. 2016. "The First Climate Change Response Strategy Plan." Edited by Ministry of Environment. [In Korean].

Green Climate Fund. Accessed November 30, 2017. www.greenclimate.fund/home

Greenhouse Gas Inventory and Research Center. 2016. "National Greenhouse Gas Inventory Report of Korea." Greenhouse Gas Inventory and Research Center. [In Korean].

Gutierrez, M., W. McFarland, and L. Fonua. 2014. "Zero Poverty, Think Again: Impact of Climate Change on Development Efforts." ODI.

Incheon Metropolitan City. [In Korean]. Accessed November 30, 2017. www.incheon.go.kr/index.do#btnGoLanguage.

Independent Commission on Multilateralism. 2016. "The 2030 Agenda for Sustainable Development and Addressing Climate Change." ICM.

Kharas, H. 2015. "Aid and Climate Finance." In *COP21 at Paris: What to Expect the Issues*. Washington, DC: Brooking Institute.

Kim, I., J. Kim, H. Lee, C. Oh, S. Park, H. Yang, and Soo-young Park. 2015. "Status and Countermeasures for Sustainable Development Goals (Sdgs)." Korea International Cooperation Agency. [In Korean].

Korea International Cooperation Agency. [In Korean]. Accessed November 30, 2017. www.koica.go.kr/

Lee, T., E. M. Markowitz, P. D. Howe, C. Ko, and A. A. Leiserowitz. 2015. "Predictors of Public Climate Change Awareness and Risk Perception Around the World." *Nature Climate Change*, 5.11: 1014–1020.

Mermer, T. 2010. "The Unesco Climate Change Initiative: Climate Change Education for Sustainable Development." UNESCO.

Ministry of Public Safety and Security. 2015. "Statistical Yearbook of Natural Disaster." Edited by the Ministry of Public Safety and Security. [In Korean].

National Law Information Center. [In Korean]. Accessed November 30, 2017. www.law.go.kr/main.html

Northrop, E., H. Biru, and M. Bouye. 2016. "2 Birds, 1 Stone: Achieving the Paris Agreement and Sustainable Development Goals Together." World Resources Institute. Accessed November 1, 2017. www.wri.org/blog/2016/09/2-birds-1-stone-achieving-paris-agreement-and-sustainable-development-goals-together

Ock, H. 2016. "Fear Grips as 4.5 Magnitude Quake Hits Southeastern Korea Again." *The Korea Herald*, September 20, 2016. Accessed October 1, 2017. www.koreaherald.com/view.php?ud=20160920000858

Oh, J., and D. Park. 2009. "Early Warning System, Disaster Recovery System and Technology Transfer Practices in Korea." *Crisisonomy*, 5.1: 102–107. [In Korean].

Organisation for Economic Co-operation and Development (OECD). "OECD Statistics on External Development Finance Targeting Environmental Objectives Including the Rio Conventions." Accessed November 30, 2017. www.oecd.org/dac/environment-development/rioconventions.htm

Organisation for Economic Co-operation and Development (OECD). "OECD. Stat." Accessed November 30, 2017. https://stats.oecd.org/

Seoul Metropolitan Government. [In Korean]. Accessed November 30, 2017. www.seoul.go.kr/main/index.html

United Nations Framework Convention on Climate Change. 2016. "Green Climate Fund." Accessed November 30, 2016. http://unfccc.int/cooperation_and_support/financial_mechanism/green_climate_fund/items/5869.php

United Nations Statistics Division. 2017. Accessed November 30, 2017. "Global Database: SDG Indicators." http://unsdsn.org/resources/publications/sdg-index-dashboard/

United Nations. "Sustainable Development Knowledge Platform." Accessed November 30, 2017. https://sustainabledevelopment.un.org

World Bank. 2015. "From Billions to Trillions: Transforming Development Finance: Post-2015 Financing for Development: Multilateral Development Finance." http://siteresources.worldbank.org/DEVCOMMINT/Documentation/23659446/DC2015-0002(E)FinancingforDevelopment.pdf

World Economic Forum. 2016. "Sustainable Development Goals and Paris Climate Agreement: Now It's Time to Act." Accessed November 30, 2017. www.weforum.org/press/2016/01/sustainable-development-goals-and-paris-climate-agreement-now-it-s-time-to-act/

9 Goal 17: partnership for the goals

Jooyoung Kwak, Eungkyoon Lee, and Steven Kyum Kim

Sustainable Development Goals (SDGs) and global partnership

Goal 17: global partnerships for the goals

The shared vision and commitment to the SDGs is best highlighted by Goal 17, to "strengthen the means of implementation and revitalize the global partnership for sustainable development" (UN 2017). This goal highlights the importance that countries have for one another in an integrated global society. Globalization has brought greater economic integration and technology has greatly reduced the barriers for social interaction and economic integration, sharing ideas instantaneously across the world.

To measure the progress of achieving global partnership as manifested in Goal 17, the UN has outlined targets in five areas of finance, technology, capacity building, trade, and systemic issues. The targets and indicators listed in Table 9.1 provide quantifiable measures of progress in achieving the goals.

The indicators provide a measurable but imprecise tool for assessing partnership outcomes. They are used to gauge the capacity level of nations to support both domestic and international partnerships. Other than the finance dimension, which looks mainly at a country's capacity to raise revenue through tax collection, the indicators in the other dimensions are geared outwardly towards official development aid (ODA) and foreign direct investments (FDI). The focus of the indicators is primarily top-down and centered around national policies and measures. Only in the multi-stakeholder partnerships are non-state actors mentioned.

However, the roles of businesses and civil society are not clearly articulated within the SDGs. Non-state actors are crucial to financing, technology transfer, capacity building, and trade in the development of sustainable economic, environmental, and social systems. Technology transfer and knowledge sharing is a critical aspect of international partnerships but is only effective if there are workers with the skills necessary for these enabling technologies and industries. Capacity building aims to support technical assistance in the development of national plans and strategies; yet top-down national policies often fail to integrate local businesses and civil society organizations (CSOs) in terms of specific

Table 9.1 Goal 17 targets and indicators

Targets	Indicators
Finance	
17.1 Strengthen domestic resource mobilization, including through international support to developing countries, to improve domestic capacity for tax and other revenue collection	17.1.1 Total government revenue as a proportion of GDP, by source 17.1.2 Proportion of domestic budget funded by domestic taxes
17.2 Developed countries to implement fully their official development assistance commitments, including the commitment by many developed countries to achieve the target of 0.7 per cent of gross national income for official development assistance (ODA/GNI) to developing countries and 0.15 to 0.20 per cent of ODA/GNI to least developed countries; ODA providers are encouraged to consider setting a target to provide at least 0.20 per cent of ODA/GNI to least developed countries	17.2.1 Net official development assistance, total and to least developed countries, as a proportion of the Organization for Economic Cooperation and Development (OECD) Development Assistance Committee donors' gross national income (GNI)
17.3 Mobilize additional financial resources for developing countries from multiple sources	17.3.1 Foreign direct investments (FDI), official development assistance and South–South cooperation as a proportion of total domestic budget 17.3.2 Volume of remittances (in United States dollars) as a proportion of total GDP
17.4 Assist developing countries in attaining long-term debt sustainability through coordinated policies aimed at fostering debt financing, debt relief and debt restructuring, as appropriate, and address the external debt of highly indebted poor countries to reduce debt distress	17.4.1 Debt service as a proportion of exports of goods and services
17.5 Adopt and implement investment promotion regimes for least developed countries	17.5.1 Number of countries that adopt and implement investment promotion regimes for least developed countries
Technology	
17.6 Enhance North–South, South–South and triangular regional and international cooperation on and access to science, technology and innovation and enhance knowledge-sharing on mutually agreed terms, including through improved coordination among existing mechanisms, in particular at the United Nations level, and through a global technology facilitation mechanism	17.6.1 Number of science and/or technology cooperation agreements and programmes between countries, by type of cooperation 17.6.2 Fixed Internet broadband subscriptions per 100 inhabitants, by speed

(*Continued*)

Table 9.1 (Continued)

Targets	Indicators
17.7 Promote the development, transfer, dissemination and diffusion of environmentally sound technologies to developing countries on favourable terms, including on concessional and preferential terms, as mutually agreed	17.7.1 Total amount of approved funding for developing countries to promote the development, transfer, dissemination and diffusion of environmentally sound technologies
17.8 Fully operationalize the technology bank and science, technology and innovation capacity-building mechanism for least developed countries by 2017 and enhance the use of enabling technology, in particular information and communications technology	17.8.1 Proportion of individuals using the Internet
Capacity-building	
17.9 Enhance international support for implementing effective and targeted capacity-building in developing countries to support national plans to implement all the Sustainable Development Goals, including through North–South, South–South and triangular cooperation	17.9.1 Dollar value of financial and technical assistance (including through North–South, South–South and triangular cooperation) committed to developing countries
Trade	
17.10 Promote a universal, rules-based, open, non-discriminatory and equitable multilateral trading system under the World Trade Organization, including through the conclusion of negotiations under its Doha Development Agenda	17.10.1 Worldwide weighted tariff-average
17.11 Significantly increase the exports of developing countries, in particular with a view to doubling the least developed countries' share of global exports by 2020	17.11.1 Developing countries' and least developed countries' share of global exports
17.12 Realize timely implementation of duty-free and quota-free market access on a lasting basis for all least developed countries, consistent with World Trade Organization decisions, including by ensuring that preferential rules of origin applicable to imports from least developed countries are transparent and simple, and contribute to facilitating market access	17.12.1 Average tariffs faced by developing countries, least developed countries and small island developing States
Systemic issues	
Policy and institutional coherence	
17.13 Enhance global macroeconomic stability, including through policy coordination and policy coherence	17.13.1 Macroeconomic dashboard

Targets	Indicators
17.14 Enhance policy coherence for sustainable development	17.14.1 Number of countries with mechanisms in place to enhance policy coherence of sustainable development
17.15 Respect each country's policy space and leadership to establish and implement policies for poverty eradication and sustainable development	17.15.1 Extent of use of country-owned results frameworks and planning tools by providers of development cooperation

Multi-stakeholder partnerships

17.16 Enhance the global partnership for sustainable development, complemented by multi-stakeholder partnerships that mobilize and share knowledge, expertise, technology and financial resources, to support the achievement of the Sustainable Development Goals in all countries, in particular developing countries	17.16.1 Number of countries reporting progress in multi-stakeholder development effectiveness monitoring frameworks that support the achievement of the Sustainable Development Goals
17.17 Encourage and promote effective public, public–private and civil society partnerships, building on the experience and resourcing strategies of partnerships	17.17.1 Amount of United States dollars committed to public–private and civil society partnerships

Data, monitoring and accountability

17.18 By 2020, enhance capacity-building support to developing countries, including for least developed countries and small island developing States, to increase significantly the availability of high-quality, timely and reliable data disaggregated by income, gender, age, race, ethnicity, migratory status, disability, geographic location and other characteristics relevant in national contexts	17.18.1 Proportion of sustainable development indicators produced at the national level with full disaggregation when relevant to the target, in accordance with the Fundamental Principles of Official Statistics 17.18.2 Number of countries that have national statistical legislation that complies with the Fundamental Principles of Official Statistics 17.18.3 Number of countries with a national statistical plan that is fully funded and under implementation, by source of funding
17.19 By 2030, build on existing initiatives to develop measurements of progress on sustainable development that complement gross domestic product, and support statistical capacity-building in developing countries	17.19.1 Dollar value of all resources made available to strengthen statistical capacity in developing countries 17.19.2 Proportion of countries that (a) have conducted at least one population and housing census in the last 10 years; and (b) have achieved 100 per cent birth registration and 80 per cent death registration

Source: UN 2017, 23–26.

economic and cultural concerns impacting their communities. Several indicators from trade focus on tariffs and trade with the least developed countries, but trade is the result of industrial and business activity. The issues of data, monitoring, and accountability are critical for both domestic and international partners. Transparency and openness of data is an essential tool for all sectors, including businesses that incorporate such information into business activities and CSOs for monitoring the performance and commitments of governments and businesses.

Partnerships

The ideal partnership can be defined as the following:

> Partnership is a dynamic relationship among diverse actors, based on mutually agreed objectives, pursued through a shared understanding of the most rational division of labor based on the respective comparative advantages of each partner. Partnership encompasses mutual influence, with a careful balance between synergy and respective autonomy, which incorporates mutual respect, equal participation in decision-making, mutual accountability, and transparency.
>
> (Brinkerhoff 2002, 216)

Partnerships can provide different benefits for the participants. The rationale for entering a partnership can be generally summarized into four areas: to enhance efficiency and effectiveness; to provide integrated solutions that could not be produced individually; to enable compromise and win–win solutions among multiple stakeholders; and to increase representation and democratic practices (Brinkerhoff 2007, 68–69). These rationales convergently suggest that partnerships can contribute to good governance through governance effectiveness, governance legitimacy, and managing conflict and competing interests.

Partnerships and collaborations can take varying forms and consist of diverse groups. Brinkerhoff (2007) notes that the governance framework does not only require the involvement of the public sector but also needs substantial roles for non-state actors. Figure 9.1 below displays the governance framework. The public sector is mainly responsible for development of public policies and allocation of public services; the private sector leads investment and employment, complementing the effort of the state, while civil society provides advocacy and accountability on behalf of the citizenry. Good governance requires all three sectors to provide input and feedback to create an effective system. Understanding the institutional structures and capacity of actors in each sector is critical for determining governance effectiveness and partnership success.

The core task in the governance model for sustainable development (SD) is to facilitate communication among the involved partners in order to draw upon a consensus. Industries are one of the major partners as they identify and support profitability and economic development in the policies for sustainable development. Firms may search for ways to generate profits from developing or diffusing

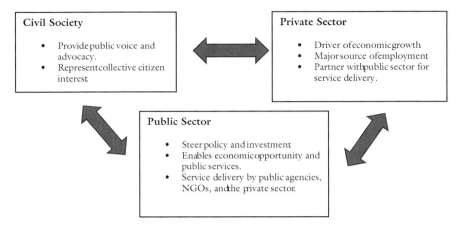

Figure 9.1 Governance framework for partnership
Source: Adapted from Brinkerhoff 2007, 98.

eco-friendly technologies with the support of other partners, including governments. CSOs expand social involvement and increase the operating capacity of organizations to act independently and autonomously. They are expected to make continuous efforts to communicate the social concerns of the public with governments and industries. Academia is also a major partner in SD since their involvement in providing research and analysis on policies and programs is essential to improving environmental and social quality, in addition to promoting regional development. International organizations mediate public pressure through support or opposition of policies and practices of governments and businesses, in addition to providing technical and financial capacity as a convener of stakeholders at multiple levels.

The governance framework highlights the importance of partnership in SD. Lessons from national and local partnership can provide invaluable governance experiences for managing competing interests and building common goals, expanding into the global context. Agyeman and Angus (2003, 357) note that sustainability has "a greater commitment to sharing of power between local governments and communities and a greater level of empowerment among citizens." The attainment of sustainable communities is determined by civil society involvement in environmental protection, since "the environmental health of a community is directly related to the civic health of its citizens" (Agyeman and Angus 2003, 358).

Partnerships have become increasingly popular to address environmental issues whose scope and scale often exceed singular jurisdictional boundaries. However, partnerships should not be viewed as a panacea. Critics quickly point out that their inability to punish or sanction often creates 'watered down' and less than ideal outcomes, such as in climate change. The lack of formal authority poses new challenges and opportunities for institutional structures that utilize informal and voluntary compliance mechanisms. Partnerships provide participants with the flexibility to build bridges and relationships of trust that can be a pathway for more effective policies and regulatory frameworks.

Although the private sector is driven by profit orientation, the motivation for partnering comes from a variety of factors. Austin (2007) notes that businesses tend to undertake collaborations beyond just profits because they face uncertainty and competition from a variety of different forces. Depending on what drives their motivation, the corresponding forces that dictate behavior will differ. In turn, the management approach and actions to be taken will be determined. In the networked age through social media, brand image and reputation influence the social and environmental practices of businesses. Consumer groups, CSOs, and international organizations have utilized market and public pressure through boycotts, divestment campaigns, and naming and shaming to influence operating behavior.

Effective partnerships that lead to good governance outcomes are highly dependent on the structure and process of collaboration. The link requires preconditions of awareness, collaborative attitude, or capacity for partners. Partnership enters into the participation process where implementation through the partnership structure is enhanced by partnership performance and project effectiveness. Positive partnership outcomes "are also directly implicated in [the] partnership structure and process" (Brinkerhoff 2007, 71). Good governance outcomes are tied to the structure (the participating actors) and the process (the participating method) (Brinkerhoff 2007, 74).

History of non-state partnerships for sustainable development

During Korea's rapid economic growth and industrial development, social and environmental concerns were pushed aside as the country sought to rebuild from the devastations of war. The post-war destruction and division made Korea one of the most impoverished countries in the world. Industrial and economic development were pursued at all cost to bring the country and its people out of poverty. Rapid industrialization and economic development of the 1960s and 1970s would lead to a radical transformation of Korea from an aid dependent recipient in the 1950s to a donor member of the OECD Development Assistance Committee in 2010.

Birth of civic environmentalism

Although SD focuses on the three pillars of society, environment, and economy, rapid industrialization and its adverse impacts on the environment and public health gave rise to the early environmental and social movements in Korea. Early environmental concerns were brought forth by rural residents seeking monetary compensation from adverse health and degradation of the land caused by industrial pollution due to rapid industrialization in the 1960s and 1970s. By the 1980s, the environmental movement had made a significant shift towards a broader anti-pollution base. Tied closely to the democratization movement taking place at the time, the anti-pollution movement was largely led by students and academia in protest of the existing power structures of the military regime (Ku 1996, 163). Academia became an important stakeholder in the social movement but took a protesting stance rather than partnership formation. The "environmental movement's political empowerment parallels the political empowerment of civil social movements in general and yields important insights into the relationship between the state and civil society" (Lee 2000, 133).

Highly publicized environmental disasters such as the phenol spill in the Nakdong River, which threatened the drinking water supply and the mass fish kills due to the release of industrial effluent, did not only magnify the environmental awareness of citizens but also led to the institutionalization of more formalized environmental CSOs, such as establishing of the Pollution Research Institute (1982) and Korean Anti-Pollution Movement Association (1988) (Heo 2013, 464). Democratization in the late 1980s marked a shift in the governance approach from protesting industrial corporations and autocratic government-oriented problem solving to a more conciliatory approach towards a mainstream environmentalism that focused on advocacy and collaboration with government and industry to influence public policy (Ku 2009, 53; Yoon 2000, 58).

Bottom-up sustainable development

SD in the Republic of Korea has a unique history, starting with the 1992 Earth Summit, in which a bottom-up collaboration approach with local CSOs, businesses, and local governments began a local autonomy and environmental movement with *Local Agenda 21*. The result of these efforts was the establishment of the Local Councils for Sustainable Development (LCSDs) in 1995, creating a wide network of local CSOs and governments (ROK 2016b, 2). "As of 2016, around 90% of local governments have [instituted Local Agenda 21] and 50% of the local governments established LCSD with an exclusive secretariat" (Cho-Ahn et al. 2017, 36). The early success of the movement in Korea resulted in international recognition at the 2002 World Summit on Sustainable Development as a successful global case (Yoon 2016, 2).

The recognition of CSOs and local governments led to national institutional mechanisms with the Presidential Commission on Sustainable Development (PCSD) and Local Sustainability Alliance of Korea (LSAK). Consensus building with CSOs and businesses were critical for the passing of the Framework Act on Sustainable Development in 2007. In addition, civil society had the pivotal role of nominating the PCSD chair for approval by the president and the commission members, including affiliates from civil society, business, and government (Yoon 2016, 2). The LSAK provided an institutional platform for a national network of LCSDs, supporting capacity building in policies and implementation through forums, conferences, and best-practices awards in collaboration with the Ministry of Environment (MOE) (ROK 2016b, 28). As of 2016, the alliance had around 200 organizations across 17 provinces (ROK 2016a, 3).

Civil society-centered sustainable development[1]

On the world environment day in June 2005, the Korean president, Moo-hyun Roh, made a declaration for a National Vision for Sustainable Development. The emphasis on civic participation reflected the importance of the social dimension of SD as well as the presidential commitment towards participatory governance. Civic experts and academia were well represented in the PCSD and provided consultation to government departments in the preparation of the National Strategy for Sustainable Development (NSSD) (KEI 2014, 21; Heo 2013, 466). Additionally, CSOs and business representatives in the PCSD played a critical role in mediating between stakeholders and coordinating inter-department involvement with both government and non-government actors in the development and implementation of national strategies and plans (Huh 2014, 103).

Business-centered sustainable development

In 2009, President Myung-bak Lee proclaimed a new vision for national economic development based on Low Carbon and Green Growth (LCGG). The new president from the opposition party advocated for green growth with a focus on the win–win strategy of economic growth without environmental damage (Lee and Yun 2011, 292). The focus of this effort would be in the development and support of new economic engines of growth in green technologies that were environmentally responsible and able to share LCGG with the world. In support of the National Strategy for Green Growth, the Presidential Committee on Green Growth (PCGG) was launched in 2009 with two co-chairs, the prime minister and a presidential nominee from the private sector (Lee and Yun 2011, 303).

While the earlier SD efforts were primarily focused domestically, the green growth initiative drove the sharing of Korea's experience with the world. However, the business-centered focus came at the cost of civic interest. The early development of Local Agenda 21 as an environmental movement created some friction at the national level. New policy changes led to a national–local disconnect that was ascribed to conflicts of interest among state bureaus, CSOs, and political parties. For the past two decades, LCSDs have continued to operate with limited attention from central authorities. However, in 2015 the organization became officially charged with the promotion of local SD. The main purpose of the status change was to legally provide financial support for LCSDs, rather than developing a comprehensive policy.

International partnership initiatives

Reflecting the belief that green economic growth should be possible for the world, several new partnerships and organizations were formed to share Korea's domestic experience. Figure 9.2 epitomizes the emergence of international partnership through the integration of policy, technology, and financing. The integration was necessary for successful development of green and sustainable economic and industrial growth that can meet social and environmental objectives.

The Global Green Growth Institute (GGGI) was established in 2010 through the support of the Korean president as a Korean NGO and would convene as an international organization with the support of 18 member countries in October of 2012. GGGI framed environmental challenges as economic policy issues, taking a more expansive scope of how countries can address development and environmental concerns through more efficient use of resources based within the context of individual countries. GGGI convenes local partners and governments with academia, CSOs, and industry to share the "know-how" of successful best practices around the world.

The Green Technology Center was established in 2013 to support and promote national green technology development policy and international cooperation on climate change technology transfer. This Korea-based organization joined the UNFCCC Climate Technology Center and Network (CTCN) in 2015 and

Figure 9.2 Emergence of international partnership
Source: Adapted from GGGI 2015, 335.

supports the implementation of partnership projects related to climate technology managed by the Korean Ministry of Science and ICT.

The Green Climate Fund (GCF) was created under the provisions of the UNFCCC to provide a financial mechanism to support developing countries in their effort to address and adapt to climate change. Although the fund was agreed upon in 2010, to further support green development and financing Korea successfully bid to host the Secretariat of the Green Climate Fund in 2012. The GCF is critical for the success of the Paris Agreement, mobilizing resources to prioritize projects and activities in developing countries and providing additional attention to those most vulnerable to climate change. GCF highlights Korea's commitment to provide comprehensive support through policy, technology, and financing.

Inward and outward sustainable development through international links

In the fall of 2015, the UN member states committed to the 2030 Agenda for Sustainable Development. This ambitious agenda contained 17 goals and 169 targets, going much further than the Millennium Development Goals (MDGs) in targeting the entrenched source of poverty and creating conditions for sustainable growth and development for both developing and developed countries. As a new institutional environment is presented, Korea has made commitments to incorporate SDGs into the national discourse to create a framework for domestic and international implementation (ROK 2016b). The responsible government bodies are working across sectors and with CSOs to engage in multi-stakeholder discussions about the development of strategies and policies for SDGs. Although slowly, the SDG efforts are expanding and integrating within the global context. Through the international links, the partnership focuses on both domestic and international SDG projects.

International cooperation is critical for strengthening partnerships to achieve SDGs. Formally an aid recipient, Korea has been a donor country since entering the OECD Development Assistance Committee (DAC) in 2010. Integrating international cooperation and development support has been the primary mechanism for Korea's global implementation of SDGs. Official Development Assistance (ODA) projects with greater inclusion of civil society are key to bolstering partnerships and synergies between the two sectors (ROK 2016b, 13). Initiatives such as the Better Life for Girls, Saemaul Undong for rural development, Scientific and Technological Innovation for Better Life, and Safe Life for All offer innovative pathways for sharing knowledge and the experience of the ROK to enhance the effectiveness of ODA in the SDGs period and beyond (ROK 2016a, 6). In 2016 the Korean government, led by the Ministry of Foreign Affairs (MOFA) and MOE, delivered the Voluntary National Reviews (VNR), titled *Year One of Implementing the SDGs in the Republic of Korea: From a Model of Development Success to a Vision for Sustainable Development*. The report highlighted the progress being made in the implementation of the 2030 Agenda.

Partnership failure

The challenges of SD in Korea remain the same. The governance of SD is highly dependent on the structure and process of the partnership, whether at the domestic or international level. "Conflict is at the very heart of governance . . . the common good that binds citizens in a polity is not one that emerges from deliberation, but is the process of deliberation itself" (Brinkerhoff 2007, 80). However, not all conflicts lead to positive outcomes; individual interests need to be tempered with the greater public interest.

Korean SD has been a mix of top-down and bottom-up approaches in moving forward SD goals. While the initial SD movement was driven from the bottom up by community-based NGOs partnering with local governments to address adverse environmental effects from industrialization through the adoption of Local Agenda 21, the integration between Agenda 21 and national SD policies at the broader scale has been challenging. The participatory governance of the first NSSD led to a legislative framework that took nearly five years of consensus building but was widely accepted by multiple stakeholders (Lee and Yun 2011, 308). Democratization not only strengthened CSOs, but also led to greater democratic accountability and participation through direct elections of local officials and increased autonomy of local governments (Heo 2013, 468).

The swinging priorities of changing administrations have resulted in the fragmentation of partnerships. Business interests were pushed ahead of the participatory governance of CSOs as the government prioritized support of businesses for green economic growth. Due to the exclusion of most CSOs and the strong push by the central government, little prospects remained for serious engagement by NGOs and citizens (Lee and Yun 2011, 302). The Citizens' Coalition for Economic Justice (CCEJ) penned a strong admonishment of the handling of the third NSSD process and the unclear language of the targets and indicators. CEEJ noted the perplexity as each government department involved in national implementation made it systematically confusing and difficult for CSOs to know who the relevant departments were and what their responsibilities were (CEEJ 2016, 311).

Differing views on the definition of SD and, consequently, the competing interests of organizations have made it difficult to reach a consensus. The push for greater transparency and accountability has weakened the techno-bureaucratic autonomy of the central government and their ability to mediate between lower levels of government. The development of the national policy failed to build an overlapping area of consensus that could bring the different actors together in a meaningful way. In response to Korea's *VNR*, the Korean Civil Society Network on SDGs (KCSN), made up of 21 CSOs, issued the *Korean Civil Society Report for 2017 HLPF on Sustainable Development*. This report focused primarily on the contents of the NSSD as they relate to Korea, but noted the lack of clarity was visible in the definitions, purpose of targets, and indicators, along with the limited usefulness of global indicators and targets for Korea (Cho-Ahn et al. 2017, 39). The list of the member organizations of KCSN can be found in Table 9.2.

Table 9.2 Member organizations of the Korea Civil Society Network on SDGs

1. Energy and Climate Policy Institute	11. Korea Institute Center for Sustainable Development (KICSD)
2. Green Energy Strategy Institute	12. Korea Social Economy Network
3. Green Future	
4. Green Korea United	13. Korea Women's Association United (KWAU)
5. Korea Civil Society Forum on International Development (KoFID)	14. Korea Women's Hotline
	15. Korean Disability Forum (KDF)
6. Korea Differently Abled Federation (KDAF)	16. Korean Women's Environmental Network (KWEN)
7. Korea Fair Trade Organization	17. Kyunggi Women's Association United
8. Korea Federation for Environmental Movement (KFEM)	18. Open Network
	19. PEACE MOMO
9. Korea Health Welfare Social Cooperative Federation	20. The Korea Center for City and Environmental Research (KOCER)
10. Korea Human Rights Foundation	21. Ulsan River for Watershed

Source: Adapted from Cho-Ahn et al. 2017, 40.

Differing definitions and expectations regarding the process and outcomes of partnership have also contributed to the adversarial and disappointing relationship between partners. Huh (2014) noted the divergent views by which government was generally more focused on the process and procedure from a managerial standpoint from the more traditional top-down structure, while academia and civil society focused on participatory discourse leading to more radical transformation. While civil society understood SD as a dynamic process that can lead to transformative change and innovation, the public-sector approach was more department-oriented, seeking incremental changes and innovation (Huh 2014, 109).

Partnerships in action for waste reduction and resource recovery

One of the key challenges facing many communities and governments is the management of waste. Rapid economic growth and development greatly increased the standard of living in Korea, but with rising incomes also came increasing consumption. Growing disposable incomes and the rise of consumer culture greatly increased household waste. While the early environmental focus was on industrial pollution and waste from industrial activity, the growing density and urbanization of Korea would place greater strains on municipal waste management. The primary methods of managing waste was the use of open landfills, by which collected municipal waste would be "open-dumped rather than sanitary landfilled," and the practice would continue until the late 1980s (Nam 1993, 13; Kim and Kim 2012, 29). Only 536 landfills were operated by local governments until 1994, of which the rate of sanitary landfill was lower than 60%, and only 11 nation-wide landfills could process waste leachate (Kim and Kim 2012, 86).

Democratization and rising incomes began to dampen the unbridled industrial policy as economic interests began to shift from being purely monetary towards quality of life issues. Along with the rapid pace of waste generation and the difficulty of creating landfill sites, the opportunity cost grew with rising values of real estate in Korea (Nam 1993, 15). Placing locally unwanted land use, such as landfills, became difficult as urbanization raised the land use cost and NIMBYism (Not In My Back Yard) of residents made the siting of locally unwanted land uses increasingly contentious.

Planning for the environment began with the Fifth Five-Year Economic Plan (1982–1986). The Environmental Office was founded in 1980 and, with the celebration of the first Earth Day celebration in 1990, was upgraded to the Environment Agency, advancing to the ministry level with a cabinet position by 1995 (Kim and Kim 2012, 26). Highly publicized industrial contaminations along with growing municipal waste placed greater pressures on the government to address public health and environmental concerns.

Partnership structure – public–private partnership

The 1990s marked a significant policy shift to influence the demand for waste services. Rather than trying to maximize waste treatment capacity, efforts were made to minimize waste. The separation of waste for recycling became compulsory in 1991 (Kim and Kim 2012, 37). Even with the penalty of 1 million Korean won for violation of separation of waste ordinance, the performance of these policies was poor due to the heavy burdens placed on residents and poor infrastructure for collection (Yoo et al. 2014, 44; Kim and Kim 2012, 35).

Providing the right incentives and administration for meaningful waste reduction would require the collaboration of central and local governments with civil society and businesses. The increased autonomy of local governments also coincided with a dramatic budget increase for waste management, exploding from 3–7 billion Korean won prior to 1990 to 145.6 billion Korean won by 1995 (MOE 2011, 12). The prioritization of the environment within the ministerial cabinet positions added respectability to waste management. Local governments were directly responsible within their regions for the collection and transportation of waste and recyclable materials through direct service delivery or contracting with private haulers (Kim and Kim 2012, 69).

Replacing the original fee based on property tax, the government would move towards the user/polluter pay model with the national implementation of the volume-based waste fee system in 1995. Consumers would be required to pay for waste disposal bags based on volume, encouraging the reduction of wasteful consumption. In doing so, incentives were offered to separate waste based on the principles of reuse, recycling, or reduce. The purchase of plastic waste disposal bags funded the cost of "collecting, transporting, storing, and processing household waste" (Kim and Kim 2012, 64). The pricing is set by local districts on a per liter basis and considers "the cost of waste disposal, financial status of the local government, and residents' standard of living" (Kim and Kim 2012, 72).

Additional supporting policies were implemented to encourage waste reduction. Due to the foul odor from the mixture of general and food waste, food waste recycling was introduced in 1997; food waste has been banned from direct land-filling since 2005 (Yoo et al. 2014, 44; Kim and Kim 2012, 75). The restriction of disposable one-time use products policy was introduced in 1994. As a result, disposable utensils and products such as plastic bags, knifes, spoons, shavers, and toothbrushes were banned or cannot be offered for free at specific businesses and locations, which promoted the use of reusable and environmentally responsible materials (Kim and Kim 2012, 82).

Partnership performance – civil society

Increased collaboration between citizen groups and local governments contributed to the successful implementation of policy. Volunteers and city workers were utilized to track illegal dumpers, who were fined up to 1 million Korean won, using existing security cameras, searching the contents of the waste to identify the violator, and rewarding reports of illegal waste dumping by offering up to 80% of the fine levied.

During development and the trial period of the policy, civil society and the private sector were convened to assess the policy. Building on the strong sense of citizenship and public duty, many Koreans were becoming more involved in environmental organizations and the public media also highlighted the health and environmental impacts of waste and landfills. As a result, citizens became "actively engaged in garbage reduction and voluntary garbage sorting programs for recycling without any direct or individual economic rewards" (Kim 2004, 720). Consumers began to prefer products that generated less waste. Additionally, residents found it more convenient to recycle as many apartment complexes and community centers created separate bins for different types of recyclable materials.

Partnership implementation – business sector

In addition to waste reduction, the policy spurred economic and business opportunities in recycling and resource recovery. The initial challenge came from inadequate recycling facilities for plastics. To help develop the recycling infrastructure, support securing facilities, and establish the recycling industry, the Korea Environment and Resources Corporation (currently the Korea Environment Corporation) provided long-term, low-interest loans to ensure long-term industry support for the recycling industry. The volume-based waste fee policy was supported by 23.1 billion Korean won in investment, including establishing nine recycling facilities, as well as centers that are able to process plastics, in addition to developing more sturdy waste bags that are also decomposable (Kim and Kim 2012, 83). Due to the restriction on offering free vinyl bags, reusable vinyl bags were introduced in 2002 and sold at all the major marts to serve the dual purpose of a grocery bag to take home purchased goods and used later for waste disposal (Kim and Kim 2012, 96–97).

There are several different tools available to the government to induce industry support. Table 9.3 provides a list of different policy tools that can be used by policymakers to induce change and provide financial support for the development of supporting industries. Pricing mechanisms including fees, charges, and taxes can induce more efficient behavior by adding an additional cost for certain behavior. Subsidies can lower the cost of desirable behavior or actions, while deposit–refund collects a surcharge in advance to be refunded upon return.

In 1995, the Korea Life Resource Recycling Association was organized by the owners of recycling centers to support in the collection of

> electronic products used in households and offices (TV, refrigerator, washing machine, electric fan, etc.), furniture (electronic products, sofa, bed, desk, etc.) and sporting goods without cost, repairs and sells them as secondhand goods, or donates them to orphanages or nursing homes.
>
> (Kim and Kim 2012, 82–83)

In 2013, an online marketplace was introduced "for users and suppliers of recyclable materials and reusable products," initially focused on waste materials, home electronics, baby products, and used furniture. The program has expanded to "used machines and equipment, semi-processed goods and any other recyclable or reusable material or good" (OECD 2017, 215). The service provides four different trading options, matching system, auction, group purchase, and ordinary trading. Although the system can boast of over 50 thousand registered users, with over half being businesses and around 690 thousand trades, the recycling markets remain weak due to a "general mistrust in the quality of recycled materials and reused products" and low commodities prices (OECD 2017, 216).

Consumers have also shown a preference for products that produce less waste. Businesses have seen an added benefit by changing manufacturing systems and designing products that produce less waste, thus increasing market share. Industry has also moved towards the use of materials that are more environmentally friendly and can be more easily recycled (Kim and Kim 2012, 59). Beginning in 2004 the government implemented the green public procurement system, requiring all government institutions to purchase green products (OECD 2017, 216). A year earlier, the Extended Producer Responsibility (EPR) was implemented,

Table 9.3 Government incentives for waste reduction

Incentive type	Fee	Charge	Deposit–refund	Tax	Subsidies
Specific policies	- Waste disposal fee	- Product charge - User charge	- Surcharge then issue rebate upon return	- Landfill tax - Hazardous waste tax	- Loan and tax - Preference grant

Source: Adapted from Kim and Kim 2012.

"which sets mandatory recycling targets for producers and importers of certain packaging materials and products, and levies a recycling charge on those who do not meet their target" (OECD 2006, 83).

Partnership outcomes – legitimacy and international recognition

The OECD and UN have positively evaluated the waste management efforts of Korea and their continual innovation to reduce and recover waste. International standards in waste management have made Korea a valuable success case and have created opportunities to share their policy experience with the international community. The success of the volume-based waste fee and recycling has emboldened Korea to pursue more advanced resource efficiency policies, moving towards a "circular economy" of zero-waste that goes beyond quantitative resource recovery from recycling and waste to energy production "towards qualitative resource circulation by encouraging upcycling (i.e. recycling that upgrades the value of the materials recycled)" (OECD 2017, 199). Opening in 2017, the "Seoul Upcycling Plaza (SUP) was established to broaden people's awareness of the environmental, social, and economic benefits and cultivate an upcycling-based industrial environment" (Seoul Upcycling Plaza 2017).

The failures to develop sanitary landfills and the negative social and political implications that arose from poor waste management have resulted in the transformation of waste facilities as liabilities to opportunities. Not only has volume-based waste disposal and recycling been successfully exported, but the repurposing of waste into valuable resources by designing for the long-term reuse of landfills is garnering greater attention. The successful transformation of the Nanjido landfill into an eco-park in support of the adjacent 2002 World Cup stadium led to the development of the world's largest landfill as an eco-tourism destination with the Sudokwon Dream Park. Built on reclaimed land from the sea, the site host "a range of activities, including an eco-energy town, natural areas, sports fields, a golf course and flower gardens, and is a venue for cultural and sporting events" (OECD 2017, 218). The public–private partnership is also registered as a Clean Development Mechanism (CDM) project for landfill gas electricity generation earning certified emissions reduction (CER) credits, turning waste into an energy resource (Shin 2017).

Overall, the waste reduction case in Korea is briefly summarized in the model presented in Figure 9.3. A new initiative of waste management was led by public–private partnership, as the policy created business opportunities for the private sector. It proceeded with participation of CSOs, which continued to influence private participation and behavior, as CSOs monitor and suggest further ideas of the policy and voice public concern. National sentiment towards environmentalism and the cooperative attitude by all participants' recognition of the importance in achieving SDGs strengthened the effectiveness of the campaign. As a result, the initiative met the goal of waste reduction and resource recovery. It established legitimacy of the initiative and became internationally recognized as a successful case.

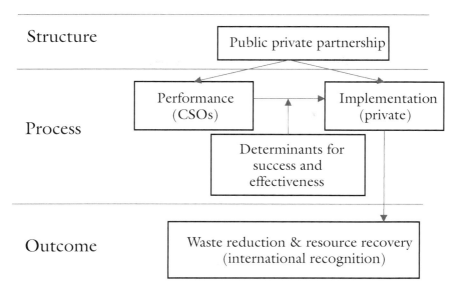

Figure 9.3 Causal chain for partnership's contributions to waste reduction and resource recovery
Source: Adapted from J. Brinkerhoff 2007, 70.

Conclusion

SD is a comprehensive movement where not only technical solutions and policies matter but also participation determines the success and the quality of development. In contrast to the technology or policy that stands politically neutral or shows a solid baseline stance, participation involves an unlimited boundary of actors from which, naturally, arises conflicts of interest over the development goal. In particular, as globalization has accelerated, SD has been undertaken at the global level more frequently than before.

This chapter illustrated the rationale of partnership and the desirable interactions among the partners, with a focus on Sustainable Development Goal (SDG) 17. It introduced the history of SD in Korea as accompanied by democratization so that mainstream environmentalism changed to a more conciliatory approach where the state, industry, and civil society organizations (CSOs) could collaborate. As environmental awareness increased in global society, the organization's ability to undertake environmental decision-making and implementation was also upgraded in status. As a result, partnership in action became more extensive and diverse, making it more important to align different interests in order to lead to effective, legitimate, and satisfactory outcomes in undertaking the SDGs.

Our case study on volume-based waste fees and resource recovery suggests that successful achievement of SDGs is never a one-way, top-down, state-oriented approach but rather the result of coordination and reconciliation among partners with different interests. In the case of volume-based waste fees, local governments, CSOs, and the private sector were major project partners. Overall, the case displays the increasing importance of partnership in making good governance in pursuit of SDGs, and demonstrates that partnership's contribution determines the quality of outcome in the SDG implementation.

Note

1 A detailed description of government policies and strategies can be found in Chapter 3.

References

Agyeman, J., and B. Angus. 2003. "The Role of Civic Environmentalism in the Pursuit of Sustainable Communities." *Journal of Environmental Planning and Management*, 46.3: 345–363.

Austin, J. E. 2007. "Sustainability Through Partnering: Conceptualizing Partnerships Between Businesses and NGOs." In *Partnerships, Governance and Sustainable Development: Reflections on Theory and Practice*, edited by Pieter Glasbergen, Frank Biermann, and Arthur P. J. Mol, 49–67. Cheltenham: Edward Elgar Publishing.

Brinkerhoff, D. W. 2007. "Enabling Environmental Partnerships: The Role of Good Governance in Madagascar's Forest Sector." In *Partnerships, Governance and Sustainable Development: Reflections on Theory and Practice*, edited by Pieter Glasbergen, Frank Biermann, and Arthur P. J. Mol, 93–114. Cheltenham: Edward Elgar Publishing.

Brinkerhoff, J. M. 2002. "Assessing and Improving Partnership Relationships and Outcomes: A Proposed Framework." *Evaluation and Program Planning*, 25: 215–231.

Brinkerhoff, J. M. 2007. "Partnership as a Means to Good Governance: Towards an Evaluation Framework." In *Partnerships, Governance and Sustainable Development: Reflections on Theory and Practice*, edited by Pieter Glasbergen, Frank Biermann, and Arthur P. J. Mol, 68–89. Cheltenham: Edward Elgar Publishing.

Cho-Ahn, C., O. Kwon, E. Kim, M. Lee, and D. K. H. Yoon. 2017. *Korean Civil Society Report for 2017 HLPF on Sustainable Development*. Seoul: Korea Civil Society Network on SDGs. Accessed July 20, 2017. Online accessible at: https://sustainabledevelopment.un.org/index.php?page=view&type=111&nr=14506&menu=138&template=1706

Citizens' Coalition for Economic Justice (CCEJ). 2016. "Republic of Korea: Implementing the SDGs." Country report in *Spotlight on Sustainable Development 2016: Report by the Reflection Group on the 2030 Agenda for Sustainable Development*, 310–312. Development Alternatives with Women for a New Era (DAWN), Third World Network (TWN), Social Watch, Global Policy Forum (GPF) and Arab NGO Network for Development (ANND). Accessed August 2, 2017. www.socialwatch.org/report2016). ISBN 978-3-943126-27-3

Global Green Growth Institute (GGGI). 2015. *Korea's Green Growth Experience: Process, Outcomes and Lessons Learned.* Seoul: GGGI.

Heo, I. 2013. "Changing Aspects of Government – Society Relations in South Korea: Evidence from the Evolution of Environmental Policy Governance." *Contemporary Politics*, 19.4: 459–473.

Huh, T. 2014. "Dynamics and Discourse of Governance for Sustainable Development in South Korea: Convergent or Divergent?" *Journal of Environmental Policy and Planning*, 16.1: 95–115.

Kim, J-H. 2004. "Sustainable Urban Waste Management System in Metropolitan Seoul, South Korea." In *The Sustainable City III*, edited by N. Marchettini, C. A. Brebbia, E. Tiezzi, and L. C. Wadhwa, 717–726. Ashurst: WIT Press.

Kim, K-Y., and Y. J. Kim. 2012. *2011 Modularization of Korea's Development Experience: Volume-Based Waste Fee System in Korea.* Seoul: KDI School of Public Policy and Management.

Korea Environment Institute (KEI). 2014. "Measuring Progress for Sustainable Development." In *Greenable Volume 2, 2014.* Seoul: KEI.

Ku, D. 1996. "The Structural Change of the Korean Environmental Movement." *Korea Journal of Population and Development*, 25.1: 155–180.

Ku, D. 2009. "The Emergence of Ecological Alternative Movement in Korea." *Korean Social Science Journal*, 2: 1–32.

Lee, J-H., and S-J. Yun. 2011. "A Comparative Study of Governance in State Management: Focusing on the Roh Moo-hyun Government and the Lee Myung-bak Government." *Development and Society*, 40.2: 289–318.

Lee, S-J. 2000. "The Environmental Movement in Korea and Its Political Empowerment." *Korea Journal*, 40.3: 131–160.

Ministry of Environment (MOE). 2011. "Waste Reduction and Recycling." In *Some Success Stories of Korean Environmental Policies, Vol. 3.* New Delhi: Ministry of Environment.

Nam, I. 1993. *Economic Incentives in Waste Management: Korea's Case.* Seoul: Korea Development Institute.

OECD. 2006. *OECD Environmental Performance Reviews: Korea 2006.* Paris: OECD Publishing.

OECD. 2017. *OECD Environmental Performance Reviews: Korea 2017.* Paris: OECD Publishing.

Republic of Korea (ROK). 2016a. *2016 National Voluntary Review – Executive Summary.* ROK: The Government of the Republic of Korea.

Republic of Korea (ROK). 2016b. *Year One of Implementing the SDGs in the Republic of Korea: From a Modal of Development Success to a Vision for Sustainable Development.* ROK: The Government of the Republic of Korea.

Seoul Upcycling Plaza. 2017. "Overview." Accessed September 10, 2017. www.seoulup.or.kr/Sup/overview.php

Shin, M. 2017. "Case Study Database: Smart Waste Management." Urban SDG Knowledge Platform, September 15. Accessed October 20, 2017. http://urbansdgplatform.org/profile/profile_caseView_detail.msc?no_case=97

United Nations (UN). 2017. "Annex III. Revised List of Global Sustainable Development Goal Indicators." In *Report of the Inter-Agency and Expert Group on Sustainable Development Goal Indicators (E/CN.3/2017/2).* New York: UN Economic and Social Council.

Yoo, K-Y., W-J. Kim, and K-K. Kang. 2014. 2014 Modularization of Korea's Development Experience: Nanjido Eco Park Restoration from Waste Dumping Site. Republic of Korea: Ministry of Strategy and Finance.

Yoon, D. K. H. 2016. "Starting Strong on the SDGs in Asia: Readiness in South Korea." (Discussion Paper for the International Forum for Sustainable Asia and the Pacific). Japan: Institute for Global Environmental Strategies (IGES).Accessed July 2, 2017. http://pub.iges.or.jp/modules/envirolib/view.php?docid=6682

Yoon, K. S. 2000. "Environmental Challenges and Local Agenda 21 Process in the Case of the Republic of Korea." In *Learning from Each Other in North and South: Local Agenda 21 in Germany and the Republic of Korea – INEF Report*, 54–61. Institut für Entwicklung und Frieden der Gerhard-Mercator-Universität Duisburg.

Part III
Conclusion

10 Conclusion

Sung Jin Kang and Jung Hee Hyun

Among the UN's 17 SDGs, this book chose to focus on the environmental aspects of the SDGs, mainly discussing clean water, affordable and clean energy, decent work and economic growth, sustainable cities and communities, climate action, and partnerships for the goal. This focus allowed for an in-depth analysis of the economic and environmental conditions of the ROK and its progress over the past three decades. By identifying the most relevant SDG targets with the ROK's unique development experience, this book has identified institutions and governance mechanisms tied to specific policies and methods of implementing each pillar of the SDGs.

This chapter serves to highlight key findings from previous chapters and synthesize the results found from analysis done separately for each goal. Chapters 4 to 7 have successfully tracked the progress of the ROK's selected SDGs using a common methodology of developing a SDG index suggested in this book. Based on the ROK's legacy of economic and social development, this chapter serves to review the progress made during presidential terms. Because the specific policies and actions implemented for individual SDGs are discussed in each chapter, the overall socio-economic context of each presidential term is provided to contextualize the overall upward trend of the ROK's SDG progress. Finally, a concluding note suggests how the ROK should improve its design for implementing the SDGs by identifying key barriers and opportunities, while also noting the applicability of the ROK's sustainable development trajectory for other countries.

The ROK's rapid economic development strategies, implemented during the period of President Jung-hee Park's export-driven industrialization (1962–1980), stand out as a model case. Yet, the repercussions of such a tunnel-vision approach resulted in calls for a more democratic and systematic development process, especially for price and labor market stabilization. During President Doo-hwan Chun's leadership (1980–1988), inflation stabilization and a foundation for a market-driven economy were successfully implemented thanks to another militaristic presidential regime despite convictions of human right violations during his rise to power along with social censorship and restriction.

President Tae-woo Roh (1988–1993) was the first president elected after enacting the restriction of the presidential rule to a single five-year term and the successful 1988 Seoul Olympics. President Roh focused on democratization, decentralization, and further liberalizing the market. Most notable policies centered on improving national welfare and human development, including the construction of 200 million housing units and the high-speed rail system and increasing R&D expenditure. President Young-sam Kim (1993–1998) began the first non-militaristic presidential regime after serving 30 years as the leader of the opposition party. His major policies included the real-name financial system, large education reforms, and improvement of ICT infrastructure. With continued efforts on globalizing and liberalizing the market, the lack of a proper monitoring system to regulate the financial sector became one of the major causes of the 1997 Asian Financial Crisis.

During President Dae-jung Kim's (1998–2003) presidency, recovery from the financial crisis, and the implementation of large structural reforms, was the first and foremost priority. Alongside macroeconomic changes, President Kim reformed the health care and pension systems in a way favorable for the social protection of vulnerable citizens. With further development of the IT and service industry, the ROK was well-suited to transition to the twenty-first century information era. To address the social fabric of the ROK, which had become much more stratified between regions, economic classes, and generations, President Moo-hyun Roh (2003–2008) introduced labor and welfare policies for the *seomin* (common people) and balanced regional development. Other major policies included the Korea–US FTA and eradication of corruption in the government.

As mentioned in previous chapters, the Myung-bak Lee (2008–2013) administration stands out for his alternative directions for economic growth beyond restructuring and reform. His commitment to green growth and technology were evidenced beyond domestic efforts to international initiatives such as the agenda on green growth at the 2010 Seoul G20 Summit and establishment of the Global Green Growth Institute. President Lee placed great significance on engaging with relevant global affairs to make space for greater participation and role for the ROK. President Geun-hye Park's (2013–2017) administration pushed for development in the "creative economy," increasing the R&D budget and providing government support for start-ups and entrepreneurs rather than continuing Lee's green growth approach. Although the ROK was quick to recover from the 2008 global financial crisis, prolonged stagnating economic growth and social problems revealed that much progress is still required in its current structural systems.

The average index values calculated for every administration, according to the results from the previous chapters, are shown by each goal. These figures show the overall progress for each goal made by each presidential administration. Chapter 4 measured the ROK's progress towards achieving safe water and sanitation by coordinating and developing indexes to monitor water-related goal indicators that align with the target, followed by identifying the ROK's key challenges and opportunities in implementing SDG 6 (Figure 10.1).

Improvements in management and availability of water and sanitation in the ROK were overall positively made throughout all administrations. Given the ROK's well-established basic infrastructure for providing quality water and sanitation to all citizens as well as ensuring efficient use of water (Targets 6.1, 6.2,

Conclusion 183

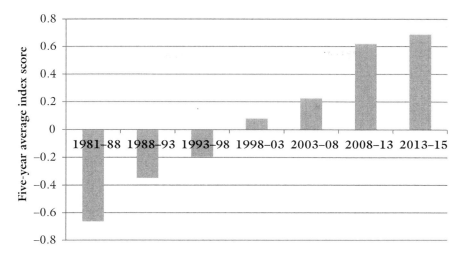

Figure 10.1 Index for SDG 6 by administration

6.4), the targets on improving the environmental aspects related to water quality and ecosystem (Targets 6.3, 6.6) served as the main differentiating indicators of the ROK's progress on achieving SDG 6. The greatest progress made on SDG 6 was between the Dae-jung Kim and Myung-bak Lee administrations (1998–2013), where the water supply and sanitation coverage and the water use efficiency increased despite slight decreases in the water quality of open bodies of water and water ecosystem. Yet, the greatest indicator of the ROK's efforts related to SDG 6 can be speculated based on the limited collection of quantitative data acceptable as per the internationally proposed indicators – much progress has yet to made.

Chapter 5 discussed the ROK's concrete actions to improve energy access through energy efficiency cooperation, policies and measures based on national circumstances (Figure 10.2).

There largest progress was between President Doo-hwan Chun and President Tae-woo Roh, and the main cause is presumed to be the improvement of energy intensity and access to electricity. Also, the second largest progress was made between President Dae-jung Kim and President Young-sam Kim; the improvement of energy intensity and the opening of the electricity and gas sector to foreign direct investment are presumed to increase the index. The progress between President Myung-bak Lee and President Geun-hye Park was similar to the progress made between President Dae-jung Kim and President Young-sam Kim, possibly explained by the introduction of Renewable Portfolio Standard.

Chapter 6 aimed to provide a solid framework of indicators to monitor progress of the ROK in incorporating decent network and economic growth goals into national economic sustainability (Figure 10.3).

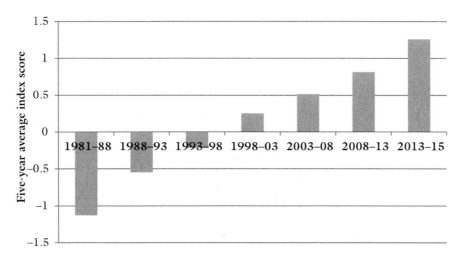

Figure 10.2 Index for SDG 7 by administration

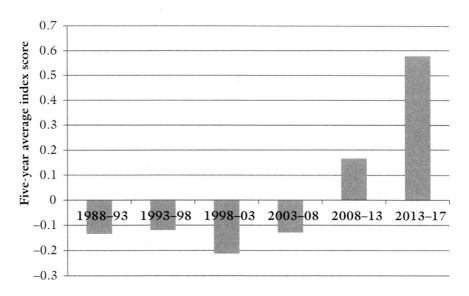

Figure 10.3 Index for SDG 8 by administration

Goal 8 is unique in that it is the only index with a negative growth rate between administrations. It is not surprising that the decreased development was the effect of the 1997 Asian Financial Crisis. Besides the Dae-jung Kim administration, all other administrations delivered positive progress. Under the Lee (2008–2013) and Park (2013–17) administrations the greatest progress was achieved, with continuous increase in GDP per capita (target 8.1), strengthened financial institutions (target 8.10), and increased spending for trade ODA (target 8.a).

Chapter 7 proposed a devised framework to track the urban sustainability of the ROK and identify some possible constraints of national and local contexts, suggesting the formulation of better-informed policies in a more systematic manner.

According to Figure 10.4, there was significant progress between President Moo-hyun Roh and President Myung-bak Lee from 2000 to 2010. This improvement is almost twice of that of the 1990s. The main cause is presumed to be the improvement of residential environment (target 11.1), protection of cultural property (target 11.4), and improvement of the environment (target 11.6).

Chapter 8 provided a range of the ROK's initiatives as means of implementation and integrated measures into national policies and strategies including climate finance, national disaster risk reduction strategies, and awareness-raising on climate change mitigation and adaptation. Although Korea showed progress in terms of mitigating climate change owing to Myung-bak Lee administration's Green Growth Strategy, the Geun-hye Park administration did not build upon the previous administration's legacy due to the deteriorating national and international situation. However, Chapter 8 anticipated that Korea's climate change policy will play an active role in the future as the current administration is engaged in taking various climate actions, including countermeasures against domestic fine dust.

Chapter 9 discussed the ROK's global partnership in various aspects, linking its development cooperation towards coherence and coordination to fuel synergies between all the stakeholders. Chapter 9 in particular focuses on SDG 17 to discuss the rationale of partnership and desirable interactions among the partners.

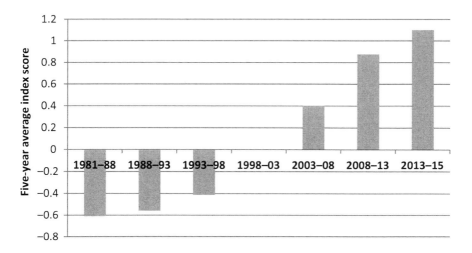

Figure 10.4 Index for SDG 11 by administration

As the global society further acknowledges and prioritizes the environment, the partnerships for action can become more extensive and diverse in undertaking the SDGs. By conducting a case study about volume-based waste fees and resource recovery, Chapter 9 proved that only with coordination and reconciliation among partners with different interests can the SDGs be achieved successfully. Moreover, the case indicated an increasing significance of partnership in pursing SDGs and demonstrated that the quality of outcome in SDG implementation depends on partnership's contribution.

While each chapter in this book showed a consistent improvement in the ROK government's progress in achieving the SDGs, one of the major barriers was that each administration's policies were not coherent, and those policies did not always lead to actual implementation and expected results. Even so, the ROK has potential to demonstrate more progress, since many action-oriented practical programs are being implemented owing to increasing awareness of environmental NGOs and citizens in Korean society. Also, the current administration's action plan to implement Renewable Energy 2030, which aims to increase the country's reliance on renewable energy sources to 20% by 2030, suggests the country's persistent efforts to promote the SDGs. This country-level effort to integrate sustainable development concepts into national and international development strategies, which began in the early 1990s, could be a good model for other developing countries in a similar development process to the ROK, suggesting the applicability of the ROK's sustainable development trajectory for other countries.

Bibliography

Chang, H. J. 1993. "The Political Economy of Industrial Policy in Korea." *Cambridge Journal of Economics*, 17.2: 131–157.

Cho, C., and Y. Kang. 2013. "Korea's Stabilization Policies in the 1980s." Korea Knowledge Sharing Program: KSP Modularization, KDI School of Public Policy and Management.

Cho, D. 2015. *Growth, Crisis and the Korean Economy*. Abingdon: Routledge.

Moon, H. C. 2016. *The Strategy for Korea's Economic Success*. New York: Oxford University Press.

Index

Page numbers in *italics* indicate figures and in **bold** indicate tables on the corresponding pages.

Act on the Maintenance and Improvement of Urban Areas and Dwelling Condition for Residents 116
Act on the Prevention of Sexual Assault and Protection 130
Agenda 21 *see* Local Agenda 21 (LA21)
Asian Financial Crisis 73, 105, *105*, 184–185
Asian Games, 1986 57
Automatic Rainfall Warning System 146

Ban, Ki-Moon 5, 140
banking, commercial 97–100, *98–99*
Bank of Korea 100
Basic Plan for Dissemination and Development of Alternative Energy Technologies 68
Basic Plan for Resource Circulation 87
Basic Plans for Sustainable Development 86
Basic Roadmap for National Greenhouse Gas Reduction 2030 144
Better Life for Girls 168
biochemical oxygen demand (BOD) 43, 46, *46*
bottom-up sustainable development 165–166
Brundtland, Gro Halel 3
Bureau of Cultural Property Organization 122
business-centered sustainable development (SD) 166
business sector implementation of partnerships 172–174, *173*

Car-free Commuting Day 156
Cell Broadcasting Service (CBS)-based Phone Disaster Notification Broadcasting System 146
chemical oxygen demand (COD) 43, 46
Chun, Doo-hwan 181, 183
cities and communities, sustainable: conclusions and implications 133–135; cultural and natural heritage in *122*, 122–123; data on 113; environment and 124–127, *125–127*; factor analysis 131, 131–133, *132–133*; growth of urbanization and 110–111, *111*; housing in 113–116, 114–117, *117*; introduction to 110–111, *111*; natural disasters and 123–124, *123–124*; public space in 127–131, 128, *128–130*; relevant policy overview 111–112, *112*; results 113–133; sustainable urban management in 118–122, *120–121*; transport in 117–118, *119*
Citizens' Coalition for Economic Justice (CCEJ) 169
civic environmentalism, birth of 164–165
civil society organizations (CSO) 22, 158, 163, 164, 165, 175; bottom-up sustainable development (SD) and 165–166; civil society-centered sustainable development and 166; partnership failure and 169
Clean Development Mechanism (CDM) 174
clean water *see* water

climate action: conclusion on 155–156; improving education, awareness-raising and human and institutional capacity on climate change mitigation, adaptation, impact reduction and early warning 146–155, 147, *151–152*; integrating climate change measures into national policies, strategies and planning 142–146, *144*, 145, *146*; introduction to 138–140; and strengthening resilience and adaptive capacity to climate-related hazards and natural disasters in all countries *140–141*, 140–142, *143*; trends in achieving Goal 13 140–155
Climate Policy Initiative (CPI) 149
Club of Rome 21
collaboration between local governments and citizen groups 172
Commission of Sustainable Development (CSD) 24, 30–31
conservation and efficiency, energy 72–76, *75*
consumer groups 164
cooperation, water 52–53, *53*
Countermeasures against Natural Disasters Act 142
Countermeasures against Typhoons and Floods Act 142
creative economy 182
Creative Economy Action Plan 86, 87
CSD *See* Commission of Sustainable Development (CSD)
cultural and natural heritage *122*, 122–123
Cultural Properties Protection Law developed 122
Cutting 1 Ton of GHGs Per Person Campaign 156

data analysis: economic growth trend 89–100, *90*, *91–92*, 93, *94–101*, *96*; SDG 11–13; water 55–59, *56–57*, *57–58*
data collection, SDG indicators 11–12
democratization 165, 171, 181–182
Disaster Notification Board System 146
disasters, natural *see* natural disasters
domestic material consumption (DMC) 91–92, *94*
drinking water 39–41, *40–41*
dumping problems 44

early warning systems 146–155, 147, *151–152*
Earth Day, 1990 171
Earth Summit, 1992 21, 22
economic growth, sustainable: Asian Financial Crisis and 73, 105, *105*; conclusion and implications 105–107; data on 89–100, *90*, *91–92*, 93, *94–101*, *96*; introduction to 85; relevant policy overview *86*, 86–89, *88*; results from trend 102–105, *103*, *103–104*
ecosystems, water 51–52, *52*
education, awareness-raising and human and institutional capacity on climate change mitigation, adaptation, impact reduction and early warning 146–155, 147, *151–152*
efficiency: energy 72–76, *75*; water-use 47–49, *48–50*, 49
electricity, access to 66–67, *67*
Electric Power Industry Foundation Fund 71
empirical studies on Sustainable Development Goals (SDGs) 8
energy: access to electricity and 66–67, *67*; analysis on performance of ROK goal by target 66–77, *67*, *69*, *71*, *72*, *75*; conclusion on 79–80; conservation and efficiency of 72–76, *75*; foreign direct investment in 77, *77*, 77–78; infrastructure and technology for modern and sustainable energy services 76–77, *77*; international cooperation to promote clean technologies for 76; introduction to 65–66, *66*; policy development in ROK related to 65–66, *66*; renewable 67–72, *69*, *71*; results from factor analysis 77–79, 78, *79*
Energy Use Rationalization fund 75
Energy Use Rationalization Law (formerly Heat Management Law) 73
environmental impact of cities 124–127, *125–127*
environmentalism, civic 164–165
European Union (EU) 11
Extended Producer Responsibility (EPR) 173–174

factor analysis 13–14; economic growth 89–100, *90*, *91–92*, 93, *94–101*, *96*,

Index

04, energy data
102–105, 103, ...ex building ..., 16–17, 18;
77–79, 78, 79... communities
9–11, 14–15... 2–133;
sustainable
131, 13... 169–170, 170
water ...ect investment (FDI) ...) 68–71
failure ... Rationalization Plan
FDI ...
... Economic Plan
...) 171
...tutions, capacity of
98–99
...te Change Response Strategy
2
...gy use rationalization plan 73
...onal strategy for sustainable
...evelopment (2006–2010) (NSSD) 23–24
Five-Year Plan for Green Growth 86
Five-Year Plan of the Seventh Economic Social Development 86
foreign direct investment (FDI) 77, 77, 77–78, 158
Forest Statistics 51
fourth energy use rationalization plan 74
Fourth Renewable Energy Basic Plan 70
freshwater resources 48–49, 50
Future We Want, The 4

GGGI *see* Global Green Growth Institute (GGGI)
Global Competitiveness Index (GCI) 106
Global Green Growth Institute (GGGI) 25, 167, *167*, 182
global partnerships: in action for waste reduction and resource recovery 170–174, *173*, *175*; conclusions on 175–176; defined 162–164, *163*; failure 169–170, *170*; history of non-state partnerships for sustainable development and 164–170, *167*, *170*; implementation in the business sector 172–174, *173*; legitimacy and international recognition 174, *175*; performance in civil society 172; structure of 171–172; sustainable development goals and 158–164, 159–161, *163*; *see also* sustainable development (SD)

governance, water 53–54
greenbelt 119, *120*
Green Climate Fund (GCF) *167*, 168
greenhouse gas emissions (GHG) 32, 138, 155–156; and integrating climate change measures into national policies, strategies and planning 142–146, *144*, 145, *146*
Green Sharing Market 156
Green Technology Center (GTCK) *167*
gross domestic product (GDP) *91*, 185; agricultural sector contribution to 48; economic growth and 85, 89–97, *90*, *93*, *94*, *98*; energy and 75–78; natural disaster and 123, *124*; urbanization, water coverage, sanitation coverage and *39*; *see also* economic growth, sustainable

hazardous chemicals and materials 44, *47*
Heat Management Association 73
Heat Management Law 73
housing 113–116, *114–117*, *117*
hygiene 41–43, *42*

index-building, factor analysis for 9–11, 14–15; example of 15–19, 16–17, *18*
Industrial Technology Innovation Promotion Act 86
infrastructure and technology for modern and sustainable energy services 76–77, *77*
institutional framework to achieve sustainable development 30–31
integrated water resources management (IWRM) 50–51
Inter-Agency and Expert Group on SDG Indicators (IAEG-SDGs) 113
internal market index (IMI) 11
International Decade for Action 'Water for Life' 37
International Futures (IF) 8
International Labor Organization (ILO) 89, 94
International Panel on Climate Change (IPCC) 65
inward sustainable development (SD) 168
IWRM *see* integrated water resources management (IWRM)

Kim, Dae-Jung 4, 22, 182–184
Kim, Young-sam 182, 183

Korea *see* Republic of Korea (ROK)
Korea Energy Economics Institute (KEEI) 68
Korea Life Resource Recycling Association 173
Korean Anti-Pollution Movement Association 165
Korean Civil Society Network on SDGs (KCSN) 169
Korean Civil Society Report for 2017 HLPF on Sustainable Development 169
Korea Water and Wastewater Association (KWWA) 40, 44
KWWA *see* Korea Water and Wastewater Association (KWWA)

LCSD *see* Local Commissions of Sustainable Development (LCSDs)
Lee, Myung-bak 24–25, 31, 76, 149–150, 155, 166, 182–185
Limits to Growth, The 3, 21
literature of SDGs 7–9
Local Agenda 21 (LA21) 3–4, 21, 22, 30; bottom-up sustainable development (SD) and 165; on sustainable cities and communities 111–112; on water governance 53–54
Local Commissions of Sustainable Development (LCSDs) 22
Local Councils for Sustainable Development 22, 165
Local Green Growth Commissions (LGGC) 31
local participation in water governance 53–54, 54
Local Sustainability Alliance of Korea (LSAK) 30, 54; bottom-up sustainable development (SD) and 165–166
Low Carbon and Green Growth (LCGG) vision 166
LSAK *see* Local Sustainability Alliance of Korea (LSAK)

material footprint (MF) 91–92, 93
Millennium Development Goals (MDGs) 4, 5, 8, 168; on clean water 37
minimum energy performance standard (MEPS) 74
Ministry of Environment (MOE) 21, 22, 25; bottom-up sustainable development SL sanitation 43; on water services 40 166; on
Ministry of Foreign Affairs 48; on
MOE *see* Ministry of Environment (MOE)
MOFA *see* Ministry of Foreign Affairs 25 (MOFA)
Moon, Jae-in 155

National Clean Air Conservation 15, 19
National Land Planning and Utilization Act 121
National Strategy for Green Growth 3, 86–87, 112, 166
National Strategy for Sustainable Development (NSSD): First 23–24; Second 24–25; Third 25–26, 27–29
National Sustainable Development 86
National Vision for Sustainable Development 166
National Water Quality Monitoring Program 45
natural disasters 123–124, *123–124*; early warning systems for 146–155, 147, *151–152*; resilience and adaptive capacity to *140–141*, 140–142, 143
Natural Disasters Act 143
NIMBYism (Not In My Back Yard) 171
nongovernmental organizations (NGOs) 25, 30, 167, 169
non-point source (NPS) pollution 44
NSSD *see* National Strategy for Sustainable Development (NSSD)

Office for Government Policy Coordination (OGPC) 25
official development assistance (ODA) 4, 26, *151–152*, 151–155, 158, 168; water sector 52–53, *53*
OGPC *see* Office for Government Policy Coordination (OGPC)
oil shocks 73
One Heritage One Keeper campaign 122
open defecation problem 41
Organization for Economic Co-operation and Development (OECD) 26; Aid for Trade 100, *100*; Asian Financial Crisis and 77, 80; Development Assistance Committee 164, 168; economic growth and 94,

95; on energy intensity 75, 75–76; monitoring of ODA flows 151–152, 151–155; partnerships outcomes 174; on tourism 97
Our Common Future 3
outward sustainable development (SD) 168

Paris Agreement of 2015 76, 138, 144, 153, 168
Park, Geun-hye 26, 182, 185
Park, Jung-hee 181
partnerships *see* global partnerships
PCGG *see* Presidential Commission on Green Growth (PCGG)
PCSD *see* Presidential Commission of Sustainable Development (PCSD)
PM10 (fine particulate matter) 124, 127, 128, *128*
Pollution Research Institute 165
pre-establishment of national sustainable development strategies 22–23, *23*
Presidential Commission of Sustainable Development (PCSD) 21–22, 22–23, 30, 111; bottom-up sustainable development (SD) and 165–166; First NSSD and 24
Presidential Commission on Green Growth (PCGG) 24, 31, 166
public-private partnership 171–172
public safety 129–131, *130*
public space 127–131, 128, *128–130*
public transit 118, *119*
public welfare 100, *101*

Qualification System for the Restoration Engineer of Cultural Properties 122
quality, water 43–46, *45–47*

Radio Disaster Warning Broadcasting System 146
rainfall 48–49, *50*
Ramsar Convention 52, *52*, 58
recycling 126, *127*; and reuse of water 44
Regulatory Indicators for Sustainable Energy (RISE) 66
renewable energy 67–72, *69*, *71*
Renewable Portfolio Standard (RPS) 70, 72, *72*
Republic of Korea (ROK) 5–6; Asian Financial Crisis and 73, 105, *105*, 184–185; assessment of water-related SDG targets and indicators in context of 39–54; democratization of 165, 171, 181–182; economic growth, 1960s to late 1990s 21; energy policy development in 65–66, *66*; first national strategy for sustainable development (2006–2010) 23–24; Local Commissions of Sustainable Development (LCSDs) 22; Local Councils for Sustainable Development 22; Ministry of Environment (MOE) 21, 22, 25, 40, 48, 166; Ministry of Foreign Affairs (MOFA) 25; Office for Government Policy Coordination (OGPC) 25; pre-establishment of national sustainable development strategies 22–23, *23*; Presidential Commission of Sustainable Development (PCSD) 21–22; second national strategy for sustainable development (2011–2015) 24–25; sustainable development policies 22–26, *23*, 27–29, 31–32; third national strategy for sustainable development (2016–2035) 25–26, 27–29
research & development, spending on 182
resilience and adaptive capacity to climate-related hazards *140–141*, 140–142, 143
resource recovery, partnerships in action for 170–174, *173*, *175*
Rio +20 Summit 4
RISE *see* Regulatory Indicators for Sustainable Energy (RISE)
Roh, Moo-hyun 23, 166, 182, 185
Roh, Tae-woo 181–182, 183
ROK *see* Republic of Korea (ROK)

Saemaul Undong 168
safety, public 129–131, *130*
sanitation and hygiene 41–43, *42*
scarcity, water 47–49, *48–50*, 49
SD *see* sustainable development (SD)
Second Basic Plan for the Development and Utilization of New Renewable Energy Technology 69–70
Second Comprehensive Plan on Non-Point Source Management 44
second energy Master Plan 74
second energy use rationalization plan 73

second national strategy for sustainable development (2011–2015) 24–25
Seoul Local Air Environment Standard 19
Seoul Sustainable Energy Plan 156
sexual assault 130, *130*, 130–131
Sixth Industrial Technology Innovation Plan 87
small and medium enterprises (SME) 87
Special Act for Promotion and Support of Urban Regeneration 116
Special Act on the Promotion of Urban Renewal 116
stewardship-based management for area-specific risk reduction target (SMART) program 46
Stockholm Declaration 3
sustainability, definition of 7
sustainable development (SD) 7–8, 175–176; birth of civic environmentalism and 164–165; bottom-up 165–166; brief overview of policies in 22–26, *23*, 27–29; business-centered 166; civil society-centered 166; first national strategy for sustainable development (2006–2010) 23–24; governance model for 162–163, *163*; history of non-state partnerships for 164–170, *167*, *170*; institutional framework to achieve 30–31; international partnership initiatives for 167; introduction to 21–22; inward and outward, through international links 168; partnership failure and 169–170, *170*; pre-establishment of national sustainable development strategies 22–23, *23*; second national strategy for sustainable development (2011–2015) 24–25; third national strategy for sustainable development (2016–2035) 25–26, 27–29
Sustainable Development Goals (SDGs) 3–4; climate action 138–140; conclusions on 181–186, *183–185*; definition of sustainable development 5; economic growth 85–89; energy targets 65, 66–77, *67*, *69*, *71*, *72*, *75*; factor analysis for index building 9–11; framework development 5; global partnership and 158–164, 159–161, *163*; literature on 7–9; methods and scope of study 11–15; policy and funding guidance 4–5; sustainable cities and communities 110–112; water goal 37–38; water-related targets 39–54

Third Basic Plan for Sustainable Development (2016–2035) 86
Third Basic Plan for the Development and Utilization of the New and Renewable Energy Technology 70
third energy use rationalization plan 74
third national strategy for sustainable development (2016–2035) 25–26, 27–29
total suspended solids (TSS) 43
tourism 97, *98*
Transmission System for Intangible Cultural Property 122
transport 117–118, *119*
"Triple Bottom Line" approach 8
TV Disaster Warning Broadcasting System 146

unemployment rates 94, *95–96*, 96–97
United Nations Development Program (UNDP) 8
United Nations Environment Program (UNEP) 3
United Nations Framework Convention on Climate Change (UNFCCC) 76, 138, 139–140, 149–155, 167–168
United Nations Inter-Agency and Expert group 9
United Nations Millennium Declaration 4
United Nations Millennium Development Goals (MDGs) *see* Millennium Development Goals (MDGs)
United Nations Sustainable Development Goals (SDGs) *see* Sustainable Development Goals (SDGs)
urbanization, growth of 110–111, *111*; *see also* cities and communities, sustainable
urban management, sustainable 118–122, *120–121*

Verbal (Text) Notification System 146
Voluntary National Reviews (VNR) 168, 169

waste generation 126, *126*
waste reduction, partnerships in action for 170–174, 173, *175*
water: conclusion on *59*, 59–60; cooperation regarding 52–53, *53*; data analysis results 55–59, 56–57, *57–58*; data and study methodology 55, 56–57, 58–59; drinking 39–41, *40–41*; ecosystems related to 51–52, *52*; governance of 53–54; integrated water resources management (IWRM) 50–51; introduction to 37–38, *38–39*; quality of 43–46, *45–47*; rainfall 48–49, *50*; recycling and reuse of 44; sanitation and hygiene 41–43, *42*; scarcity and water-use efficiency 47–49, *48–50*, 49; Sustainable Development Goals (SDGs) water-related targets 39–54

Water and Environmental Management Plan (WEM) 51

WEM *see* Water and Environmental Management Plan (WEM)

Wetland Conservation Act 52

wetlands 52

World Bank 48–49, 150; Development Indicator 65

World Commission on Environment and Development (WCED) 3

World Summit on Sustainable Development, 2002 22, 165

World Travel & Tourism Council (WTTC) 97

Year One of Implementing the SDGs in the Republic of Korea: From a Model of Development Success to a Vision for Sustainable Development 168